Totalistic Teen Treatment

A Qualitative Analysis of
Retrospective Accounts

Marcus Chatfield

This is a paperback edition of a thesis project, *Adult Perspectives on Totalistic Teen Treatment: Experiences and Impact.* This manuscript is available online as a free PDF file. Because of differences in pagination due to reformatting, the title of this edition differs from the electronic version.

ISBN: 9781096687245

May all human programs be more humane

ACKNOWLEDGMENTS

This research was possible because of the privileges and gifts I received during the last 48 years. If anything has been accomplished, it is due primarily to luck and to the goodness of others. I'd like to acknowledge some individuals whose presence and actions brought this project to life.

This study happened because people participated in the questionnaire and the interviews. I was encouraged and grateful that so many were interested and willing. I am especially indebted to the 30 interview participants who gave their time to speak with me about their experiences and perspectives. Their narratives are the heart of this study—it was an honor to learn from their viewpoints. Above all else, I hope this work is worthy in their eyes.

My thesis committee provided exceptional guidance and support. My committee chair, David Diehl, was always interested and responsive, yet skeptical; always patient and supportive, yet demanding. And somehow, he was always available. The standard he held me to and the example he set will continue to teach. Suzanna Smith devoted hours of her time paying attention to needed revisions, calling attention to subtle meanings and loaded language. Her sensitivity to detail and her skill for listening conveyed a deep care for my topic that inspired me to examine my thinking and the quality of my voice. Jodi Lane is a masterful teacher who perfectly balances fair, frank, no-nonsense critique with an enthusiasm and realness that points exactly to the heart of the matter. Her expertise on the topic and the skill she conveys it with, are gold. Her insights made this a stronger work and I felt honored to have her on my committee. Sebastian Galindo taught me how to think about and conduct qualitative research. His methods course shaped this project and provided me with critical resources I didn't even know I needed. Throughout this project I felt I had the best committee. These people embody the skills and qualities I aspire to develop. I am so moved by the quality of their thinking and their care for my well-being as a student.

I feel a sense of gratitude for all of my professors in the FYCS department. Larry Forthun, Sarah Lynne-Landsman, Kate Fogarty,

Tracy Johns, and Mickie Swisher provided me with learning I needed and use. I feel especially grateful to Kate Fogarty and Mickie Swisher because I confided in them when I was close to giving up and they responded with affirmations and emotional support. On more than one occasion, Mickie sat and talked with me after class, telling me about her passion for critical thinking and the learning process. Her methods and theories courses were taught at a level that was just beyond my comfort. Her devotion to students, her emails, and teaching style have provided me lessons I will learn from for a lifetime.

This department is populated by exceptionally kind and brilliant scholars, and we have Gregg Henderscheidt, who takes care of everyone with helpful wisdom. In my coursework outside the FYCS department I found the work and spirit of Carolyn Tucker. I believe she is one of the greatest resources available to students at the University of Florida. Her course on health disparities would benefit every student interested in the social sciences.

Good friends also made this thesis possible. Christina supported my scholarship and provided me with a vote of confidence that continually inspires me to be a better person. In the middle of this project, Liese invited me to present my learning in Denmark and Norway. She heard me across the Atlantic and validated my work in a way that I can only hope to be worthy of. Marshall shared his genius insights, helped pilot test my instruments, and sent articles that become foundational to my thinking. Ashten gave many hours to this project as a co-coder. She helped me develop a coding structure and she helped me believe in myself. Kris and Cyndy inspired me. Zack, Ginger, Liz, Todd, Alex, and Matt reminded me of what's important.

Cindy caught me during my implosions and listened to me every day and loved me perfectly.

TABLE OF CONTENTS

8

APPENDIX

LIST OF TABLES

LIST OF FIGURES

LIST OF ABBREVIATIONS

Group H
The 15 interview participants with the highest QOE index scores.

Group L
The 15 interview participants randomly selected from a frame of participants with QOE index scores of 1.00 to 1.99.

QOE
Quality of Experience.

TPC
Totalistic Program Characteristics.

Abstract

This original qualitative research analyzes adult reports about the experiences and impacts of totalistic teen programs. In the United States a wide array of residential treatment centers, therapeutic boarding schools, wilderness/outdoor, and intensive outpatient programs provide psychological and behavioral programming to "troubled" youth in totalistic settings. These programs are characterized by insularity, autocratic power structures, and intensive group practices. Some individuals may experience genuinely therapeutic responses to such treatment while others may experience a range of negative effects. Although federal investigations and dramatic news reports provide anecdotal evidence suggesting some program types may be problematic, few empirical studies have explored the relationship between program design and quality of life within totalistic settings, and very little is known about the way such programs impact adult development.

This research used a purposeful stratified sampling technique to identify interview participants with a wide range of experiences within 25 different totalistic teen programs. Data were collected in an online questionnaire (N=223) and in one-hour phone interviews conducted nationally (N=30). Using categorical, comparative, topical, and thematic approaches to analysis, this research answers questions about the experiences, immediate effects, and long-term impacts of totalistic teen treatment methods. This thesis applies key findings to policy recommendations and concludes there is a need for multidisciplinary research toward greater protections for youth in totalistic treatment settings.

1

❀ INTRODUCTION ❀

Scope

This thesis presents qualitative research based on interviews with adults who, as adolescents, resided within a totalistic treatment milieu. The term "totalistic" refers to an array of features and methods associated with autocratic treatment programs and total institutions that utilize a closed group dynamics approach to affect fundamental personal change (De Leon, 2000; Goffman, 1961; Grant & Grant, 1959; Schein, Schneier, & Barker,1961). The term also implies the assumption that the totality of simultaneous, clustered conditions is a primary "active ingredient" within such programs (Leach, 2016). The term "residential treatment" is a matter of convenience and is not meant to exclude totalistic forms of intensive outpatient treatment.

In the context of teen programs, treatment can be defined as the attempt "to bring about directed change in a person or persons" (Anglin, 2002, p. 17). The term "totalistic" is most simply defined as the degree to which the milieu specifies and dictates the way individuals should "think, feel, and act" (Langone, 1993, p.4). This study explores the perceived experiences, effects, and impacts associated with totalistic treatment settings that are characterized by: 1) strict controls of communication; 2) peer surveillance and policing; 3) a philosophy based on the need to change the whole person; 4) a series of prescribed stages or phases of progress and privileges; 5) frequent participation in formal or informal group sessions involving confrontation, confession rituals, or prolonged interpersonal encounter methods; 6) a strict system of rules and inflexible punishments; and

7) a central authority structure that governs all aspects of life. Totalistic teen treatment programs typically begin treatment with an intensive introductory period where the initiate may be cut off from the outside world and afforded very little privacy. Advancement beyond this initial stage is typically contingent upon demonstrating an earnest willingness to participate in the milieu. Therapeutic changes are expected to progress through a prescribed system of levels, steps, or phases where basic privileges and social status are earned through demonstrations of learned behavior, internalization of program values, obedience, and genuine expressions of gratitude for the treatment. The intention behind these milieu features, whether faith-based or secular, is typically described as a need to change the whole person.

Population and Magnitude

The magnitude of this issue is difficult to estimate because there is a profound lack of information about residential treatment programs in general (Friedman et al., 2006). Adding to the difficulty, state-level data lack uniformity and are based on inconsistent definitions and reporting protocols (Overcamp-Martini & Nutton, 2009). Apparently, there is no centralized database keeping track of the total number of youth currently residing in the wide assortment of treatment programs and there is no way to calculate the number of Americans who have been treated in totalistic programs. An unknown number of American youth currently reside within an unknown number of privately-operated out-of-home treatment settings such as behavior modification programs, emotional growth centers, therapeutic boarding schools, faith-based programs, residential treatment facilities, wilderness programs, therapeutic communities, and conversion therapy programs.

Group-home foster care population estimates range from 56,000 (Izzo et al., 2016) to 212,000 (Thoburn & Ainsworth, 2015). Approximately 50,000 reside within juvenile justice facilities (OJJDP, 2014) and 36,000 reside within psychiatric hospitals (SAMHSA, 2016). In 2008, more than 200,000 youths resided in federally-funded residential treatment programs alone (GAO-08-346, 2008). The total number of youth residing in privately operated state-licensed programs is not known and even less is known about youth residing in unlicensed programs that function with little or no state oversight (Friedman et al., 2006). In 2006, the American Bar Association estimated that 10 to 15 thousand youths were placed in unlicensed programs each year (Behar, Friedman, Pinto, Katz-Leavy, & Jones, 2007).

Youth living in these settings have been placed there by parents or guardians, admitted by the foster care system, or sent by the judicial system. While living in these programs, they are treated for a wide variety of behavioral and mental health issues such as substance abuse, behavioral disorders, psychiatric disorders, developmental issues, general delinquency, or learning disabilities. For many youth, such treatments begin with a shocking and disorienting transport by hired escorts. Some practitioners recommend that parents hire professional transporters who will "legally kidnap" youth in the middle of the night and deliver them to treatment facilities by whatever means necessary (Robbins, 2014). In addition to treatment for substance use and psychological or behavioral disorders, an unknown number of healthy and functional youth are placed in programs by intolerant parents or guardians who wish to have their child's gender or sexual identity "corrected" (SAMHSA, 2015).

Problem

Many residential treatment facilities are staffed by well-trained professionals who utilize the least-restrictive, least-intrusive methods available. Many therapeutic settings allow free communication with the outside world and provide individualized care in open environments characterized by warmth, where youth experience clear boundaries and personal autonomy. However, an unknown number of teen treatment programs are staffed by professionals who attempt to direct personal change through closed group dynamic methods within a totalistic milieu. Since the early 1960s, these program methods have been compared to methods of coercive persuasion or thought reform (Beyerstein, 1992; Chatfield, 2014; Frank, 1974; Frankel, 1989; Gordon & Empey, 1962; Schein et al., 1961; U.S. Senate, 1974). Although such methods have been controversial, opinions about the potential for psychological harm in totalistic teen treatment settings based primarily on anecdotal evidence and speculation rather than empirical research. Although the milieu itself can be a source of harm (White & Kleber, 2008) there are few systematic analyses of the way totalistic "regimes of care" (Daly, 2014, p.6) are actually experienced (Chama, 2014; Polvere, 2011; Rauktis, 2016).

Although there is a growing trend toward the promotion of evidence-based practices (Boel-Studt & Tobia, 2016) only a handful of such practices are used within residential care settings (James et al., 2015). Within the juvenile justice system, some estimates find that only 5% to 11% of court-ordered youth receive evidence-based care (Walker, Bumbarger, & Phillippi, 2015). Published research on the effectiveness of programs often lack adequate descriptions about their methods (James, 2011) and many effectiveness studies fail to define the treatment they claim to measure (Bettman & Jasperson, 2009).

Most teen treatment programs utilize an eclectic and un-proven mix of methods (Fahlberg, 1990; Harder & Knorth, 2015). A privately-funded program may use any combination of labels to describe the intended effects of their milieu. Whether faith-based or secular, program practitioners are free to label their methods as they wish. Some authors claim that positive youth development principles and methods are more effective in residential settings than family settings because there are no conflicting influences (Baber, 2011) but others have noted the potential for psychological harm when unthera-peutic combinations of psychotherapeutic and behavioral meth-ods are applied simultaneously in these settings (Zimmerman, 2004). In addition to the lack of guidelines defining the safe combinations of methods, there is a lack of guidelines that de-fine the boundary between safe and unsafe degrees of emotional intensity (Barlow, 2010). Critics have noted "gross incompe-tence" (Friedman et al., 2006, p. 297) within under-regulated programs and a widespread lack of ability to define and distin-guish between appropriate and inappropriate uses of residential treatment in general (Whitehead, Keshet, Lombrowski, Dome-nico, & Green, 2007).

In addition to problems with the content of treatment, there are problems with the content of marketing devices used by some privately-operated programs. The United States Gov-ernment Accountability Office (GAO) found that some pro-grams utilize deceptive marketing practices such as exaggerated statements, undisclosed conflicts of interest, fraudulent tax-do-nation schemes, and false claims regarding individualized re-ferral services and accreditation procedures (Cases of Abuse, 2008; GAO-08-713T, 2008). There are no federal laws pertain-ing to the content or methods used in marketing by program operators (GAO-08-713T, 2008).

Since the early 1980s, an industry of contracted referral agents, transport companies, and online advertisers has grown up around thousands of licensed and unlicensed private programs in the United States (Szalavitz, 2006). In 2008, federal investigations by the GAO documented numerous confirmed and reported cases of abuse and deaths within private programs (GAO-08-146T, 2008; GAO-08-346, 2008; GAO-08-713T, 2008). Some first-hand accounts of life inside totalistic programs describe "cruel and dangerous uses of thought reform techniques" (Cases of Neglect, 2007, p. 76) similar to those described by Lifton (1963), Schein et al. (1961) and Singer and Ofshe (1990). Such methods are designed to elicit fundamental changes in attitudes, beliefs, behavior, and identity through the constant application of therapeutic social pressure (Frankel, 1989). Controversial and potentially dangerous behavior modification methods, often applied within totalistic settings, are also legal in most states (Woodhouse, 2002) and may be used for a variety of purposes including "conversion therapy" (Byne, 2015; SAMHSA, 2015).

Federal legislation to prevent institutional child abuse, unsuccessfully proposed in the early 1980s (Interstate Consortium, 1980), has apparently been re-introduced annually since 2005 but has yet to be enacted. There are no federal safety standards or federal data-reporting requirements for privately operated programs and state level requirements vary (GAO-08-346, 2008, i; Overcamp-Martini & Nutton, 2009). Some states do not have licensing requirements for certain types of programs and other states provide an array of licensing exemptions (Friedman et al., 2006; GAO-08-346, 2008).

The failure to provide safe and appropriate therapeutic care across this wide assortment of programs may indicate the existence of a "systemic illness" (Whitehead et al., 2007). The inconsistent definitions across state agencies, the absence of

22

federal standards, and limited state oversight are structural features that interact to enable harm visited upon youth who have little or no legal right to refuse treatment (Liegghio, Nelson, & Evans, 2010). In the United States, harm in the name of help is rarely subject to systematic research (McCord, 2003; Mercer, 2017; Smith, 2010).

Empirical studies specifically examining abuse and unintended effects associated with residential teen programs are scarce. Descriptive research is limited also but indicates a need for more attention to systematic forms of maltreatment arising in the context of treatment. These are described in the GAO investigations mentioned above, congressional testimony (Cases of Abuse, 2008; Cases of Child Neglect, 2007), exploratory studies (Behar et al., 2007; Chatfield, 2014; Nunno, Holden, and Tollar, 2006), journalism sources (Reamer & Siegel, 2008; Szalavitz, 2006), historiographies (Clark, 2017; White, 2014), and numerous memoirs, news reports, and court transcripts. A small number of critical reviews raise concerns about the prevalence of harmful practices associated with residential programs (Byne, 2016; Friedman et al., 2006; McCord, 1999; Mercer, 2017; Robbins, 2014; Woodhouse, 2002; Zimmerman, 2004) but very few empirical studies explore topics specifically related to systemic forms of institutional maltreatment within the United States. Blake's (2003) dissertation, which found no relationship between state licensing and youth safety, is a rare example.

Anecdotal evidence suggests that intensive methods applied within totalistic settings may be experienced as repeated, inescapable traumatic injuries. Harm arising from such experiences may be associated with long-term symptoms of complex post-traumatic stress disorder (Ebert & Dyck, 2004; Herman, 1992). This type of stress syndrome is characterized by symptoms that are known to predict future problematic behaviors that often persist into adulthood (Kerig, Moeddel, & Becker, 2011). This raises questions about the danger youth may face when the treatment itself is experienced as a vicious dynamic and the effects of such "treatment trauma" (White, 2016) contribute to silence among victims (Whitehead et al., 2007). The prevalence of problematic methods and iatrogenic harm in the United States is not known (Farmer, Murray, Ballentine, Rauktis, & Burns, 2017) and is beyond the scope of this study. The goal here is to propose systematic research that can contribute to our knowledge about the subjective experience of those who were directly impacted by totalistic teen treatment programs.

Purpose

The purpose of this study is to explore retrospective first-hand accounts by adults who, as adolescents, spent weeks, months or years of their lives inside a totalistic treatment program. The primary focus explores how such intensive treatment methods were actually experienced and how the cumulative impact and meaning of those experiences is perceived and described by interviewees. Using methods informed by scholars of multiple approaches to qualitative research, the data collection and analysis are informed by grounded theory and phenomenological perspectives that privilege the subjective nature of meaning-making processes. This study intends to illuminate important topics, analyze emerging themes and common patterns, and report participants' narratives in their own words. This type of research is relevant to the discourse on improving safety and quality of care within licensed and unlicensed treatment settings.

This research is guided by three main questions. How are totalistic teen treatment methods experienced? How do participants describe the immediate effects of the program? How do participants describe the long-term impact of the program?

The design of this study is informed by two theories that are used as a deductive conceptual framework. George De Leon's theory of therapeutic community (2000) is perhaps the most-widely accepted model of totalistic treatment and may be the closest to a universal model of intensive programming in the United States. It is generalizable even to programs that do not self-identify as therapeutic communities and for practitioners, it is flexible enough to allow for modifications while maintaining a set of essential elements (Dye, Ducharme, Johnson, Knudsen, & Roman, 2009). A well-known weakness with De Leon's theory is that although the model is shown to be moderately effective for some populations, it does not fully explain the active mechanisms of individual change (De Leon, 2000). In order to conceptualize this change process, Kurt Lewin's theory of group dynamics, which is an extension of field theory (Lewin, 1947; Schein et al., 1961), is perhaps the most adequate and simplest model that makes the fewest assumptions. Lewin explains the way group dynamics can be orchestrated to elicit individual changes in attitudes, beliefs, and behaviors by identifying three phase states: Unfreezing, Change, and Freezing (or Re-Freezing in Schein et al., 1961). In this model, internally maintained resistance to change must be "softened" and the personality structure "melted" so that the adoption of new changes can be adopted and then internalized through "re-freezing."

Rationale

Current ethics of care assume that treatment providers will rely on the least-restrictive and least-intrusive therapeutic change methods. Although this standard is widely known, its usefulness is questionable because measures of restrictiveness and intrusiveness are typically framed by the adults who deliver such methods rather than by the targets who receive them (Polvere, 2011). Opinions about the usefulness and benevolence of such methods are typically viewed from the standpoint of programmatic intent (DeLeon, 2000) rather than the actual lived experience of youth (LeBel & Kelly, 2014). Qualitative research that systematically collects and synthesizes data relevant to the experience of totalistic change methods may help shine a light behind the closed doors of some of America's total institutions. By giving voice to this underrepresented and often stigmatized population, such illuminations will hopefully contribute to ongoing efforts toward ensuring that intensive teen treatments have a beneficial impact on youth and adult development.

There is a need to know more about the way totalistic teen treatment programs affect adult development. Meta-analytic reviews (Bettmann & Jasperson, 2009; Boel-Studt and Tobia, 2016; Harder & Knorth, 2015; James, 2011; Lipsey, 2009) reveal that many studies seek to quantify program effectiveness using limited outcome measures without considering the full range of effect or the potential for negative impact. This thesis is driven by a set of assumptions about the need to understand the potentially harmful impacts of intensive treatment milieus. It assumes that harmful outcomes documented in the literature (Dishion, McCord, & Poulin, 1999; McCord, 2003; Mercer, 2017; White & Kleber, 2008) as well as preventable, willful acts of cruelty and neglect in care settings, constitute institutional maltreatment because they are likely to impair development (Rabb & Rindfleisch, 1985). This thesis assumes that institutional maltreatment does exist (Hanson, 1982; Stanley, Manthorpe, & Penhale, 1999), that it is a global phenomenon (Burns, Hyde, & Killet, 2013), an ill-defined phenomenon (Rabb & Rindfleisch, 1985), and that it is preventable (Harell & Orem, 1980; Mercer, 1982). However, because it is "tricky," difficult to locate, and persistent in spite of our best efforts at prevention, it is rightfully considered a "wicked," as opposed to a "tame," problem (Burns, Hyde, & Killet, 2013; Smith, 2010). Because it is unrealistic to assume that it can be attributed to a few bad apples (Zimbardo, 2007), this study will attempt to understand "the barrels"—how they look from the inside, how they have been experienced, and how they have impacted adult lives.

Although it is important to be able to predict the effectiveness and beneficial impacts of any intervention, this study assumes that it is equally important to be able to predict and prevent negative side-effects and harm. This type of prevention science would require theoretical knowledge and the capacity for prediction through "dark logic" models (Bonell, Jamal, Melendez-Torres, Cummins, 2015). These models would need to be developed and studied with a wide range of data, including rigorous, systematic analyses of first-hand accounts and subjective experiences (Smith, 2010). This thesis assumes that in order to predict unwanted outcomes, such outcomes must first be understood from the standpoint of the individuals who have direct knowledge about them. Only then can meaningful generalizations about themes, constructs and causal relationships move beyond polemic reactions (Smith, 2010; Zablocki, 1997) and simplistic dominant narratives (Polvere, 2011).

Since the late 1970s, scholars in child welfare have targeted four different levels of institutional maltreatment: interpersonal, systematic, systemic, and complex (Gil, 1982; Stanley et al., 1999). Some adverse interpersonal incidents may be prevented through staff training and supervision (Izzo et al., 2016). However, systematic forms of maltreatment are imposed by design and are typically delivered with overtly benevolent intent (Harell & Orem, 1980; Mercer, 1982; White & Kleber, 2008). Systemic forms of abuse refer to policy-level or enforcement failures, lack of effective licensing and oversight, and insufficient data-reporting procedures (GAO-08-713T, 2008; Stanley et al., 1999; Stop Child Abuse, 2016). Complex forms of institutional maltreatment may refer to overlapping levels (Smith, 2010), complex psychological abuse (Moran et al., 2002), cumulative, simultaneous impacts of milieu features (Chatfield, 2014), the totality of conditions (Leach, 2016), and the experience of group psychological abuse (Rodríguez-Carballeira et al., 2015).

Significance

The potential significance of this study's contribution can be organized around a unifying but vexing question: When is residential treatment comparable to thought reform? This question is explored by numerous experts who describe a wide range of perspectives. Jerome Frank, in *Persuasion and Healing* (1974), and Barbara Frankel, in *Transforming Identities* (1989), both conclude that the difference lies not in any essential set of methods, but in the individual's freedom to exit the milieu. Their perspectives raise immediate questions about the implications of coerced treatment, the inability of youth to refuse such treatments, and court ordered placements. Some of these concerns are discussed in their analyses but they both imply the differences are often superficial.

George De Leon, the towering expert on therapeutic community (TC) theory, distinguished the two according to the benevolence of the TC practitioner on the one hand, and the malevolent intention of cultic organizations on the other (De Leon, 2000). He also points to the fact that the essential technologies for transforming the "whole person" are ancient, saying that similar prototypes of the TC model exist throughout history wherever communal groups practiced such methods. However, this may not be an entirely accurate comparison. Australian ethologist and political scientist, Frank K. Salter (1998), describes six crucial differences between ancient practices and methods associated with thought reform in modern organizations. Specifically, ancient milieus did not include systems of: 1) routine obedience, 2) interrogation, 3) accusation, 4) mild degradation—self-revelation, 5) intense degradation—confession/apology, and 6) punishment/reward (Salter, 1998, p. 444). These six methodological characteristics are described as some of the essential features in therapeutic community theory (De Leon, 1991; 1995; 2000; Dye et al., 2009) and Ofshe and Singer's (1986) and Singer and Ofshe's (1990) descriptions of thought reform programs.

Commenting on the general discourse surrounding the central question posed here, Benjamin Zablocki (1997) argued that scholarly discussions about thought reform were severely lacking in objectivity and marked by emotional polemics. He explains how social scientists had effectively "blacklisted" the concept, preventing meaningful discourse. Early experimental practitioners such as Lamar Empey (1962) explicitly compared totalistic teen treatment of American "delinquents" to "brainwashing." And military researchers such as Schein et al. (1961), assured the public that there is no essential difference between totalistic treatment and coercive persuasion: "It could just as well be argued that the Communists are using some of our own best methods of influence" (p. 269). Considering the military origins of "guided group interaction" (Abrahams & McCorkle, 1945; McCorkle, 1952) and the "total psychotherapeutic push method" within totalistic programs for delinquent soldiers (Knapp & Weitzen, 1945), Schein's frank assessment may be the most astute.

This thesis is unique in the way it places this unresolved and controversial question in a central position in order to contextualize historical and ethical considerations of reformation alongside a wide base of relevant knowledge and information about teen treatment programs. This study seeks to explore residential treatment experiences with a lens and scope that is not typically employed in design, data collection, and analysis related to the topic. Instead of examining program effectiveness, this study intends to examine the effects of programming.

As a graduate of a behavior modification facility that provided family treatment for substance using teens, the author is aware of the strengths and weaknesses that come with being an "insider" (Eppley, 2006; Matthews & Salazar, 2014). The benefits of having first-hand experience must be tempered with the ability to step back, to look with detachment, and to think critically about what is seen as well as how it is seen. This ability to shift between perspectives can be a valuable source of insight and rapport with participants if it is cultivated with due diligence. By intentionally striving to make issues of bias and accuracy fully transparent and subject to self-reflexivity, the role of the insider can be a source of rigor and depth, rather than compromised integrity.

The design of this study is informed by an appreciation for a wide range of opinions and evidence relevant to this topic. Although the guiding question may be unanswerable, it is posed in order to unify a highly relevant body of literature that has been omitted from much of the discourse. By proposing this wider conceptual framework and by raising unanswered ethical questions about social technologies and our ability to conceive of and address their implications (U.S. Senate, 1974), this study aims to locate findings within an ethical and historical context that is relevant to multiple disciplines and areas of research.

There is a conspicuous gap in our knowledge about the way intensive program methods may affect youth and influence adult development. This gap in the literature may reflect a polemic chasm between professionals who, on the one side, are under increasing pressure to demonstrate the effectiveness of such methods (Walker et al., 2015), and on the other, their critics, who decry their use as inappropriate (Dozier et al., 2014). If the current research gap reflects the space between those two poles, this study assumes it would be helpful to know how that middle range is described by those with first-hand experience of it. Their voices are currently absent from the academic discourse.

Social scientists may not know enough about intensive program methods to be able to explain the active mechanisms of change (Harper, 2010; Parent, 2003) or to make meaningful generalizations about the side-effects of such treatment. If the measured outcome variables are but small slices, removed from a whole spectrum of possible side-effects, how useful are the findings of even the most-rigorous meta-analyses? Few outcome studies explore the lived experience or the full range of impact. This research addresses that knowledge gap by taking a unique approach and by going beyond questions about whether or not intensive methods "work." By considering a fuller range of experience and perceived effects, future research can begin to produce new theoretical knowledge about social dynamics and individual change. Such advancements in theory might be relevant to those who wish to improve the quality of care wherever orchestrated social methods are applied to the reformation of identity, personality, and behavior patterns in youth.

2

❧ REVIEW OF THE LITERATURE ❧

Therapeutic Community Theory

Context

George De Leon's therapeutic community (TC) theory describes a modality of treatment that is used in more than 60 countries worldwide (Bunt, Muehlbach, & Moed, 2008) and has been one of the most influential treatment modalities in the United States (Clark, 2017; Dellums, 1997). Federally funded research in this modality of treatment began in the 1960s with grants from the Law Enforcement Assistance Administration (LEAA) and the National Institute of Mental Health (NIMH) and have steadily continued through the National Institute on Drug Abuse (NIDA) and the National Development and Research Institutes (NDRI) (Clark, 2017; De Leon, 2000).

The TC modality is a dominant paradigm with humble beginnings in an organization known as Synanon. A small group of adult heroin addicts in the late 1950s, formed the Synanon organization in Santa Monica, California. Through trial and error, they "rediscovered basic social-learning or behavioral science laws" (De Leon, 1991, p. 1555) and created a radical way of changing an individual's lifestyle and identity

(De Leon, 2000), sparking a recovery revolution (Clarke, 2017).

George De Leon developed TC theory based on his many decades of observations and research in Integrity Therapy sessions, the Synanon organization, and second generation Synanon offshoot programs such as Daytop Village and Phoenix House (De Leon, 2000). These programs were originally developed for the treatment of adult heroin addicts who lived together in communal settings where they engaged in all aspects of life and recovery together (Casriel, 1963; Sugarman, 1974). Because TC group therapy sessions typically utilize psychoanalytic and behavioral concepts within a social learning environment, TCs are considered a social-psychological treatment (De Leon, 1995). TC theory views addiction as a symptom of the "real problem," which is the "whole person" (De Leon, 2000). Modified TCs operate with the same core technology but extend treatment to youth, the homeless, psychiatric patients, and to those with issues other than addictions (De Leon, 1995; 2000).

The methodology is in use all over the world and millions of people have been treated with this methodology since the 1950s. TC theory is based on the philosophy of "Alcoholics Anonymous, and the religious reform and temperance movements" (De Leon, 1995, p. 1604) but the therapeutic community prototype "is ancient, existing in all forms of communal healing and support" (De Leon, 2015b, p. 511). De Leon emphasizes that there are two distinct types of TCs and his theory describes the autocratic model, as opposed to the democratic TC model, which developed in English psychiatric hospitals during the 1940s. He notes that the democratic TC model has shown little effectiveness in the treatment of addictions and although the two modalities share the same name, they evolved independently and are distinctly different forms of treatment (De Leon, 2000).

Constructs

Because TC theory views addiction as a disorder of the whole person, treatment requires a process of restructuring the whole personality (De Leon 2000; White, 2014). In order to elicit genuine transformation, TCs address the core issue: the whole range of identity, attitudes, beliefs, and behavior patterns that contribute to substance abuse or other targeted issues (De Leon, 2000). The essential elements of TC theory are organized into four main construct domains: 1) program perspective, 2) program approach, 3) program model, and 4) treatment process (De Leon, 1995; 2000). The "core technology" of the TC model (Dye et al., 2009, p. 276) contains many essential elements that can be found in a wide range of programs that do not define themselves as therapeutic communities. These essential elements include: the goal of global change; required participation in group confrontation and confession sessions; a strict system of rules and punishments; peer policing; required completion of progressive levels or phases; restrictions on communication; and a centralized authority structure (De Leon & Melnick, 1993).

Program Perspective

According to TC theory, the disordered person typically presents characteristics of psychological dysfunction, social deficit, and low tolerance for frustration, discomfort, or delay of gratification. In this perspective, residents are typified as having low self-esteem, problems with authority, and problems with responsibility. In TC theory, residents are characterized as generally impulsive, unrealistic, unable to cope, dishonest, manipulative, self-deceiving, guilt-ridden and lacking in reading, writing, attention, and communication skills. The intended effects of treatment are global changes in lifestyle and identity. Treatment involves close adherence to the essential precepts, beliefs and values of the program (De Leon, 1995).

Program Approach

Residents are "active participants in the process of changing themselves and others" (De Leon, 1995, p. 1612). Each resident is responsible for the well-being of the peer group and this is demonstrated by providing "feedback"—observations and authentic reactions to individual peers. Each resident is expected to act as a role model of the change process. By helping to modify each other, individual change occurs through social intercourse guided by strict rules and norms to protect the community. Self-development involves learning through skills training, "adherence to orderliness of procedures and systems, in accepting and respecting supervision, and behaving as a responsible member of the community upon whom others are dependent" (p. 1612). Group therapy occurs in formal and informal settings. "The private inner life of the individual, feelings and thoughts, are matters of importance to the recovery and change process, not only for the individual but for other members. Thus, all personal disclosure is eventually publicly shared" (p. 1612). The social network created in the TC is needed to sustain recovery upon reentering society. Residents in this network share special words and phrases that facilitate and demonstrate progress in the milieu.

The argot is the special vocabulary used by residents to reflect elements of its subculture, particularly, its recovery and right living teachings. As with any special language, TC argot represents individual integration into the peer community. However, it also mirrors the individual's clinical progress. The gradual shift in attitudes, behaviors, and values consonant with recovery and right living is reflected in how well residents learn, understand, and use the terms of the glossary and the argot in general. Residents' use of the argot of the TC is an explicit measure of their affiliation and socialization in the TC community (De Leon, 1995, p. 1612).

Program Model

In residential TC programs, "clients remain away from outside influences 24 hours a day for several months before earning short-term day-out privileges" (p. 1613). The inner environment is a communal space that promotes a sense of commonality. Often there are reminders hung on the walls displaying the essential messages of the program to help promote affiliation. Almost all activities are collectively programmed in a daily schedule. All members of the community are expected to "maintain the integrity of the community and assure the spread of social learning effects" (p. 1613). Residents typically work to take care of the facility but work roles depend on the program setting. Treatment involves prescribed phases of incremental learning that are marked by successive increases in responsibilities and expectations. Higher phase residents typically enjoy more status privileges than those on lower phases. The curriculum has formal and informal aspects but all activities are meant to teach the TC perspective. "The concepts, messages, and lessons of the curriculum are repeated in the various groups, meetings, seminars and peer conversations, as well as in readings, signs and personal writings" (p. 1614). One of the most important activities is the encounter group, meant to "heighten individual awareness of specific attitudes or behavioral patterns that should be modified" (p. 1614). These group sessions teach residents to identify and manage their emotions "through the interpersonal and social demands of communal life" (p. 1614). Completion of primary treatment is a stage in the recovery process. Aftercare and peer support are critical.

Treatment Process

The "evolution of the individual as a member" (p. 1618) occurs within two related sub-domains: affiliation and role model. Progress is assessed by the peer group and staff in "how well they walk and talk the behavioral expectations of the community" (p. 1618). The "evolution of the individual as a prosocial member of society" occurs within three related sub-domains: social deviancy, habilitation, and right living (p. 1618). This is assessed by the peer group and staff in the demonstration of "mainstream social skills, attitudes, and values" (p. 1618). The "evolution of the individual in terms of personal growth" occurs within two related sub-domains: maturity and responsibility (p. 1618). This is assessed by the peer group and staff and is demonstrated in a resident's ability to demonstrate self-regulation and "consistency in meeting obligations to self and the expectations of others" (p. 1618). The development of psychological skills enable change in the other three dimensions and occur within three sub-domains: cognitive, emotional, and psychological well-being. Enduring change requires improvement in cognitive and emotional skills and an absence of the "typical signs or symptoms of emotional and mental disturbance" (p. 1618).

Relevance

Since the 1960s, the core technology of TC theory has been applied in many contexts within modified TCs (Dye et al, 2009). Empirical research in the "core technology" of the TC model has been organized into 6 fundamental domains: reliance on confrontational group therapy, a prescribed series of treatment phases, hierarchy of tenure and roles, philosophy of "right living," emphasis on work or education, and "community as method" (Dye et al., 2009). The term, "community as method," refers to the totality of conditions in the milieu that contribute to the process of changing the whole person (De Leon, 2000). These characteristics have been developed in order to assess the degree to which current TCs have remained faithful to the original Synanon model. A modified TC may place a varying degree of emphasis on each category and still remain true to the original TC model (De Leon, 2000; Dye et al., 2009). These variances result from the adaptability of the theory and to the context of treatment scope and population served. For example, although TCs for adolescents focus less on work as therapy, they use more disciplinary action than most other TCs and more confrontational practices than all other TCs (Dye et al., 2009). Many residential programs in the US that do not identify as a TC may be characterized by the essential features of the traditional or modified TC, making the theory generalizable to a broad range of treatment settings.

Strengths

De Leon's TC theory utilizes concepts of cognitive behaviorism and social learning theory to describe a type of social engineering. The theoretical constructs of behavioral theories alone do not "capture the complexity or distinctive features of these settings" (De Leon, 1995, p. 1553). "The social organization of the TC, its structure, and its systems essentially constitute an environment for engineering social learning" (De Leon, 1995, p. 1548). The theory's main strength is that it is based on many decades of observation and it describes a modifiable system that can be adapted to specific contexts without losing its core technology. The theory describes a comprehensive set of dimensions that are crucial to understanding organizational structure and program design wherever group dynamics are used as treatment.

TC theory was developed to explain a modality of treatment already in use all over the world. Knowing that "technologies often develop without the benefit of science" (De Leon, 1991, p. 1555), the question is: How well do abstract theories explain these technologies? In application, although the traditional and modified TC model are generally known to be effective for some individuals (De Leon, 2015b; De Leon & Wexler, 2009; Nielsen, A. L., & Scarpitti, 1997), George De Leon notes that some critics question whether the TC model is an evidence-based practice because of a lack of research through randomized control trials (De Leon, 2015a). Conclusions drawn from complex social experiments can be tentative for many reasons but most relevant to this thesis is the lack of causal explanations. This is a weakness of residential treatment in general; even if effective change is demonstrated, explaining such change may implausible due to a lack of adequate theoretical knowledge (Harper, 2010), or to the fact that such theories are still in their infancy stages (Gilligan, 2015), or because existing theories of change have atrophied (Whittaker, del Valle, & Holmes, 2015).

Weaknesses

The weaknesses in TC theory go beyond its inability to explain the mechanisms of individual change. The theory does not address the potential for harm related to a fundamental paradox of reeducation in TC settings and it does not define the boundaries of "positive coercion." TC theory is also weak in its failure to distinguish itself from coercive persuasion. A fundamental paradox of using TC methods in total institutions is articulated by Fritz Redl (1957) who gives seven levels of meaning implied in the term "therapeutic" and then points out that when a therapeutic milieu is used in "reeducation for life," the intention may be contradictory to the practice. On the one hand, the intention is to provide a substitute for the real world and an alternative to the normal demands of social life because of an individual's developmental need. At the same time however, when the peer group and staff expect normal skills and normal reactions to be demonstrated within an engineered environment so that more-intensive demands can be delivered than would be possible in open society, the practice may be "contradictory to the very idea of using a "special" milieu in the first place" (Redl, 1957, p. 513). "It seems to me that on this level, the term "therapeutic" needs the most careful examination of all, for the custom of making demands out of both sides of our salvation-greedy mouths, requesting opposites which cannot be delivered in one package at one time and place, is all too widespread already" (p. 513). To Redl, the term "therapeutic" means that a milieu is free from counter-therapeutic agents while meeting developmental needs with flexibility, competence, and safety.

41

TC theory describes a modality of treatment that has been compared to "brainwashing" by anthropologists (Frankel, 1989), addictions experts (Beyerstein, 1992), sociologists (Ofshe & Singer, 1986), and by early members of Synanon (Yablonsky, 1962). De Leon's theory would be improved if it addressed these similarities by distinguishing treatment from coercive persuasion and thought reform, as described by Schein, Schneier, and Barker (1961), Lifton, (1963) and Singer and Ofshe (1990). Confrontational peer encounter sessions meant to heighten "a client's awareness of image, attitudes, and conduct that need modification" are the central foundation of TC treatment (Nielsen & Scarpitti, 1997, p. 280). The ability to define safe uses of interpersonal force in therapeutic settings is crucial because even relatively mild forms of group encounter methods in noncoercive therapy settings have been linked to psychological distress and harm (Yalom & Lieberman, 1971).

If practitioners assume that their power and opinions are always benevolent, the autocratic TC perspective may be dangerous, especially if the subjective experience of anything contrary is dismissed as a symptom of an individual's disorder. This source of institutional power would be in keeping with Lifton's discussion of "doctrine over person" (Lifton, 1963), which always assumes that the program perspective is infallible and that there is a "right" way to experience the treatment and a "wrong" way, equated with resistance, defiance, and the need for punishment. Practitioners view the use of force and confrontation in positive terms assuming the manipulation of guilt and shame will make residents more aware "rather than becoming a source of resentment and anger" (Neilsen & Scarpitti, 1997, p. 287). In TC theory, the subjective "self, feelings, thinking and awareness are viewed as real dimensions of the individual" but they "are always evident in, or inferred from, observable behavior" (De Leon, 1991, p. 1552). If such group inferences deny the validity of the individual's perceptions, opinions, or experience, a double-bind may be created, demanding that an individual choose between compromising their own personal integrity by seeking internal stability through loyalty to the invalidating group or through mental contortions of dissonance reduction (Festinger, 1957) or repression (Skoll, 1991).

De Leon's theory describes the use of "continuous observation in the 24-hour regime," which "provides the steady input of data" to the group about an individual's issues that must be "addressed and modified" (De Leon, 1991, p. 1554). Reminiscent of communist cadres and struggle sessions (Chen, 1960; Whyte, 1974), and in keeping with the essential elements of total institutions (Goffman, 1961), De Leon emphasizes that in TCs, "practically all learning occurs collectively in peer groups" (p. 1554). Therapeutic community theory emphasizes the use of repetition where the "concept of recovery and right living is continuously reiterated in virtually all of its activities" in order to strengthen motivation through "mutual encouragement to remain in the learning process" (p. 1554). De Leon explains the causal links in these processes using a circular logic: "The efficacy of these methods is dependent upon the individual's receptivity to the TC's demanding regime. Skills training, role conditioning, and trial-and-error learning unfold because of perceived membership in (i.e., affiliation with) a community of similar others" because "in the TC, affiliation increases the client's amenability to remain in the learning situation" (p. 1554).

The strengths of TC theory are that it describes a dominant paradigm, it is based on decades of observation, it is comprehensive in its description of organizational structure, it is adaptable in practice, and generalizable to the analysis of a broad range of programs. The weaknesses are that it fails to address the paradoxical potential for harm in using therapeutic communities for reeducation, it does not define "positive coercion," does not distinguish between treatment and persuasion, and it relies on a circular logic that presents new arrivals, not with treatment, but with repetitive reasons to believe there is need to stay in treatment (De Leon, 1991). Finally, TC theory does not adequately explain the mechanisms of personal change.

Group Dynamics Theory

Context

Kurt Lewin's (1947) theory of group dynamics describes a way to conceptualize how and why group processes can influence individual change. George De Leon (2000) alludes to the usefulness of Lewin's theory to explain personal change processes but it is Edgar Schein who extends the three main constructs in his model explaining change in thought reform programs (Schein et al., 1961). Lewin's three phases of change model (Unfreeze, Change, and Freeze) was developed during WWII when worker productivity, enhanced teamwork, and popular morale were a research priority. Lewin believed that the capacity to predict and change social behavior might "prove to be as revolutionary as the atom bomb" (Lewin, 1947, p. 5). He also saw that this capacity was crucial to ensuring human survival if we were to win "the race against the destructive capacities set free by man's use of the natural sciences" (p. 5). Like De Leon, Lewin noted that although the social sciences had exploded with rapid growth, "theoretical progress has hardly kept pace with the development of techniques" (p. 5). During the war, Lewin's goal was to design factory systems that maximized production through modifying the social field and influencing individual change processes that affected perceptions, attitudes, beliefs, and behavior, thus improving team spirit and ultimately, helping war-era factories to keep up with quotas (Lewin, 1947).

He discusses the need for social science to evolve more quickly and to move beyond simple behaviorism that denies the relevance of subjective experience. Lewin was one of the first to propose cognitive behavioral approaches to eliciting permanent positive changes in identity, thought, and behavior patterns. His approach emphasized the role of subjective experience as an interlocking variable in group dynamics and social change processes that hinge upon the benevolent manipulation of perception, goals, and values.

Constructs

Lewin's theory of group dynamics is rooted in his general field theory explaining why group dynamics can be orchestrated to elicit individual changes in attitudes, beliefs, and behaviors (Bach, 1954; Lewin, 1947; Schein et al., 1961). Group dynamics theory identifies three phase states of change: Unfreezing, Change, and Freezing. In the unfreezing phase, internally maintained resistance to change must be "softened" and the personality structure "melted" so that new changes can be adopted and then internalized through "re-freezing." Rather than using an economic model that focuses on human attributes in terms of social capital or deficit, Lewin uses a physics model that considers change through social force processes that go beyond individualistic psychoanalytic concepts. Group dynamics theory is useful in that it keeps "the observer's eyes open to various aspects of interdependency that other concepts simply have no way of expressing" (Bach, 1954, p. 340).

In explaining the way group processes affect permanent change within individuals, Lewin first distinguishes between two dynamics: change and resistance to change. Using the factory as an example, he explains that if social conditions change but production levels do not, this would indicate a resistance to change, measured as rate of production. In analyzing group dynamics, he refers to the role of the "social field" as the totality of social forces, entities, relative positions, barriers, channels of communication, and available choices (Lewin, 1947). In considering the way group dynamics affect individual behavior he relies on concepts of force and force fields. One example he uses to consider the rates of aggression in autocratic groups is to conceive of higher levels of aggression as an increase in "the strength of forces toward more aggression" or as a lessening of "forces towards less aggression" (p. 20).

Influencing individuals by modifying the social field requires knowledge of two basic concepts: 1) increasing force toward desired levels or 2) diminishing the opposing forces. In the application of force in social fields, he considers the way increasing the amount of tension toward change is accompanied by fatigue, aggression, emotionality, and lower constructiveness—therefore, unfreezing through diminishing forces of resistance is preferable to increasing the pressure to change. These two forces may be used simultaneously where intense affiliation and emotional intimacy is used to lessen the resistance to change within the insular, totalitarian cadre, as Schein, Schneier, and Barker (1961) describe at length in the context of thought reform.

On the creation of permanent inner personal changes, Lewin begins with a discussion on the way force fields can be modified in order to influence levels of change. To explain these levels of change as movement from one phase state to the next, he uses the analogy of a river—to modify the rate of flow, you cannot simply isolate one factor and focus on it singly. The whole river and riverbed must be taken into account before it is narrowed or widened, deepened, or cleared of rocks. In a similar way, in order to bring about sustained change, the "total circumstances have to be examined" and "the constellation of the social field as a whole has to be studied and reorganized so that social events flow differently" (p. 32). In groups, he refers to resistance to change using the term, "social habits," because in spite of the application of force, the social process does not respond equivocally and therefore indicates the presence of inner-resistance to change. "In order to overcome this inner resistance an additional force seems to be required, a force sufficient to "break the habit," to "unfreeze" the custom" (p. 32).

In considering the force required to initiate the unfreezing process, he alludes to forces that also contribute to the post-change freezing processes based in affiliation: "the greater the social value of a group standard, the greater is the resistance of the individual group member to move away from this level" (p. 32). This theorem seems close to the heart of TC theory and helps to explain the need to develop intense affiliation and to repeat value messages as well as painful reminders of the past. The role of value levels also helps to explain TC theory's emphasis on nurturing the individual's perceived need to remain in the group and the reason treatment begins with shaping the newcomer's beliefs about the need for treatment (De Leon, 1991).

Lewin's theorem on the role of group affiliation predicts that resistance to individual-level changes of standards will be diminished by altering the degree of group-level values of those standards. By modifying the field, the individual is more modifiable because individual values tend to correlate with changing social values. This helps to explain the central tenant of "community as method" (De Leon, 2000) because, "if the group standard itself is changed, the resistance which is due to the relation between individual and group standard is eliminated" (Lewin, 1947, p. 34).

In describing commitment to new changes, Lewin argues that simple explanations about motivation are inadequate (p. 37–38). Lewin finds that motivation alone does not explain change, for that would presuppose an unexplained link between motivation and action. "This link is provided by the decision which links motivation to action and at the same time, seems to have a "freezing" effect which is partly due to the individual's tendency to "stick to his decision" and partly to the "commitment to a group"" (p. 37–38). Internalizing permanent change as a means of maintaining consistency between outer behavior and inner meaning is described at length in Volkman and Cressey's (1963) observations of differential association dynamics in Synanon's group therapy sessions. The fifth principle of differential association postulates that "resident A" is changed most effectively when attempting to change "resident B" (Volkman & Cressey, 1963 p. 139). This is consistent with Lewin's emphasis on the role of group standards and expectations of consistency in freezing new levels of change.

Lewin meant for his theories and research to be applied toward commercial uses and toward developing ways to affect social evolution to help ensure human survival in the face of totalitarianism. Although Lewin may have meant for his work to be applied toward the strengthening of democratic economies, one of the most comprehensive uses of his group dynamics theory is in explaining totalitarian "brainwashing" (Schein et al., 1961). In explaining applications of the three main constructs in group dynamics theory, Edgar Schein provides the most comprehensive analysis. He extends Lewin's work to explain Communist thought reform and also describes how such methods could be used in the reform of adult prisoners and juvenile delinquents in the United States (Schein et al., 1961; Schein, 1962).

Schein's theoretical framework explaining coercive persuasion (1961) relied on Lewin's (1947) field theory theorems linking group values to individual change processes. Schein used these concepts to explain the psychological processes, the effects of coercive change, and the way these effects are "organized around a person's self-image or self-concept" (p. 117). Schein expands Lewin's work by recognizing that the adoption of new identity characteristics hinges on the individual's perception of the social field and the perception of ability to choose greater safety and stability through internalizing the new values, attitudes and beliefs modeled in the milieu. The role of controlling available choices in cultic thought reform programs is developed at length by Janja Lalich in her theory of bounded choice (Lalich, 2004) and in Barbara Frankel's ethnographic study of totalistic treatment milieu (1989).

Edgar Schein and colleagues (1961) explain Lewin's use of the term "forces" to mean the "totality of external and internal events which the person perceives at a conscious or semi-conscious level as pulling or pushing him in some direction: needs, motives, desires, impulses, restraints, demands, questions, orders, temptations, [and] goals" (p. 118). Interacting with these forces are the individual's own cognitive mechanisms driven by the need to maintain a consistent self-image, to reduce uncertainty, and to preserve psychological equilibrium. Schein, like Bach (1954), finds utility in Lewin's model because of its ability to explain complex interactions of social forces that are not explained in behavioral or psychoanalytic models. "The utility of this model derives in part from this point – it focuses attention on the many forces which underlie beliefs, etc. and therefore on the manifold strategies which the agent of influence can and usually does apply. It thus serves to steer us away from oversimplified explanations of the influence process" (p. 119). Schein's definitions of the three main constructs in Lewin's theory of group dynamics are perhaps the most relevant to the study of therapeutic change processes.

> *Unfreezing.* An alteration by the agent of influence of the forces acting on the person such that the existing equilibrium is no longer stable. Subjectively, one can think of this as the induction of a need or a motive to change; i.e., the person who has been unfrozen with respect to some belief desires to change or abandon that belief (p. 119).

> *Changing.* The provision by the agent of influence of information, arguments, models, to be imitated or identified with, etc., which provide a direction of change toward a new equilibrium, usually by allowing the person to learn something new, redefine something old, re-evaluate or reintegrate other parts of his personality or belief system, etc. Subjectively this would be experiences of "seeing the light," having insight, seeing that the other fellow's viewpoint has a lot of merit, beginning to understand how someone else thinks about things, and so on (p. 119–120).

> *Refreezing.* The facilitation by the agent of influence of the reintegration of the new equilibrium into the rest of the personality and into ongoing interpersonal relationships by the provision of reward and social support for any changes made by the person. Subjectively, this would be experienced as discovering that others shared one's view, that they were pleased with the change, that the new belief was quite congenial with other parts of the self-image and other beliefs, etc. (p. 120).

Relevance

One of Kurt Lewin's students, George R. Bach, adapted Lewin's theory of group dynamics to the practice of intensive group therapy and helps to explain its relevance to De Leon's TC theory and residential teen treatment:

> The practical importance of field theoretical research to the group therapist is obvious when one considers that many of the studies of group dynamics are concerned with changing some behavior pattern within the individual, such as his productivity, by changing the nature of his social field. This is no different from the use of the social field of the therapy group (Bach, 1954, p. 340).

This complex process requires knowledge about social forces that may not be adequately described in developmental models that focus on risk and resiliency factors. Schein's emphasis on the complexity of eliciting internal change is important in understanding the process but also in explaining the lack of knowledge related to intensive teen treatment experiences. The individual is changed by "surviving" within the environment (Schein, 1962), but quantitative research that measures only a few outcome variables might ignore the full complexity of the subjective experience as well as the factors that may contribute to the potential for harm.

Before efficacy can be empirically studied, plausible theory explaining the construct relationships in the individual change process must be explicit (Harper, 2010). Empirical studies using an economic model may not provide a logical explanation of change processes and may be limited in their explanatory power. Demonstrating associations between deficit characteristics and poor outcomes does raise important questions about the relationship between social capital and outcome measures but does little to explain causal directions. The complexity of the change process may be directly related to the unpredictability and potential for harm in residential treatment and the reason such potentials have not been adequately explored.

Addressing the difference between thought reform and residential treatment, Schein is explicit: "What distinguishes coercive persuasion from other kinds of influence processes is the degree to which the person who is to be influenced is physically or psychologically confined to a situation in which he must continue to expose himself to unfreezing pressures" (p.139). This is very similar to the tentative conclusions offered by Jerome Frank (1974) and Barbara Frankel (1989) and it is relevant to discussions about teen programs and a youth's inability to refuse treatment. Schein's reference to confinement in the unfreezing process might help explain systematic forms of institutional child abuse. It may be that harm is most often visited during the "unfreezing" processes that are systematically designed to break through defenses (Chatfield, 2014).

Relevant to the use of confrontation therapy in TCs (De Leon, 2000; White & Miller, 2007), Lewin notes that unfreezing may require "catharsis to break open the shell" of an individual. In a similar vein but perhaps describing the more widely accepted practice of unfreezing as a therapeutic relaxation of defenses, Lewin acknowledges that "it is sometimes necessary to bring about deliberately an emotional stir-up" (p. 35). And relevant to the control of communication and connection (Lifton, 1963) and to the logic of isolating therapeutic community residents from the macro society (De Leon, 2000), Lewin explains: "Sometimes the value system of this face-to-face group conflicts with the values of the larger cultural setting and it is necessary to separate the group from the larger setting" (p. 36–37). Such isolation is crucial because "the effectiveness of camps or workshops in changing ideology or conduct depends in part on the possibility of creating such "cultural islands" during change" (p. 37).

Strengths

The strengths of Lewin's theory of group dynamics is that it is one of the most plausible explanations of therapeutic change in totalistic settings. It explains not only how, but why social fields influence individual change processes. Lewin's work is strengthened by Schein's extension to explaining ideological reform and identity shaping processes and by Bach's extension to intensive group therapy methods. Schein and Bach emphasized that Lewin's theory was adequate in complexity and depth to explain dynamics that are unexplained by behavioral and psychoanalytic theories of change. By utilizing a physics model, rather than an economic model, its simple logic makes few assumptions and lends itself to generalization.

Weaknesses

The most relevant weakness in Lewin's theory may not be in the power of the theory itself but in the way his work, and social engineering in general, have been equated with wild and exaggerated stories of "brainwashing" and "mind control" or simply ignored as irrelevant by clinicians interested in residential teen treatment. Just as De Leon's theory is strong because it is so widely accepted in practice, Lewin's main weakness may be that his ideas threaten our sense of free will and all that is good about American notions of freedom. Edgar Schein, as well as neuroscientist Walter J. Freeman (2000), and evolutionary psychologist Hiram Caton (1998), contend that these processes are not only morally neutral, but that they are the foundation of human connection and our ability to yield and love and bond. The ideas Lewin proposes are not guilty of being un-American but rather guilty of making Americans uncomfortable. This is unfortunate because practitioners who blacklist such theories or reject Lewin's ideas also reject their usefulness in explaining change and in improving the safety of change processes.

Military research in coercive persuasion found that coerced changes in some westerners "wore off" soon after repatriation (Schein et al., 1961). However, for the westerners who were able to find support for their new beliefs and attitude changes, they persisted. Because of this, Schein suggests the need to consider coercive persuasion in terms of a general theory of influence rather than a "peculiar, uncommon, or bizarre set of procedures designed to make man do something "against his will" (p. 138–139). He emphasizes their usefulness in eliciting beneficial change and then built his career on adapting these methods to corporate training and industrial applications.

It is possible to use the theoretical lens provided by Edgar Schein (1962) to consider the mechanisms of change reflected in the descriptions of many youths' experiences of totalistic programs. Schein used Lewin's group dynamics theory to explain how therapeutic change occurs in the resocialization of delinquents and adult prisoners: supports to the old patterns must be undermined, emotional ties to past connections must be broken, the total environment must provide rewards and punishments in terms of desired behaviors, attitudes and new beliefs, and provide models and new emotional supports within the environment. In this treatment process, new beliefs and attitudes are learned as a response to adapting to the milieu and driven by the basic need to maintain personal equilibrium.

David Bromley (1998) describes these mechanisms in similar terms and lists more than 30 different social theorists whose work is applicable to the study of this resocialization process. He is perhaps most interested in the legal rights of new religious movements but he generalizes his analysis to describe change processes within psychotherapy organizations, summarizing four essential elements that distinguish therapy from the process of coercive persuasion: 1) the process is distinct from spontaneous persuasion, salesmanship, conversion, and normal education 2) the process has an encapsulating effect that makes it emotionally difficult or impossible to exit, 3) it involves the elements of thought reform, 4) and it produces psychological disruption after the process has ceased.

Like Janja Lalich's theory of bounded choice (2004), Bromley emphasizes imbalances of power in the ability to shape perceptions of context, grievances and the ability to raise disputes. He argues that the term "brainwashing" is problematic and unnecessary because there are so many relevant theories available for explaining individual change mechanisms in the resocialization process. If we extend Bromley's argument to this thesis we can see the importance of systematic qualitative data collection and analysis. In order to utilize these contrasting theories for exploring the therapeutic effects occurring in the resocialization process and the unintended iatrogenic impacts, researchers would need to consider the first-hand accounts of those who have experienced them.

Baber and Rainer (2011) describe the way Positive Youth Development (PYD) theory is conceptualized and applied in an authoritative therapeutic community serving mostly upper-class adolescents. The authors argue that when PYD principles are applied within a controlled environment they are more beneficial than when used by parents in a family because there are no conflicting social values to contend with and there is no confusion about the expected behavioral responses when youth "violate standards" (Baber & Rainer, 2011, p. 322). The

55

authors do not address possible differences between the way adults label their practices and the way youth experience them.

Zimmerman (2004) describes three faulty assumptions the evidence-based paradigm rests upon: that there is such a thing as an average patient with average cases of a known disorder; that teaching, or treatment inevitably progresses in a prescribed series of pre-ordained progressive phases; and that youths will eventually give up their symptoms eagerly whether or not they initially are able, or want to. The power in these false assumptions is translated into word choices that privilege the perspective of the practitioner over the youthful target. By framing the outcomes exclusively in positive terms without considering the potential for harm, practitioners imply that the only possible or valid experiential outcome is beneficial. These assumptions may translate into approaches and perspectives that have the potential to deny or invalidate a youth's sense of integrity, credibility, and self-worth (Zimmerman, 2004).

The potential for harm in designing phase-like milieus assumes that spontaneous human development can be orchestrated in a one-size-fits all progression. When individualized treatment plans are designed to fit with the demands of the milieu, they may be little more than a token gesture, further objectifying and ignoring the full range of subjective experience out of necessity to maintain the schedule and order of the program (Zimmerman, 2004). Finally, where there is a lack of explicit criteria for determining the safe boundaries of persistent therapeutic pressures applied within totalistic settings there can be little assurance that safe degrees of stress are applied (Chatfield, 2014). These potentials for harm must be made explicit if antitherapeutic effects are to be mitigated (Zimmerman, 2004).

Early studies on encounter group methods among healthy adult volunteers found that some adults experienced long-term harm after short exposure to group sessions (Yalom

& Lieberman, 1971). How and when intensive encounter methods can be used safely upon youth in closed treatment settings is unknown. Our aversion to considering the similarities between thought reform and treatment has not only hindered the development of crucial program assessment tools, it has allowed us to assume that such dynamics do not arise spontaneously. Should we assume that it is only the therapeutic uses that will be unintentionally rediscovered? In his definitive work on therapeutic communities, George De Leon (2000) begins by acknowledging that many programs have inadvertently rediscovered the power of socially driven change methods by trial and error. Wherever programs engage youth in a change process that resembles Lewin's "unfreezing," "change," and "refreezing" phases, there is a need to ensure the process is genuinely therapeutic, even if inaccurately named.

Review of Research

Overview

In discussing what is known about residential treatment, a number of caveats must accompany even the simplest of statements. The term itself is problematic; like "brainwashing," it does not refer to anything specific (Lifton, 1957) but at the same time it is used to label several contrasting methods of resocialization, rehabilitation, reeducation, and reformation. This array of methods makes up a "pharmacopeia" of practices applied with any number of intended effects (Redl, 1957). Effectiveness studies measuring program outcomes often fail to define what they mean by "residential treatment" (Bettman & Jasperson, 2009). Very few outcome studies adequately describe program features or explain how and why their program works (Harder

& Knorth, 2015). The term "residential treatment" refers to an amalgamation of ill-defined methods (Whitehead et al., 2007) that are used upon a wide range of different groups of young people who have been placed for a wide variety of reasons to live within a wide range of treatment settings. Residential treatment settings are often referred to as "black boxes" because so little is known about what goes on in these milieus (Harder & Knorth, 2015; Palareti & Berti, 2009).

Considering the variability of populations, reasons for placement, types of placements, lengths of stay, types of treatment, targeted outcomes, and the range of care quality, it is not only difficult to make meaningful generalizations about what is known, it may be "bad science" to try (James, 2011, p.319). Numerous authors have noted the widespread problems with research quality and the limited amount of evidence to support residential models, but others argue that it is unfair to make blanket statements without considering the nuances of efficacious practices that are sometimes applied with fidelity and used for very specific purposes (Boel-Studt & Tobia, 2016). The percentage of "residential treatment" programs that fit this description is unknown.

Evidence-supported residential programming, such as the Teaching Family Model, the Sanctuary Model, and the Stop Gap model, have been shown to be effective but there is little evidence showing that these models are implemented with fidelity (James, 2011). The Positive Peer Culture model is also evidence supported but along with implementation problems, some authors point to concerns over the iatrogenic effects associated with peer-culture programs (Dishion et al., 1999; James, 2011; Mercer, 2017). It may be that large-scale trends in evidence-based practices make more sense the farther back you stand but it is difficult to know how useful such findings can really be. This review will summarize some of the findings of meta analyses on residential treatment, empirical studies examining the mechanisms of change, ethnographic studies on therapeutic community practices, and qualitative studies that examine youth experiences in a variety of residential treatment settings.

Meta Studies

Harder and Knorth's (2015) review of reviews and meta-analyses summarizes the findings of 110 outcome studies on residential programs examining the quality of research published between 1990 and 2005. They found that 83% of the studies described treatment components inadequately, without explaining the theoretical link between the content of treatment and intended outcomes. Their review identifies a range of outcome variables but they found that the studies in their review only utilized an average of 2.7 different measures. They note that past reviews and meta-analyses found modest improvements in psychosocial functioning while youth actually resided within the residential setting, but after release, the longer the follow-up period, the less convincing the findings. This general conclusion contrasts with Boel-Studt and Tobia's (2016) finding that when considering child welfare group care programs specifically, reviews show post-treatment improvements. However, a review by Lee, Bright, Svoboda, Fakunmoju, and Barth (2011) found that outcomes for group care programs are often worse than alternative interventions; tentatively concluding that some programs are more promising than others. Harder and Knorth (2015) also conclude ambiguously that "residential treatment might be equally effective as other types of treatment if evidence-based treatments are applied to youth during residential care" (p. 223).

Lipsey's (2009) meta-analysis of 361 primary research reports, dating from 1958 to 2002, compares juvenile justice treatment outcomes by modality and intervention type. His analysis finds that post-treatment recidivism rates, which ranged from 43% to 54%, were significantly impacted by youths' pretreatment characteristics. Overall, a significant amount of the variation in program effects was due to methodological differences in the various studies analyzed. And although the outcomes varied by modality, across the various types of programs there was little difference. Discipline modality programs were less effective than therapeutic programs, while counseling, multiple-service, and skill-building were most effective. In comparing the effectiveness of different modalities, there were more differences within each category than there were between types. Variations in dosage were not related to effects and most striking was how few of the variables were related to recidivism rates. Reflecting the theme of ambiguity in the literature, Lipsey concludes that good effects can occur even within lower-quality treatment environments and it is reassuring that effective treatment is not context-dependent.

Bettmann and Jasperson (2009) review the effectiveness literature and summarize some of the same critiques of residential treatment noted by Boel-Studt and Tobia (2016), James (2011), and Harder and Knorth (2015). There are methodological and definitional issues with research, as well as a general lack of theory. In practice, there are concerns about iatrogenic effects, unpredictable reactions to treatment, traumatic reactions to placement, and abuse or misuse of disciplinary measures. Bettman and Jasperson also note inaccuracies in diagnostic and placement criteria as well as failure to utilize less-restrictive milieus. Their review does find that family engagement is linked with outcome success but they focus their review on the deficits in the literature. They find that individual, group, family, and milieu treatments are not assessed independently and programmatic elements are not isolated or studied individually. They find a widespread lack of definition of the term "residential treatment" and find that program approaches are often labeled as "therapeutic community" or "cognitive behavioral" etc., without any actual verification.

Reviewing the trends and conclusions in these reviews, many authors seem to agree that there are widespread methodological problems, a broad lack of theory, and numerous ill-defined concepts. Additionally, outcome studies typical fail to sample among those who dropped-out or may have had negative experiences. Data are generated typically through self-report measures, which ask youth for information that could be self-incriminating. This raises the question of whether or not effect sizes could be biased in the positive if what is known is primarily based on the self-reports of youth who were successfully "treated." It is difficult to draw firm conclusions about residential treatment because what is known is mixed and ambiguous. Noting the potential for harm in some residential programs, in 1999, the U. S. Surgeon General concluded it was impossible to predict for whom the potential benefits outweighed the risks and therefore, residential treatment could not be recommended (USDHHS, 1999). There may be more evidence-based practices available today than there were in 1999, but our knowledge about the impact of substandard practices remains weak.

Explaining the Mechanisms of Change

Nielsen and Scarpitti (1997) conclude that although therapeutic community methods are effective, it is not clear why TC methods work. They present a speculative conceptual model (Appendix A) of the dynamics of personal change but these constructs have not been empirically tested. The inability to explain mechanisms of change in residential programs is a relatively new issue and new field of study (Edelen et al., 2007) that is becoming increasingly important as more and more states link continued funding to the demand that practitioners produce empirical evidence proving that their methods actually work (Pew Charitable Trust, 2015). Although more and more publicly-funded programs need to be empirically proven and theoretically sound, privately operated and religious programs may have less incentive to adopt evidence-based practices.

Edelen and colleagues (2007) attempts to measure individual treatment components within state-funded adolescent therapeutic communities using the Dimensions of Change Index (DCI). They find that three out of eight dimensions were associated with program retention but none affected youth outcome measures. Contradicting Lipsey's (2009) meta-analysis, they found that very few pretreatment characteristics affected retention rates or outcomes. Higher change-rates in three of the measured dimensions were associated with program retention but none of the dimensions were associated with treatment outcomes. The authors note that although the TC model is considered effective for adolescents, there is a limited understanding of how the treatment process is linked to outcomes. They do not comment on the lack of relationship between their eight dimensions of change and treatment outcomes.

Explaining change in adult TCs, Neville, Miller, and Fritzon (2007) conducted an empirical study to assess the reliability and appropriateness of using action systems theory (Shye, 1985) to explain psychological and behavioral change in therapeutic communities for adult prisoners in the United Kingdom. They analyzed observational data tracking the progress of

68 individuals in therapy groups during an 18-months period to track observable behavior over time. They emphasize the point made by Edelen and colleagues (2007) and Harder and Knorth (2015), that there is a need to know the theoretical model of change underlying the intervention in order to validate the assertion that treatment is logically linked to prosocial change and beneficial outcomes.

Action systems theory is based in personality theory, which assumes that although we alter our behavior according to context, there is a core consistency that defines an individual's "true nature" or style. Action systems theory presents a way to categorize personal changes that occur due to an individual's attempts to modify some aspect of their external or internal world. The authors conclude that the dimensions of action systems theory are reliable for use in describing and categorizing behavior change in TC environments. Like therapeutic community theory, it is more of a descriptive rather than predictive, explanatory framework.

Using a contrasting theoretical framework, Stevens (2012) describes change in TCs as identity reconstruction through a process of narrative reframing within a "psychologically informed planned environment" (p. 541). The author explains identity as "narrative consistency" and claims that narrative identity theories are more appropriate to developmental perspectives on the resocialization process. These theories describe the way an individual's self-narrative changes in order to fit their social environment and in this process of adapting, a new person is born through the creation of a new story, or "storied self." It is through internalizing this new self-narrative that unity, purpose, and meaning conjoin in a socially-acceptable way within the prison TC.

Gowan and Whetstone's (2012) ethnographic study of treatment in Arcadia House, a TC in the United States, explains changes to identity as a complicated set of responses to the demands of life within a "strong-arm rehab." Their study highlights the incongruence between the way program staff conceptualize their practices and the way residents actually experience them. Their observational study involved a six-person team of researchers over a two-year period analyzing data from more than 50 episodes of participatory observational fieldwork and 60 interviews. Arcadia House is a Synanon-type residential treatment center for men in a Midwestern state. Most of the residents there had been sentenced to treatment by the criminal justice system. The authors use the term, "strong-arm rehab" to characterize the mutual surveillance, regimen of group therapy sessions, formal sanctions, and confrontations associated with autocratic therapeutic communities.

For each resident, therapeutic change in Arcadia House began with public testimony about their acceptance of the criminal addict label. After this initial testimony, members in Arcadia House were expected to undergo a total identity transformation process. In keeping with therapeutic community theory, rehabilitation at Arcadia was equated with rebirth, and addiction was viewed as a symptom of a total personality disorder. As one staff member explained, "Arcadia was not in the business of constructing dual selves, but brand new people….a full resocialization" (p. 80). Peers were expected to regularly police and reprimand each other and success was equated with having the right attitude—expressed as constant "submission to the institution and the group, coming forth with the expected response in meetings, completing chores according to the many micro-rules, and suppressing any elements of cultural style likely to cause offense" (p. 83).

The authors note that autocratic TC culture demands that participants "submit to the program, without any sense of injury" while also "collaborating with the system that holds their lives at ransom" (p. 85). Alternatively, they might split themselves into two, "talking the talk" but "holding apart a more authentic self that was suppressed within the facility" (p. 85). Their interviews found that many men floated between the two extremes with ambivalence and deep confusion. During their two-year study, some clients were returned for treatment up to 18 times but staff at Arcadia refused to discuss the high failure rate. "The truth is, no (they can't make it). And that's difficult, because we're trying to sell them this philosophy that if they do the right thing, put in the work, things will change" (p. 79).

Subjective Experiences of Youth

The dominant trend in research literature examines residential teen treatment from the perspective of adults (Polvere, 2011) but there are a handful of studies that examine accounts of the actual lived experiences of youths. Rauktis (2016) is among the first to explore how youth perceive behavior management status-level systems within various types of out-of-home settings. The author notes a gap in the existing research about youth experiences of such systems and a need for more research that includes youth perspectives in evaluating out-of-home care.

The study collected data from six focus groups in Pennsylvania to analyze retrospective accounts from 40 adolescents aged 18 and over who had exited from child welfare services and had been in at least one out-of-home placement in the last five years. Treatment settings described included: foster care, treatment foster care, shelter, kinship foster care, boot camp programs, campus style residential, small group homes, and homeless shelters. Sixty-four percent were female and 62%

were African American. Youth described point and level systems that typically began with no points, maximum restrictions, and few privileges.

"I think you had three phone calls a week....kind of crazy, like limited you to the number of times you could speak to your family" (Rauktis, 2016, p. 96). Points were earned to buy privileges and toiletries, and to advance to the next level. Participants described loss of individual agency, lack of control over their personal schedule, and lack of access to basic hygiene items.

> You're just nobody...they control you, you feel no privacy, you feel not at ease. No one gets that, I mean we are people...we have feelings...they said that they're gonna take every kid-individual—and they're gonna break them down and they're gonna build them up the way they want them to be (p. 97).

Rauktis concludes that although youth need freedom and autonomy for development, in these settings, even the most personal levels of choice were impacted by ineffective behavior management systems that restricted appropriate opportunities for growth.

Polvere (2011) analyzes interviews with 12 participants to explore how young people, aged 16–23, describe the way they experienced restrictive residential treatment. The author presents youth experiences and perspectives as a counter narrative to dominant themes in the literature. The author states that these voices are important because those with direct experience have valuable insights on how practices should be improved. Findings describe problematic treatment practices such as traumatizing forms of physical restraint and distress in witnessing restraint procedures, disappointment with quality of treatment, and lack of reentry support. Participants described frustrating, hostile, and abusive interactions by staff and conflicts with peers, the experience of stigma and alienation due to lost relationships, a sense of being invisible, and feeling ashamed of their placement. They discussed the way stigma in social interactions shapes identity, "limits their humanity" and affected how people treated them on the outside.

They reported multiple conflicting diagnoses and being medicated for disorders they were later determined not to have. They also reported being diagnosed for normal childhood behaviors that were misdiagnosed as illness. They described how institutionalization itself can contribute to a youth's behavioral problems. Some discussed the relief they felt when they finally received a diagnosis because it gave their behaviors and experiences a name. Polvere describes the complex relationship between youth and institutional power dynamics revealing a depth of perspective into the way perceptions and insights mediate the intended effects of treatment. The author concludes that this type of subjective information should be considered when assessing the actual impact, outcomes, and ways to improve quality of care.

Haynes, Eivors, and Crossley (2011) is a qualitative study from the UK that is similar to Polvere (2011) in illuminating the experience of restrictiveness in residential settings. Differences between the two studies might be due to the contrast between U.S and U.K. treatment environments. The authors note that although reviews of the literature often conclude that adolescent psychiatric stays are beneficial to symptom change and relationships, less is known about adolescents' subjective views of treatment. Satisfaction surveys report generally positive findings but, as noted by Polvere (2011), the complexity of subjective accounts of authority relationships complicates such findings.

The authors conducted interviews with 10 adolescents aged 13–19 who had been in residential psychiatric care for at least two weeks within the last 18 months. Youth who were deemed not healthy enough to participate by hospital staff were excluded from the study and the authors note an important question this raises about the need to balance a youth's right to be heard with considerations about protecting their best interests by excluding them from participation in research. The main theme found in their analysis was the sense of "living in an alternative reality."

"It was just like completely different to anything else I've ever experienced, it's like I don't know, I just can't put it into words, how different it was" (p. 152). They reported a range of emotions such as fear, disgust, and confusion, triggered by witnessing violence, aggression and self-harm throughout their stays. They felt unnerved by unusual rules and felt restricted and disconnected, amplifying the sense of living within an alternative reality.

Contributory themes reflected feelings of restrictiveness and disconnection, and the challenges of new relationships in an alien environment. They reported boredom and annoyance with rules and routines, but the worst aspect was the loss of freedom and privacy. Participants felt scrutinized, infantilized, and increasingly restricted but as they made progress, they reported a new perspective and understanding of the need for tight controls. Regaining freedom and autonomy within the milieu was reported as an important part of recovery and associated with increased self-esteem.

They all felt disconnected from family, friends, and from their everyday lives, had missed out on special events, and were affected by how the stay impacted their educational opportunities. Relationships with staff were polarized. Like Polvere (2011) they reported value in being in proximity to each other's problems as it helped them feel less alone and provided perspective. Reciprocal and nonjudgmental friendships, and the simple process of talking and listening, were important for coping with negative aspects of hospitalization. These relationships helped them manage their anger and aggression. Also helpful were coping mechanisms such as mental strategies to normalize and rationalize the experience in ways that helped them look forward and to think positively.

The authors refer to Eric Erickson's (1968; 1980) theories of development to explain how hospitalization can be a threat if it impacts identity cohesion or moves them to an overly narrow and negative identification. They allude to a potential contradiction between the need to draw boundaries against their peers in the milieu as a protective mechanism against negative identity development while at the same time finding protection in bonding with these peers. They note that participants were constantly reacting to and dealing with their experiences in an active and responsive way. Avoidance was also an important coping strategy discussed. "It's hard when you're living with all that violence. I would just try and shut off. I'd disappear into my own little world, my own bubble and just exist in that bubble" (Haynes, Eivors, & Crossley, 2011, p. 154).

In addition to qualitative studies of group homes and residential mental health care experiences, one study examines youth accounts of treatment within a faith-based behavioral health care facility. Chama and Ramirez (2014) present a retrospective study describing program atmosphere, interactions with staff, punishment practices, counseling issues, the role of spiritual development, and re-entry issues. The authors cite a lack of research exploring the lived experience of this population and the lack of adequate services provided nationally in a wide array of settings. Their qualitative study focuses on a random sample of 30 adults who experienced residential teen treatment for treatment of Attention Deficit and Hyperactivity Disorder (ADHD). Participants described a "tearing down program" within a punitive, prison-like treatment environment. They described frustration with the incongruence between the program goals and the staffs' attitudes and behaviors. Although they described staff members as disrespectful and lacking in integrity, many expressed dislikes for the executive director and blamed the staff's morale and inappropriateness on the director's unprofessionalism.

Interviewees described systematic forms of psychological and physical abuse. "I did not like how the staff would like try to tell the kids that their parents didn't care. Or that they're gonna be in a facility like that for a long time. It kind of tears you down" (p. 125). Punishments included withholding food, public humiliation methods, and punitive actions. Participants were dissatisfied with the quantity and quality of services provided by counselors who were uninterested and untrained. Rather than addressing family problems, the staff only focused on youth behavior. "Maybe, you know, if they spent more time trying to figure out what the problem was in the home instead of, like, trying to change the person completely, you know what I'm saying?" (Chama & Ramirez, 2014, p. 127).

Some participants complained about the coercive nature of the religious practices but others felt the coercion was positive. "The week of prayer thing. That was very beneficial. They should always keep that and . . . they should have maybe like two or three instead of just one" (p. 128). Participants also discussed dissatisfaction with reentry preparations. "Once you're fixed you don't know what to do with your new [self] so you go back to the old because that's all that you know. So, once they fix them they should help them know what they should do when they're fixed. I know that would help me out a lot" (Chama & Ramirez, 2014, p. 128).

Conclusion

The literature on residential teen treatment is ambiguous. Many studies attempt to create knowledge out of ill-defined data with little explanation of how theoretical constructs relate to each other. There is often not enough information to verify the fidelity of implementation or the link between treatment and outcomes. Research and practice is dominated by the perspectives of adults who are the deliverers and measurers of what they imagine to be treatment. What is known is often filtered through the needs of adults who are driven by narrow questions about effectiveness that ignore the full range of effects.

Comparing the ambiguous findings of meta reviews and outcome studies to qualitative measures of the subjective experience, the relevance of first-hand accounts becomes clear. Adults describe residential treatment the way they imagine such methods work. However, there is a difference between the way practitioners conceptualize their methods and the way their targets experience them. This is one of several unresolved dichotomies that present ongoing potentials for psychological harm in residential treatment settings (Zimmerman, 2004). The potential for iatrogenic effects can be obscured by the recurrent use of words and phrases that enhance institutional power while invalidating the subjective experience of harm (Thomas, 1982).

Systematic abuses in residential care (Behar et al., 2007) may be dismissed as overdramatizations by news reporters (Boel-Studt & Tobia, 2016) or as a thing of the past (Reamer & Siegel, 2008). When researchers fail to adequately describe their treatment practices they also fail to distinguish their methods from coercive persuasion. Some autocratic programs utilize group treatment dynamics that are comparable to dynamics associated with group psychological abuse (Rodriguez-Carbarlliera et al., 2015). Institutional abuse is a "wicked" problem, defying simplistic explanations; requiring systematic research if it is to be understood (Smith, 2010) and theoretical approaches that address all of its dimensions if it is to be prevented (Burns, Hyde, & Killet, 2013; Gil, 1982; Rittel, 1973).

The research proposed here is informed by a set of difficult questions arising from noticeable gaps in the literature. When is residential treatment comparable to thought reform? Is there a relationship between our inability to explain the mechanisms of change in intensive treatment settings and the inability to predict outcomes and address systemic forms of institutional abuse? What are the safe boundaries of coercive persuasion? Whether or not intensive methods within totalistic programs can be used effectively, there is a need to understand how, or if, practitioners can use such methods safely. By exploring the way adults describe their treatment experiences and the impact of totalistic programs, researchers may be better-able to consider the potential for harm as they evaluate programs of all types.

3

❀ METHODS ❀

Overview

This retrospective study utilized two types of data collected during two different stages. First, an online questionnaire was used to collect descriptive and quantitative data for the creation of an interview sampling frame. Second, an in-depth phone interview was used to collect qualitative data provided by 30 participants. Chapter 3 explains the methods and instruments used in these two stages of the research. The methodological steps taken are listed as chapter sections in Table 3-1.

Table 3-1. Chapter Sections and Steps Taken

Review and Purpose	Three Research Questions
Research Design	Quantitative Data Collection, Creation of Sampling Frame, Two Groups, 13 Interview Questions and Follow Up Questions
Data Collection and Preparation	30 Interviews: Recorded, Transcribed, Edited, Formatted
First Round of Coding	450 Pages of Qualitative Data, Coded with 5 Primary Categories and Development of Subcategories
Second and Third Rounds of Coding/Sorting	2,354 Codes, Sorted Into 85 Sub-Subcategories Under 38 Subcategories
Analysis of Explicit Patterns	31 Topics Distilled by Counted and Qualitative Comparisons
Analysis of Implicit Meanings	Exploration of Topical and Thematic Patterns
Theoretical Themes	3 Themes Describing 6 Concepts

Review and Purpose

The purpose of this study is to explore retrospective first-hand accounts by adults who, as adolescents, spent weeks, months or years of their lives inside a totalistic treatment program (such as residential treatment centers, behavior modification facilities, therapeutic boarding schools, or boot camps). The goal of this study is to learn how adolescent residents experienced totalistic treatment programs and to understand the effects and impacts of those experiences. Three research questions were posed:

> RQ1: How are totalistic teen treatment methods experienced?
> RQ2: How do participants describe the immediate effects of the program?
> RQ3: How do participants describe the long-term impacts of the program?

The term "totalistic" is used here to describe an array of simultaneously applied features within a treatment milieu that include: strict controls of communication; a peer "policing" culture; intent to reform the "whole person"; regular participation in group sessions; strict rules and inflexible punishments; a prescribed system of levels or phases; and a central authority structure that governs all aspects of life. The present research is informed by literature that emphasizes the need to examine the lived experiences and perspectives of treatment recipients (Chama & Ramirez, 2014; Gilligan, 2015; Haynes et al., 2011; LeBel & Kelly, 2014; Polvere, 2011; Rauktis, 2016; Smith, 2010; Zimmerman, 2004). Although individual outcome measures are important to assessing effective practices, it may be equally important to understand the relevance of subjective factors such as the totality of conditions, how they relate to the quality of the treatment experience, and the full range of impacts (Farmer et al., 2017; Holden, Anglin, Nunno, & Izzo, 2015; Gilligan, 2015). This study is designed to explore a wide range of treatment experiences in a way that allows for a nuanced, critical analysis. Critical approaches to qualitative research seek to understand and challenge dominant ideologies and structures that impair and silence those who do not benefit from them (Glesne, 2011, p. 10–12).

Research Design

Design Overview

In the first stage, an online questionnaire generated information on six domains: Demographics, Treatment Overview, Treatment Experience, Opinion of Experience, Totalistic Program Characteristics, and Interest in Participating in an Interview. This questionnaire was used to create an interview sampling frame comprised only of participants who rated their program as totalistic. To screen out participants who experienced a less-totalistic program, an index variable was created. It was calculated as the mean score of each participant's responses to items in the domain, Totalistic Program Characteristics (TPC). From the sampling frame of participants who experienced life within a totalistic teen program, thirty interview participants were selected and divided into two subgroups based on their scores for quality of experience (QOE). To assign participants to subgroups, an index variable was calculated as the mean score of each participant's responses to items in the domains of Treatment Experience and Opinion of Experience. This comparative, cross-participant design (Yin, 2016, p. 256) was meant to ensure that a wide range of experiences and perspectives would be represented in the interviews. The subgroup comparisons were meant to highlight similarities, differences and patterns in the data to explore the topic (Bryman, 2012, p. 73–74) and to enable thematic analysis (Harding, 2013, p. 5).

Pilot Testing

The invitation, online questionnaire, and interview protocol were pretested for clarity, ease of comprehension, bias, and validity, using cognitive interviewing techniques (Willis, 2005). The questionnaire was pre-tested by five participants who fit the eligibility parameters for the study and were familiar with the content area or had previous academic training in research methods. The interview protocol was pretested by three participants for flow, phrasing of interview questions, adequate content, probing questions, and needed transitions. The first 7 pilot tests used a "think aloud" method, where participants were asked to speak their thoughts as they first responded to the questionnaire items. The final pilot test used a probing method that reviewed the responses from earlier pilot tests to ask specific questions ensuring that identified problems with clarity, phrasing, and comprehension had been adequately corrected (Priede & Farrall, 2011). Leading questions, double-barreled items, awkward statements, and missing topics were corrected prior to final expert review conducted by the supervisory committee. The invitation, full questionnaire including the consent agreement, and interview protocol are shown in the Appendices.

Recruitment

The study was approved by the University of Florida Institutional Review Board (IRB) Office in September 2017; IRB approval number UF-IRB201701655. Invitations to participate in research (Appendix C) described the nature of the study and were shared with numerous professional organizations, individual experts, clinicians, academicians, and authors who have written about this topic and related topics. The invitation contained an online link to a Qualtrics questionnaire hosting website. It was shared widely on numerous types of social media platforms and by individuals who shared it through their personal email accounts.

At the end of the planned month-long data collection period, the quality of experience scores were extremely skewed. In hopes of obtaining a more even distribution of positive and negative scores, the first stage of data collection was extended an additional six weeks to allow more time for recruitment of participants. An earnest attempt was made to distribute the invitation to all known professional organizations that might have access to potential participants with more positive treatment experiences.

Data Collection and Preparation

Screening

A total of 235 completed responses to the online questionnaire were collected. Twelve responses were immediately screened out: 3 responses by participants who were over the age of 17 when they were placed in treatment, 1 response by a participant who was 17-years-old when they completed the online questionnaire, 2 duplicate responses identified by the participant's IP address, and 6 responses failing the quality assurance test question shown in Appendix B.

A total of 223 adult participants who were 11 to 17 years old when they entered the treatment program, remained in the sample after the initial screening process. Sixty-six percent identified as female, 28% as male, and 9% as non-gendered, "some other gender identity," transgender, preferred not to answer, or did not respond. Of the 212 who reported on race, 89% were white and no participants identified their race as black or African American. All statistical data analyses were conducted using SPSS version 25.0 (IBM Corporation, 2017).

Participants who were placed in more than one program were asked to respond to the questionnaire based on their time within the one program that has had the most impact on their life. A wide range of program types is represented in the screened sample, but when asked to check all that apply, the majority selected "Therapeutic Boarding School," and almost half selected either "Residential Treatment Center" or "Ranch/Wilderness Camp or Outdoor Program." When asked to check all that apply, the four highest ranked reasons for placement were: "Family Problems" (77%); "Behavioral Problems other than criminal activity and substance abuse" (61%); "Problems at School" (53%); and "Substance Abuse" (41%).

Index Variables

To measure participant's perceptions about the totalistic nature of their program, the term was operationalized by identifying seven key totalistic program characteristics (TPC), shown in Table 3-2. These items were identified in the review of De

Leon's theory of autocratic therapeutic community (2000) and Goffman's classic ethnographic research on total institutions (1961), and informed by closed group dynamics theory (Grant & Grant, 1959; Lewin, 1947; Schein et al., 1961). Based on participants' per-item mean scores, an index variable was created to represent "how totalistic" they rated their program. Participants with a TPC index score of 4.0 and above were included in the interview sampling frame. These seven items had a strong internal validity (Cronbach's Alpha = .849) and when testing alpha with items removed, each item contributed to the discriminatory power of the combined set.

Table 3-2. Items Measuring Totalistic Program Characteristics (TPC) and Sample Mean Scores

	Sample Mean
Residents in the program were expected to hold each other accountable and/or report on each other for rule infractions.	4.87
Almost all forms of communication between residents, and with people in the outside world, were controlled or governed by rules.	4.85
For at least some amount of time in the program, all aspects of life, such as school, therapy, meals, and recreation, took place in program or by permission of the program.	4.85
Progress through the program required the completion of prescribed stages, phases, or levels of treatment progress.	4.83
Everyone was required to participate in group sessions that involved confessions and/or confrontations.	4.83
The program had a detailed and strict system of rule enforcement and punishment procedures.	4.82
The program philosophy emphasized a need to totally change, to be completely saved, or to be transformed.	4.74
Sample Mean for Combined TPC Index Variable	4.83
	Cronbach's Alpha=.849 (N=219)

Note. Items were scored on a 1 to 5 scale; 1=strongly disagree/5=strongly agree. Mean per-item score range: 1.00 = least totalistic/ 5.00 = most totalistic. Items are ranked here by the sample's mean.

An index variable measuring overall quality of experience (QOE) was created by operationalizing items identified in the review of evidence-based practices. The term "quality of experience" refers to recipients' subjective experience of treatment quality. In this study, operationalization of the term is informed by evidence-based practices such as the Residential Child Care Project's "Children and Residential Experiences" (CARE) model (Holden et al., 2010; Holden et al., 2015) and a review on the concept of quality in residential treatment by Farmer et al. (2017).

This index score was created by combining participant scores for Program Experience and Opinions of Experience. These domains differed primarily in the phrasing of response options and all items were measured on a five-point Likert-type scale. For the domain, "Program Experience," participants are asked to rate six items measuring how helpful, safe, fair, and reasonable the program felt to them. They were also asked how equally the staff treated residents and how easy it was to adjust to life after the program. For the domain, "Opinions of Experience," participants were asked to rate nine items to measure how strongly they agreed or disagreed with statements related to quality of experience. Together, these 15 items had a very strong alpha (.938) with each item contributing to an increase in this score. These items are shown in Table 3-3.

Table 3-3. Items Measuring Quality of Experience (QOE)

Program Experience	Sample Mean
How safe or unsafe did you feel in this program?	2.15
Overall, how helpful or harmful was this program for you?	2.00
How equally or unequally did the staff members treat the residents?	1.90
How fair or unfair were the punishments in this program?	1.59
How reasonable or unreasonable were the rules of this program?	1.58
How easy or difficult was it to adjust to life after this program?	1.51

Table 3-3. Continued.

Opinions of Experience	Sample Mean
*In this program, my basic physical needs were neglected.	2.59
I trusted the staff members to act in my best interests.	1.99
I received an appropriate and adequate education while in this program.	1.90
The program's long-term impact on my life has been positive.	1.84
*Overall, I had a negative experience in this program.	1.80
This program helped me to be a happier person.	1.76
*I experienced negative side effects from treatment while I was in this program.	1.67
This program provided me with high-quality treatment.	1.62
*I often felt a sense of dread while I was in this program.	1.45
Sample Mean	
Combined QOE Index Variable	1.82
	Cronbach's Alpha=.938 (N=219)

Note. Items were scored on a 5-point scale: Program Experience, 1=most "negative" and 5=most "positive." Opinions of Experience, 1=strongly disagree and 5=strongly agree. * indicates reverse scoring. Items ranked by mean score.

Each participant was ranked according to their mean QOE score. This score was calculated as an index variable assumed to represent each participant's overall perceived quality of experience.

Creating the Sampling Frame

The second stage of the study began with the creation of a stratified, purposeful sampling frame (Pidgeon & Henwood, 2006, p. 635) of potential interview participants who rated their program as "totalistic," as indicated by a score of 4.00 or higher. Measured on a five-point scale, those with a mean TPC index score of 1.00 to 3.99 were screened out to ensure that qualitative data were collected only from those who had experienced a totalistic teen treatment program. A total of 212 participants rated their program as highly totalistic. Seventy-four different program facilities were represented in the original sample of 223 participants and 71 programs were rated as highly totalistic.

These programs were located within 25 different states and participants named 4 different American-owned program facilities located outside the US. A diagram showing the first two screening processes is shown in Figure 3-1.

The two subgroups described below in Table 3-3 were created based on participants' ranked index scores for overall quality of experience (QOE). The higher QOE index score group was identified first. This group is called "group H" and it consisted of the 15 highest scoring participants who were also willing to be interviewed. Their mean quality of experience (QOE) index scores, measuring their overall reported quality of experience, were between 4.60 and 2.60. Five participants (33%) in this group scored their QOE below 3.00. The range was determined by the needed number of participants decided in the proposal stage of the study. A low-score cut-off point of 2.50 was determined to be the minimum for the higher scoring group, and 15 participants above this cut-off were willing to be interviewed. The low-scoring group of 15 participants, "group L," rated their quality of experience much lower and within a narrower range. Their QOE index scores were between 1.80 and 1.00. All index scores were measured on a five-point scale.

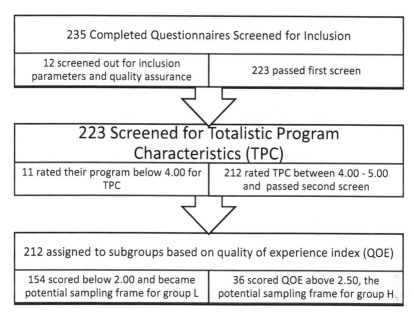

Figure 3-1. Diagram of First Two Screening Processes

The lower scoring group included 15 participants randomly sampled from those whose QOE scores were below 2.00 (n=154). In selecting higher scoring participants, a random subgroup sampling approach was not possible because so few scored QOE above 2.50 (n= 36). To help ensure that the two subgroups were distinct, those scoring between 2.00 and 2.50 had been identified as a middle scoring group (n=22) and were screened out of the interview sampling frame. A diagram showing how the two subgroups were created after the first two screening processes is shown in Figure 3-2.

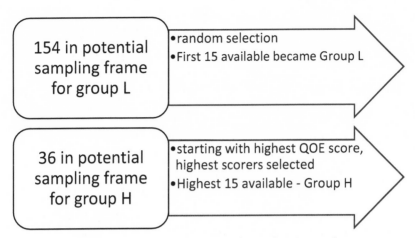

Figure 3-2. Diagram of Subgroup Creation After Screening.

Sample Description

The final sample of 30 interview participants is described in Table 3-4 and Table 3-5, which show each participant's alias and subgroup assignment, gender, age, intake year, program type, state the program was located in, graduate status, mean index scores for totalistic program characteristics (TPC), mean index scores for quality of experience (QOE), their answer to question number 34, intake age, and number of months they were in the program. Responses to question 34 are included because this question asked how strongly they agreed or disagreed with the statement, "The program's long-term impact on my life has been positive."

The higher scoring group, Group H (Table 3-4), included 9 males, 4 females, one "non-gendered" person, and one who checked "some other gender identity" when reporting gender. Their QOE scores ranged from the second-highest ranked participant to the 33rd. All but one answered "agree" or "strongly agree" to question 34. Group L, the low scoring group, consisted of 13 females, one male, and one person who identified their gender as "some other gender identity."

Table 3-4. Higher Scoring Group of Interview Participants Descriptive Data

Alias	Gender / Age	Intake Year	Program Type: State	Gr.	TPC	QOE	Q 34	Intake Age	Mos In
Lawrence	M, 31	2002	Wilderness: ID	Y	4.86	4.60	5	16	3
Ann	F, 38	1995	RTC/Outdoor: TN	Y	4.86	4.00	5	16	12
Greg	M, 48	1985	RTC/TBS: ME	N	4.86	3.93	4	16	18
Cee Cee	F, 44	1985	TBS: TN	N	5.00	3.93	4	12	72
Frank	M, 23	2009	TBS: MT	Y	4.71	3.67	4	15	24
Howard	M, 51	1982	Int. Outpatient: OH	Y	5.00	3.60	4	17	18
Yvonne	NG, 19	2012	RTC: UT	Y	4.71	3.60	5	14	7
Barry	M, 29	2004	TBS: MT	Y	4.86	3.20	4	15	22
Xander	M, 48	1985	Int. Outpatient: FL	Y	4.00	3.20	4	16	12
Uriah	M, 36	1995	Outdoor/JJ: FL	Y	4.29	3.13	4	14	14
Valorie	O, 28	2004	TBS: MT	N	4.43	2.80	4	14	26
Nathan	M, 29	2003	RTC/TBS: UT	N	5.00	2.73	3	16	14
Iris	F, 42	1991	TBS: ID	Y	4.86	2.67	4	16	28
Wilma	F, 20	2011	TBS: IA	Y	4.71	2.67	4	14	30
Aaron	M, 53	1982	TBS: ME	Y	4.86	2.60	4	17	16

Note. RTC = Residential treatment center; TBS = therapeutic boarding school; Int. = intensive; JJ = Juvenile Justice. Gr.=Compete treatment or Graduate. Mos. in = # of months in the program.

Table 3-5. Lower Scoring Group of Interview Participants
Descriptive Data

Alias	Gender/Age	Intake Year	Program Type: State	Gr.	TPC	QOE	Q34	Intake Age	Mos In
Carmen	F, 41	1989	Int. Out: TX	N	4.71	1.80	2	15	36
Tony	M, 42	1991	RTC/TBS /Outdoor: OR	Y	5.00	1.73	3	16	24
Mary	F, 21	2010	Wild/Outdoor: OR	Y	4.14	1.73	1	14	3
Dee Dee	F, 27	2004	RTC/TBS UT	Y	5.00	1.60	2	13	37
Elsa	F, 31	2004	TBS: Mexico	N	5.00	1.60	1	17	12
Bobbi	F, 39	1994	RTC/TBS /Outdoor: AL	N	5.00	1.53	2	16	22
Pat	F, 30	2001	RTC/TBS UT	Y	5.00	1.53	1	14	27
Kam	F, 31	2003	TBS: MT	Y	5.00	1.40	1	17	20
Joan	F, 19	2016	TBS: MT	Y	5.00	1.40	1	17	18
Sebrina	F, 27	2006	RTC: UT	Y	4.86	1.33	2	16	10
Quill	F, 22	2009	TBS: MT	Y	4.86	1.27	1	14	24
Ozzie	F, 24	2010	RTC: PA	Y	4.14	1.27	1	15	11
Ziggy	F, 39	1994	Int. Out: FL	N	5.00	1.20	1	15	16
Donnie	O, 19	2012	RTC/TBS IA	Y	5.00	1.00	1	13	21
Rudi	F, 44	1989	Wilderness: UT	Y	4.71	1.00	1	15	3

Note. RTC = Residential treatment center; TBS = therapeutic boarding school; Int. Out. = Intensive Outpatient; JJ = Juvenile Justice. Gr.=Compete treatment or Graduate. Mos. in = # of months in the program.

Group L (Table 3-5) was created by randomly selecting 15 participants from the 135 questionnaire respondents who indicated interest in being interviewed and whose QOE index scores were below 2.00. Among these 15, all but one answered "disagree" or "strongly disagree" to question 34. By chance, each subgroup included one participant who rated their response about positive long-term impact as "3," the middle value defined as "neither agree nor disagree." Also by chance, each subgroup of 15 contained 11 participants who completed treatment and formally graduated from the program.

In the final sample of 30 interview participants, the age range was 19 to 53 years old and each group had a relatively even mix of ages. The average number of months in the treatment program was 19.97 months. A total of 25 different program facilities located in 12 different US states, and one American-owned program located in Mexico, were represented in the sample of 30 interview participants. Their year of intake dates ranged from 1982 to 2016. Two interview participants (7%) were placed in treatment by state authorities: Uriah (group H) was court ordered through the juvenile justice system and Ozzie (group L) was placed by the state foster care system.

Table 3-6. Sample and Subgroup Comparisons of Means and Percentages

Means	Total Sample	Group H	Group L
TPC	4.83	4.73	4.83
	(SD = .41)		
QOE	1.83	3.36	1.43
	(SD = .78)		
Current Age	34.10	35.93	30.27
Intake Age	15.30	15.20	15.13
Number of Months In	16.58	21.07	18.87
Percentages			
Female	.66	.27	.87
Male	.28	.60	.07
Non/Other Gender	.05	.13	.07
White	.89	.87	1.00
Some Other Race/ Ethnicity	.09	.07	.00
Percentage Graduates	.59	.73	.73
	(N = 223)	(n = 15)	(n=15)

Twenty-eight interview participants (93%) were placed in privately-operated, privately-funded programs by their parents. Greg and Aaron, in group H, and Bobbi, in group L, were placed in treatment by their parents after receiving a judicial order. A comparison of mean scores and percentages across the total sample and the two subgroups is provided in Table 3-6. A comparison of reasons for placement is summarized in Table 3-7.

Table 3-7. Reasons for Placement (check all that apply)

	Total Sample	Group H	Group L
Family Problems	.77	.80	.93
Behavioral Problems Other Than Criminal Activity or Substance Abuse	.61	.73	.60
Problems at School	.53	.60	.40
Substance Abuse	.41	.60	.47
Psychological Problems	.40	.40	.53
Sexual Activity	.26	.20	.27
Other	.18	.13	.20
Court Ordered for Criminal Activity	.06	.20	.07
Religious Reasons	.05	.00	.00
Sexual Orientation	.05	.00	.07
Gender Identity	.02	.00	.07
	(N=223)	(n=15)	(n=15)

The Qualitative Approach

In keeping with the pragmatic qualitative research principles described by Harding (2013) and Yin (2016), the design of this study is unique to the research questions, available data sources, and temperament of the researcher. In this perspective, there is no single "right way" to conduct a qualitative study and what seems like the "best way" may change as the research evolves

(Creswell, 2007, p. 47). Strength in the design and implementation of qualitative research requires thoughtful "methodicness" (Yin, 2016, p. 14), a progressive sequence of deliberate procedural choices that evolve "organically" as researchers identify and engage with patterns across the data to develop themes that answer their research questions (Braun & Clarke, 2016, p. 741). Weighing these choices as options as the research develops requires an understanding of the logic of qualitative ideals so that informed choices and modifications can be made (Glesne, 2011, p. 3).

Each project is unique: the types of choices a research team makes in each stage of a study determine the shape, direction, and conclusions of the project (Yin, 2016, p. 84). The value of a qualitative research project accumulates as each choice along the way is balanced against the ideal. The researcher's knowledge is like a pivot point that the judgement "scale" rests upon. But rather than a dichotomous tilt between "left" and "right," these choices emerge on a multi-directional continuum, like a plate balanced on a ball. In this approach, quality is developed as researchers strive to understand the way each choice is a trade-off that may affect the decisions already made and the choices yet to come. Robert Yin (2016) describes this series of flexible choices as a "logical blueprint" that helps to increase the accuracy of qualitative research (p. 83). The objectives are to provide the reader with a level of transparency that would allow for reproducibility; to demonstrate consistent "methodic-ness" to allow for some degree of credibility; and to maintain a close adherence to the evidence (p. 13-15). These three objectives and principles of rigorous research design informed each decision at all stages of the project.

Qualitative Data Collection

Qualitative data were collected nationally in semi-structured phone interviews with all 30 participants. Each interview was recorded with permission, and each was approximately one-hour long. The interviews were loosely structured around the same set of twelve open-ended questions and followed the same basic protocol, and participants were encouraged to speak to what was most important to them. Prior to each interview, the participant was provided with a list of the interview questions (Appendix E) and a copy of the interview consent agreement (Appendix D), which was read aloud before the interview. This potentially redundant decision was meant to maximize their comfort by avoiding any unexpected surprises and by ensuring that each participant had an equally clear picture of the scope and purpose of the interview. To reduce the chance of a technical failure, each interview was recorded using two devices simultaneously: a Sony digital recorder and the voice recorder function on the interviewer's cell phone. All interviews were conducted by the primary investigator.

Regardless of subgroup assignment, each participant was asked to respond to the same set of interview questions, but each interview was flexible and unique. Some participants indicated that they gave some prior thought to the interview questions and made notes that they referred to when responding. Some followed the protocol closely without being asked to do so, some chose not to read the questions in advance, and one spent more than 30 minutes answering the first question. The interview protocol was developed as a "funneling" questioning route that starts from broader, general topics and gradually approaches topics more central to the research questions (Stewart, Shamdasani, & Rook, 2007). The interviews began with a general question about the participants' strongest memories about

90

their time in the program. The interview questions were organized into sections according to the research question they were meant to explore. After the interview, participants were provided with a $15 gift card as a token of gratitude.

Data Transcription

Each interview was transcribed through dictation using voice recognition software in a process described by Cabral and Sefton (2013). This process begins by listening to the recording at a slow rate of playback speed and while listening through headphones the entire recording was spoken out loud into a microphone using Nuance, Version 13, Dragon Naturally Speaking Premium Student/Teacher Edition software (2014). During a second listening session, the software's output draft was edited by the primary investigator for accuracy and then formatted in preparation for coding. The accuracy of the transcripts was improved as content errors were corrected but some punctuation marks and vocalizations such as "Um," were left out of the transcription process. Participants' tone of voice, the mood of the interview, their rate of speech, speech patterns, and emotional undertones were described in memos but left out of the transcripts. Long pauses and strong emotions were noted in brackets in the transcript. This method of transcription by listening, saying aloud, and then editing while listening again, added an important dimension of engagement with the data. The final word count for the 30 transcribed interviews was 281,048 words and a similar amount of data was collected from each group. The total count for group H was 139,498 words and the total for group L was 141,550 words.

Steps in Qualitative Data Analysis

Qualitative analysis began during data collection in the form of memoing in a research journal (Yin, 2016). Memos about the interview protocol, the tone of each interview, surprising findings, and emotional reactions were jotted in notes, in a research notebook, and in a research journal Word document. After the second interview, a comparison matrix identifying participant-driven topics was created. After the first five interviews, a comparative matrix of topics was expanded in a single table. This method of comparing and contrasting during the early stages of data collection led to further refinements in the interview protocol and the code categories. Throughout the data collection process, notes about possible coding structures and notes comparing similarities and differences were entered in the research journal. All analysis was conducted manually in Word documents and on paper, without the use of qualitative data analysis software.

First, Second, and Third Rounds of Coding

After transcriptions were complete, each participant's interview was formatted in a separate Word document so that a left-hand column of codes could be developed alongside the text. In the first round of coding, each code was assigned a subcategory label under one of five primary code categories: Context, Structure, Lived Experience, Immediate Effect, or Impact. The second round of coding involved sorting all codes into further, sub-subcategories, and sub-sub-subcategories. The five main categories were identified deductively, according to the research questions, but the subcategories were developed inductively, according to the content of the transcripts. These were refined and defined throughout the coding process.

The first two transcripts were coded with a coding partner to assess consistency in identifying codable statements and consistency in the code labels applied. Codes were applied through a series of deductive questions, first identifying the primary code category, then the subcategory. In the second round of coding, sorting to sub-subcategories involved questions about the context of the participant's statements, the perspective they were explaining when they made the statement, and what the emphasis of each statement was. This required the subjective judgements of the researcher and frequent referrals back to the transcript to ensure that codes were applied as faithfully as possible. In a very few instances, where two codes were applied to the same statement they were labeled as such in the transcript and either clarified or noted throughout subsequent analyses.

Each transcription was coded line-by-line and each code consisted of five parts: the subgroup initial "H" or "L," referring to high or low QOE scores; the first initial of the participant's alias; a code number; an abbreviation for the category and subcategory the code belongs to; and a very brief note about the content the code refers to. When all transcriptions were fully coded, a master list of codes was assembled into one Word document. Then, five separate Word documents were created, one for each of the main category headings.

Subcategories were identified inductively during a process of reading lists of codes, organizing them by category, rereading the lists of codes, and refining the coding process. In this process, overlapping categories, notes about category boundaries, and subcategory refinements were noted in a research journal where memos were kept throughout the coding processes. After the second round of coding, 38 subcategories,

85 sub-subcategories, and 7 sub-sub-subcategories were created. The outline showing this coding structure is shown in Appendix F.

In the sorting process, each subcategory heading was listed in two columns, one for group H and one for group L. As each code was taken from the master list and organized with other codes with the same categorical identifier, they were also kept organized by participant rank within each of the two subgroup columns. This created the ability to read each list of codes within each subcategory, by subgroup, alias, alias rank, and order of occurrence within the transcript.

After sorting each code into subcategories, they were counted to compare the number of codes in each transcript, each subgroup, and in each subcategory. Counting was used to check for researcher bias as well as comparative representativeness across the two groups. By comparing representativeness within each subcategory, it was possible to scan for the most obvious similarities and differences between the two groups. Counting of codes is not a robust means of qualitative analysis (Yin, 2016, p. 212) but in this study it was useful, providing an initial comparison of group-driven topics. The initial list of codes, organized by category and subcategory, was printed, laid-out in an 8-foot by 4-foot table and taped to a wall for easy viewing. By viewing and comparing all the codes at once, it was possible to see the most obvious contrasts and the most striking similarities within each category, facilitating an initial, superficial comparison between subgroups.

Participant responses to direct questions asked in each interview led to the need to distinguish between subcategories that were driven by the interview protocol and categories that reflect participant-driven responses. In developing themes and in interpreting the content of each subcategory, participant-driven topics were given special attention. For example, each participant was asked to describe their strongest memories of the program, the daily schedule, and changes in their relationships with parents. These are not participant-driven topics because they were prompted to respond to these questions directly. Within these interview-driven headings, the types of memories, types of daily routines, and types of relationship changes were introduced by participants and were noted as such. Participant-driven topics such as improved communication skills, witnessing unfair punishments, and medical neglect, were topics that many participants brought up without specifically being asked. In coding, analyses, and in developing themes, participant-driven topics were distinguished from those prompted by the interview protocol.

The total number of codes assigned in group H transcripts was 1,084 and for group L, 1,270 were assigned, with a total of 2,354 codes in all. This difference in the number of codes assigned is partly explained by two factors: One transcript in group L, coded early in the process, contained an unusually large number of codes; and two transcripts in group H contained an unusually small number of codes because the participants chose to speak at length about topics that were unrelated to the research questions. The number of participants represented in each subcategory was compared by counting the total number of participants who were represented and by comparing the number between the two groups. The code counting tables are included in Appendix H.

The Coding and Category Structure

Coding is a "disassembly and reassembly process" of identifying, naming, and organizing data in a movement toward interpretation and abstraction (Yin, 2016, p. 184-217). In this study, a deductive approach using four main categories of Structure, Lived Experience, Immediate Effect, and Impact, were developed to explore the three research questions posed in the study. A fifth deductive category, Pre-Program Context, does not directly answer any of the three research questions but is the code that was given to information about participants' lives before their placement in the program and is meant to help explain differences and similarities in subgroup comparisons, especially when considering family status, reasons for placement, and attitude toward placement across the two groups. In first-round coding, each segment of qualitative text was assigned one of five code labels, shown in Figure 3-1.

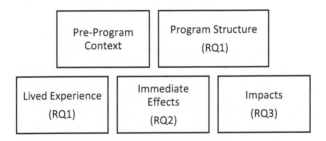

Figure 3-3. The Five Deductive Code Categories

In answering the Research Question 1, data describing the experience of totalistic teen treatment methods were labeled as one of two categories, Structure and Lived Experience. Structure refers to what was experienced, and lived experience refers to how the structure was experienced. This distinction between "what" and "how" is informed by phenomenological qualitative research methods (Cresswell & Poth, 2018, p. 137; Usher & Jackson, 2014, p. 191). Structure refers to more-objective details about the program while Lived Experience refers to the more-subjective experience of the program structure.

Research Question 2 explores the Immediate Effects of the program and this category does overlap with Lived Experience. Statements that described a felt, somatic, subjective reality or feeling were coded as Lived Experience and statements that described a personal change that occurred while in the program were coded as Immediate Effect. The category, Immediate Effect, contained the smallest number of codes because it refers exclusively to changes participants went through while they were in the program.

Codes identified under the category, Impact, are meant to help answer Research Question 3. Codes in this category refer to the way participants describe the short-term and long-term impacts of the program after release or graduation. The Impact category was loosely conceptualized as the way participants perceive the influence of the structure, the lived experience, and the immediate effects on their lives since exiting the program. Several participants acknowledged the difficulty in saying exactly what causes might have contributed to their life decisions and subsequent outcomes. The assumption that an interwoven combination of complex factors would need to be considered simultaneously, and from the subjective perspective, was one of the reasons a qualitative study was deemed appropriate to this topic.

Figure 3-2 shows the content domain for each of the five deductive coding categories. All coded qualitative data fit within one of these five categories. Statements about things that were unrelated to the interview protocol were left un-coded.

Statements about life before their intake were coded as *Pre-Program Context*	**What** they experienced in the program was coded as *Program Structure*
How they experienced the program structure was coded as *Lived Experience*	Changes they went through in the program were coded as *Immediate Effects*

Descriptions about the influence of the program after exiting were coded as *Impacts*

Figure 3-2. Content Domain for Each of the Five Deductive Code Categories

There are overlapping and interwoven meanings inherent to these five main code categories and these overlaps were resolved as the inductive coding structure and boundaries evolved. When a segment of data was relevant to multiple categories but exemplified a participant's current perspective, such statements were coded under Impact. Descriptions of how they understood complex causal relationships were given the subcategory heading, "Impact: pathways." Statements that provided rich insight, often after years of reflection on the way they have linked personal experiences to outcomes that involved multiple categories simultaneously were given the subcategory heading, "Impact: pearls." An introduction to code subcategories is provided in the introduction to each relevant section below.

Explicit Patterns and Implicit Meanings

The comparative design of this study was meant to ensure that participants with more-positive as well as more-negative experiences and opinions of totalistic treatment would be included in the interviews. This maximized the range of the data and enabled the ability to identify similarities and differences between groups. Although there were two subgroups of higher scoring and lower scoring participants, their experiences defy "good" and "bad" classification. In the lower scoring group, it was common to hear that some positive experiences were mixed in with an overall negative program experience. In group H, five participants (33%) made it clear that they had a low, or extremely low, opinion of the design of their respective programs.

Those in group H who reported that they experienced and witnessed multiple forms of institutional abuse reported that they eventually found meaning and gratitude for the program experience, but not necessarily gratitude for the program. These five attributed program benefits to growth they had engaged in as a response to more-negative treatment experiences. This attitude is reflected in their more-positive questionnaire responses. At the same time, they, and many others stated that their responses would have been quite different if they had been questioned right after exiting the program. These five are not treated as distinct subgroup within group H but they seemed distinct, as if they have "redeemed" a traumatic experience through their own healing processes.

Also making a simple dichotomous grouping difficult were the participants in group L who have a keen appreciation for the good they gained from intensely negative treatment experiences. Over the years, they have identified positive outcomes even though they describe the program design, the staff, and/or the general experience as abusive or potentially harmful.

99

This complexity emerged as the qualitative analysis developed, after the dichotomous subgroup comparative design was developed and the sampling frame was created. Due to limited resources, complex design decisions, and the sheer amount of data collected, the discrepancy between quantitatively-driven and qualitatively-driven group differences is one of many aspects of the project that is not fully developed.

The code counting tables in Appendix H present the number of participants represented within each code subcategory. This shows the most obvious contrasting differences and the "most-populated" code subcategories. These tallies reveal multiple types of information about factors shaping the research: potential coding biases; which tallies may have been driven by interview questions; and actual differences and similarities between group H and group L. This analysis led to the creation of the topic headings presented in Chapter 4, where each topic heading is introduced with summary tables showing the results of the code counting analyses.

The tables provide an initial overview of the amount of qualitative data that each topic is based on. For example, ten participants (67%) in group L described being recruited or transported to the program by deceitful or professional agents, or deceived and tricked by their parents, compared to five (33%) in group H. To be explicit about the meaning of such numbers when providing these counts, a caveat must be added here. One of the participants in group H mentioned that he had been tricked into the program by deception, but he only mentioned this in passing as if the experience was unimportant. A second participant in group H mentioned that the glossy brochures his parents saw before deciding to send him to the program obscured the reality of the place. These two are counted in the code subcategory for forcible and deceptive transport experiences. This caveat is meant to remind the reader that the counts provided in the tables do not measure or indicate the presence of the same value; they measure the number of times a code was applied by the researcher. Counts provided in the textual descriptions do refer to actual numbers of instances.

The categorical and comparative analyses were not the end goal and are not meant to provide conclusive numerical results. Throughout the analysis processes, comparisons of variables were constantly drawn across the transcripts (Miles, Huberman, & Saldaña, 2014) and noted in research memos. Each code was clearly defined but no attempt was made to define and list every variable mentioned. Where code subcategory counts are provided, they should be interpreted as the number of times codes were assigned. Such counts often refer to complex, loosely defined variables within the code definition that cannot be contained accurately enough to provide a formal numeric, or mixed-methods analysis. Counting was one part of the categorical and comparative analyses that were developed in order to identify summary topics and themes in the data.

4

❧ FINDINGS ❧

Overview

In an effort to present complete, fair, accurate, valuable, and credible findings (Yin, 2016, p. 221), two types of summaries will be presented for each of the three research questions: categorical and comparative. A thematic analysis, based on an interpretation of the findings reported below, is presented separately in Chapter 5. Findings in Chapter 4 are organized by research question, topical headings, and code subcategories. Tables introducing each topic heading summarize the code subcategories and the most striking contrasts and similarities between subgroups. The coding structure outline showing the hierarchy of primary code categories, subcategories, and sub-subcategories and how they informed the creation of topic headings is shown in Appendix F. There is some level of interpretation involved in any organizational structure but in Chapter 4, findings are presented with the minimal interpretation required to develop the topic headings.

Table 4-1. Chapter Four Topic Headings

Pre-Program Context (C)	Program Structure and Lived Experience (RQ1)	Immediate Effects (RQ2)	Impact (RQ3)
1. Reasons for Placement	1. Intake and Introduction	1. Changing relationships with parents	1. Memories
2. Parents and Home life	2. The Staff	2. Personal Growth	2. Social Impact
3. Prior Placements	3. Social Environment	3. Practical benefits	3. Trajectory
4. Educational Consultant/ Forcible transport service/ Deceptive Intake	4. Program Philosophy	4. Negative changes	4. Personal Impact
5. Attitude toward placement	5. Learning the Ropes	5. Making Progress	5. Social Skills: Improved and Impaired
	6. Program Design		6. Knowledge
	7. Personal Autonomy		7. Perspective
	8. Controlled Communication		
	9. Deprivation of Basic Needs		
	10. Emotional Intensity		
	11. Witnessing		
	12. Ultimate terms, frames of reference		
	13. Escape		
	14. Program Fit		

In introducing each section's code subcategories, a table is provided showing the actual number of participants who reported on a topic. As mentioned in Chapter 3, these quantitative findings are reported to help explain the code subcategories each topic is based on, but these counts should be interpreted with caution. In many instances, the complexity of the dynamics discussed by participants may refer to any number of qualitative elements that are not explained by tallies in the charts. The degree of importance expressed by the participant and how they mention the topic is not explained by counting, making the numeric value less clear. Some qualitative value can be interpreted through counting, but how much or what type of value the number represents can be unclear and possibly misleading to the reader.

Additionally, when coding and labeling complexly interrelated concepts, the researcher's judgement is an inherent factor to consider when assessing numbers. Reported numbers reflect the number of times a code was assigned according to the subjective judgement of the researcher. In these ways, the numbers reported are not accurate in an objective, absolute sense.

Counting, as a means of assessing the prevalence of topics, was one of the primary methods of identifying the topical headings shown in Table 4-1, but counting is not a robust means of qualitative analysis (Yin, 2016). It was used as an entry point into the most obvious trends in the data and as a more objective way to determine which trends were strong enough to be presented as topic headings. This study was informed by several resources on qualitative methodology, including the work of Jamie Harding (2013), who explains that although counting can be useful in analysis, there are reasons to avoid counting as a means of reporting qualitative findings. Under the heading "Find ways of expressing trends that avoid the use of numbers" (p. 100), Harding states that it is rare for qualitative findings to be reported as quantitative values even though counting is an inherent part of identifying themes. Quantitative values are reported in tables and in the text to provide numeric comparisons in an attempt to increase the validity of selected findings and their interpretation (Yin, 2016).

Where direct quotations are provided, the participant's alias is cited as well as their subgroup abbreviation, high (H) for high quality of experience, or low (L) for low quality of experience. The number included after the subgroup abbreviation is the unique code identifier number also giving its location in the transcript. A full review of the similarities and differences between group H and group L is provided in Chapter 3.

Quotes are presented exactly as they were stated in the transcript except in a few instances indicated by (....) to mark edited gaps in the transcript, omitted content such as unrelated side comments, or utterances such as "ah, wow," or "Uh-huh." In a very few instances, repetitive verbalizations were deleted without indication. Code numbers are included when citing transcripts to allow the reader the ability to identify the few instances where quotes are not continuous due to an edited gap or editing decision.

TPC and QOE acronyms. The subgroups, group H and group L, are referred to extensively in Chapter 4 and for the sake of clarity, it may be worth repeating an explanation of these acronyms. Group H includes the 15 adults with higher, more-positive quality of experience (QOE) index scores. Group L includes the 15 adults with lower, more-negative QOE scores. All 30 interview participants rated their respective programs as highly totalistic. The term "highly totalistic" is based on each individual participant's assessment measuring "how totalistic" their program was, based on the totalistic program characteristics (TPC) index score. This score was based on the items shown in Table 3-1. All 30 interview participants rated their program at 4.00 or above on a 5-point scale measuring TPC.

Pre-Program Context

The findings pertaining to participants' lives before the program are presented as contextual factors. The primary code category, Pre-Program Context, helps to explain some of the background leading up to their entrance into a program. These data were collected to provide an opportunity for participants to explain anything that might have been important to them in explaining their reasons for placement. It also helped to provide a starting point as they discussed personal changes they went through in the program.

Interview Questions and Subcategories

The main interview question exploring contextual factors was: What was your life like before the program? And the follow ups were: Where did you live and what was your family relationship like? And: Why did you end up in this program? Contextual codes were organized into five subcategories: Reason for Placement; Parents and Home Life; Prior Placements; Educational Consultant/Transport Service; and Attitude Toward Placement. Code counting comparisons by subgroup, for each pre-program context topic heading, are provided in Table 4-2.

As shown in Chapter 3, Table 3-5, when questionnaire participants reported the reasons they were placed in the program, the most common responses by female participants were conflicts with parents, depression, substance abuse, and self-harm. These reasons for placement were consistent with those described in the interviews. Systemic-level failures, such as predatory recruitment and marketing strategies or placement by child protective services, were also reported in the interviews as reasons for placement. Five (17%) (Ann, Cee Cee, Sebrina, Carmen, and Ziggy) identified sexual assault and trauma as relevant factors to their placement in the program. One participant's parents placed her in a drug rehabilitation program upon learning that she had been raped; another reported she was "thrown away" by her mother after being raped by her father.

For males, the main reasons for placement reported in interviews were conflicts with parents, rebellion, and substance abuse.

Table 4-2. Pre-Program Context: Summary of Topic Headings with Comparison Code Counts

Topic Number and Heading	Group H (N=15)	Group L (N=15)	Difference	Total
C1 Reasons for Placement	11	12	1	23
C2 Parents and Home Life	6	5	1	11
C3 Prior Placements	7	5	2	12
C4 Educational Consultant/Transport Service/Deceptive Intake	5	10	5	15

Note. C=Context

In describing their home life, four (13%) mentioned that one or more of their parents had mental health issues. Others described their parents as unreasonable, overly protective, or as having failed them in some profound way. Twelve participants (40%) reported a prior placement in an earlier program that was ineffective, harmful, or simply less impactful than the one program they discussed in the interview. The most common type of prior placement was in a wilderness-type program, designed to be a preliminary stage preparing them for intake into a therapeutic boarding school. Their attitudes toward placement ranged from generally positive, to being blindsided and attempting to leave upon learning they had been tricked into an intake room.

The strongest contrast in contextual factors between group H and group L was in the number of participants who were forcibly transported to the program by professional agents. Only one participant in group H (Frank) described a forcible transport to the program; however, six (40%) participants in group L reported that their intake involved physical force by adults. Forcible transport was described as a traumatic kidnapping experience that occurred in the middle of the night. Typically, participants were taken from their beds by hired professionals while their parents stood by, witnessing the removal.

> I was woken up in the middle of the night by strangers in my bedroom and my parents were in there too and just said, "Hey you're going to this school in Mexico," you know, it's kind of this blur of "wait…what?" (Elsa, L2292).

> I was kidnapped to be taken out there, my parents hired a transporter that came into my room and like, woke me up and searched me and took me away (Rudi, L299).

> I was terrified when I went because they grabbed me out of my bed in the middle of the night, you know (Pat, L1557).

Program Structure and Lived Experience:
RQ1: How Are Totalistic Teen Treatment Methods Experienced?

Two primary code categories were developed for data pertaining to Research Question 1, Structure and Lived Experience. The Structure category of codes was used when labeling what participants experienced. Statements describing how they experienced the structure were coded as Lived Experience. Even though the "what" is perhaps inseparable from the "how," the two were kept distinct in the coding process. Reporting on Structure, participants described four main types of totalistic programs: therapeutic boarding schools, residential treatment centers, wilderness therapy programs, and intensive outpatient programs. The program structure code categories refer to participant descriptions about: Program Philosophy, Program Design, Rules and Consequences, and the Setting and Conditions of the program.

Code subcategories under the primary category of Lived Experience include: Introduction to the Program; Internal, Felt; Connection and Communication; Meaning Making; and Harm, Punishment Contexts, Escape. The entire coding structure is shown as an outline in Appendix F.

Interview Questions

The first question asked at the beginning of each interview was: When you think back and remember your time in the program, what are some of your strongest memories? The second question was: What were some of your first impressions of the people in the program? This question was usually followed with a prompt to clarify which people, starting with staff and then later asking about residents. In some interviews, participants were asked if they noticed a difference between new arrivals and residents who had been there longer.

Data about program Structure and Lived Experience were often collected in responses to a single question, such as: When you first got there, did they explain the way the program was supposed to work? Or: How were the rules and expectations conveyed to you? And: Did you have the option of leaving? Almost all participants were asked to give a snapshot of a typical day: What was your daily life like there? What was the daily schedule like? If they had not yet discussed group therapy practices, or if they mentioned them only in passing, they were asked: Could you tell me more about the group sessions?

Because of the overlap between Structure and Lived Experience, participants described much of their subjective experiences while describing the structural elements of the program's philosophy, design, rules, consequences, setting, and conditions. In addition to the interview question listed above, if participants had not described their lived experience at length, one additional question and one follow-up were asked: What did it feel like to live in that environment? And: Did you understand the reasons for _____?

Research Question One Topic Headings

The topics listed in Table 4-3 were selected because in counting the number of participants in Research Question 1 code subcategories, they were the most prevalent subjects reported on in the interviews and/or were topics that showed the strongest contrasts between the two subgroups.

Table 4-3. RQ1 Topic Headings

1. Intake and Introduction	8. Controlled Communication
2. The Staff	9. Deprivation of Basic Needs
3. Social Environment	10. Emotional Intensity
4. Program Philosophy	11. Witnessing
5. Learning the ropes	12. Ultimate frames of reference
6. Program Design	13. Escape
7. Personal Autonomy	14. Program Fit

The numeric comparisons between group H and group L in Table 4-4 refer to the number of participants counted within the code subcategory that this topic is based on. Summary comparison tables are provided to help introduce each topic and to provide numerical evidence justifying their inclusion in this report. Before the name of each topic heading is a number: the first number refers to the research question and the second number refers to the topic heading number. These numbers are provided for easy cross-referencing between three documents: the introductory tables reported here, the code counting tables (Appendix H) and the codebook (Appendix G).

RQ1.1 Intake and Introduction

Table 4-4. Intake and Introduction: Comparison of Code Counts

Topic Number and Heading (Primary Code Category in Parentheses)	Code Subcategory	Group H (N=15)	Group L (N=15)	Difference	Total
1.1 Intake and Introduction (Lived Experience)	Introduction to Program: Intake, First Few Days	8	12	4	20

Only two participants (7%) described a comfortable intake process, saying that new arrivals were treated kindly by friendly staff. Eight in the higher scoring group (53%) and ten in the lower scoring group (67%) described their introduction to the program in negative, or strongly negative terms, saying it was traumatizing, shocking, disorienting, or upsetting. A total of 15 (50%) experienced a physically forceful intake or were brought willingly by parents but deceived or tricked into an intake room. They described a moment of realizing where they were and that they were to be held there against their will. Upon arrival, the introduction process typically involved a strip search and then a sudden, steep learning curve about an entirely new culture. The process was described as overwhelming, horrifying, and often tinged with betrayal and abandonment.

> The first thing when you get in there they take away your pants and shoelaces and see, you're wearing long underwear and shorts and shoes with no laces, basically, so you can't run away is the main idea, and just kind of seeing that people were wearing signs

111

and dunce caps and that kind of stuff, it was pretty shocking (Greg, H1218–1219).

I'm like, having a panic attack and crying, hyperventilating, and I like throw up on the way in because that's what happens when I have a panic attack (Donnie, L118–120).

We pull into these huge gates and that's when it kind of hits you, panic sets in and it's like "What is going on?" and I immediately was taken in to this tiny little room... I'm totally confused, and I really don't know what's going on or what to expect...it's like I'm strip-searched in like, this room full of, you know, strangers (Elsa, L2293–2294).

I went from getting admitted to right into a [group therapy] room with some kid screaming at the floor and it looked like his face was melting, it was just disgusting, and you know just talking about things that are horrific (Iris, H1401–1402).

RQ1.2 The Staff

Table 4-5. The Staff: Comparison of Code Counts

Topic Number and Heading (Primary Code Categories in Parentheses)	Code Subcategories	Group H (N=15)	Group L (N=15)	Difference	Total
1.2a The Staff (Structure)	Settings and Conditions: Staff	7	11	4	18
	Program Design: Staff	4	5	1	9
1.2b The Staff (Lived Experience)	Introduction to Program: Staff	7	9	2	16

In all types of programs, the staff members shaped the tone and social dynamics of the program. Both higher and low-scoring

112

subgroups reported a similar range of responses in describing the way they perceived staff members. In group H, the most positive examples included glowing statements.

> The staff was actually what I really liked. I had been in and out of therapy pretty much my entire life before then and I had never met adults who were so open about talking about how they've been through similar things. The staff were really open and trustworthy right out of the gate (Lawrence, H1130).

Three participants (10%) described program staff generally in positive terms. Overall, it was most common to hear that only one staff member had earned their respect and trust. Iris and Yvonne reported that feeling seen and heard by just one adult made all the difference.

> His name was [staff member], when he came onto the scene I was just kind of like—he was just very soft and gentle with me and instead of like, trying to yell at me in raps to get me to yell back and fight, fight, fight, he just was—you know a lot of times I say that we could've saved all these programs if somebody would of just given me a fucking hug but that's not the way it's set up, and so, he's the guy that gave me a hug (Iris, H1444).

But even the higher scoring participants rarely described their relationships with staff in ways that were obviously ethical and therapeutic. Yvonne's experience as a transgender person of color is also unique in this way (prefers pronouns "they, them, their"). Yvonne reported that it was their relationship with one therapist at the program that helped them learn to connect with others in intimate relationships while also maintaining healthy boundaries.

> I am one of the few cases. Few people will say that the program did help them greatly. There were a lot of people, a lot of people that I'm still in touch with, who were glad to leave and never look back on it because I don't believe that it did anything for them, and then they are also continuing to go in and out of other treatment programs currently. One of the things that I feel helped me the most in the facility was a therapist that I was placed with. Not all of the therapists at that facility were, I'd say, as good as the one that I got. The therapist that I was placed with was very, very experienced with a variety of groups and was always very, very explicit with me, very real with me rather than, I don't know, dancing around issues. I'm not sure where everybody else was with their therapist on that but I feel like that was one of the reasons I got as much help as I did (Yvonne, H652–653).

When speaking in general terms, participants in both groups used a range of mixed, luke-warm, or acutely negative phrases to describe staff, therapists, and program owners. "Some were not great, some were great" or "they were not supportive or empathetic." They used cryptic phrases when speaking in general terms: "I knew something wasn't right." When providing specific examples, they described a range of inappropriate or abusive practices. In both groups, there were clear examples of abuses of power and ridicule by staff, therapists, and program owners.

I think a lot of us were traumatized by that school, but some were a lot more traumatized than others. Like, the headmaster hated me and that was pretty traumatic and I never knew why he hated me. I guess I was a whole lot like him when he was younger, that's the only way it makes logical sense to me, he said I was a lot like him. He took great joy in publicly filleting me and in group therapy, if he decided to, he took great joy in explaining what was wrong with me and why I would never amount to anything in my life. He should not have been a therapist. He went to school for forestry and then ended up—I don't know how he ended up working with troubled teenage girls but I don't think he should've been (Valorie, H2238–2240).

Among the lower scoring participants, it was common to hear that most of the professionals working in the program were not trusted. Sebrina was in a program that provided individual counseling, but youth who were uncomfortable with their therapists were not always able to switch, or found that speaking up made things worse.

I had actually requested to be switched to a different therapist because we just didn't—it just wasn't a good fit, and that was like my first week there, and then she came in and pulled me out of class and actually yelled at me in the living room for wanting to switch, and she said that she wasn't going to let that happen, and then from then on out, almost a full year that I was there, she was not the greatest after that. So, some of the girls really liked their therapist and that was great for them, and other people were not so lucky (Sebrina, L687).

Participants in group H also reported complicated interactions with professional therapists. Seven (Wilma, Frank, Howard, Yvonne, Barry, Lawrence, Ann) participants in group H (47%) reported a great deal of immediate benefit from participation in the program but five of them (33%) also described unethical or questionable practices in neutral or positive terms.

> I guess staff members, you know, would have favorites, you know, like any human would, you know. They would play me against the others, you know, the ones, you know, who gave them a hard time. Of course, you're going to be more strict with them, so it really depends on like who you are as a person and how you work, because you're going to get into hard trouble every day. It gets annoying after a couple years, so yeah, so, and really it depends, but I didn't see any bad, anything bad with the staff members, they were doing what they were told to do (Wilma, H963–964).

RQ1.3 Social Environment

Table 4-6. Social Environment: Comparison of Code Counts

Topic Number and Heading (Primary Code Categories in Parentheses)	Code Subcategories	Group H (N=15)	Group L (N=15)	Difference	Total
1.3a Social Environment (Structure)	Settings and Conditions (SC): Soc. Environment	11	13	2	24
	Program Design: Soc. Environment	9	9	0	18
	Social Conditions: Peers	7	5	2	12
	Rules and Consequences: Group Contingencies, Peer Policing, Self-Reports	3	4	1	7
1.3b Social Environment (Lived Experience)	Meaning Making: Privileges	3	5	2	8

An additional factor shaping the settings and conditions was the social environment: the culture, tone, and power dynamics shaping interactions. More than two-thirds of all participants slipped into using program jargon to describe social dynamics and unique methods that do not have specific names in the outside world. Direct confrontations were referred to as "getting your feelings off;" staff-directed cuddle sessions were called "smooshing;" isolation practices were called "ghost challenges" or "being slept;" dorm rooms were called "pros;" and the super-secretive seminars in some therapeutic boarding schools were described with numerous cryptic phrases, such as "The Propheets," which do not have any meaning outside of the program.

Screening of questionnaire participants ensured that all interview participants had characterized their program as highly totalistic. Both subgroups described social environments that were marked by direct confrontation sessions, fear of confrontation, hyper-scrutiny by peers, and numerous simultaneous extreme demands coupled with chronic deprivations of privacy and autonomy. Spontaneous activities were rare, and when mentioned, they were noted as exceptions to the rule. In one program, spontaneous activities were actually planned into the schedule and called "spon time."

Only one participant reported that her parents had a good understanding of what was actually going on in the program. All other participants who spoke directly to parent knowledge indicated that their parents did not have full or adequate knowledge about daily life in the program. It was common to hear that parents knew the basic schedule but knew nothing about the seminar practices, group sessions, and abuses of power. In the programs that scheduled parent visit days, conditions in the program could be modified to improve appearances and three participants described this as a deceptive practice. Iris reported that the group sessions were "very watered down" when parents visited. Quill reported that although she was required to snuggle with adult male staff members as part of her treatment, she was told not to snuggle with any adults on parent visit days. Dee Dee reported that she thinks her parents were given a false sense of daily life because the schedule was altered for parent visits.

Parent knowledge was described as minimal, superficial, and controlled by staff surveillance and restrictions on parent/child communications. These settings and conditions all combined to create "a place of many extremes" (Nathan, H1775), characterized by overwhelming amounts of control that extended into every aspect of life, juxtaposed by lack of emotional and personal boundaries.

> They made everybody do disclosures of any bad thing that you've done in the past and most children that were there hadn't really done any drugs or had any sexual experience and that resulted in a lot of like false confession. We felt so pressured to have disclosures that we would make them up. Even if you didn't for some reason, they claimed that if we were overwhelmed with whatever our judgment was what would make it go away, so it was just a bunch of kids screaming things like "you're a piece of shit," like that is somehow therapy. Yelling at us definitely never made sense to me, it made everybody feel more disoriented because we never understood what the purpose of the exercises actually was (Quill, L1472).

RQ1.4 Program Treatment Philosophy

Table 4-7. Program Treatment Philosophy: Comparison of Code Counts

Topic Number and Heading (Primary Code Category in Parentheses)	Code Subcategory	Group H (N=15)	Group L (N=15)	Differ- ence	Total
1.4 Program Philosophy (Structure)	Program Philosophy	11	12	1	23

The most common phrase used to describe the treatment philosophy was some version of "they tear you down and build you back up." But participant understandings and perspectives on the process varied. Twenty-three participants (77%) made explicit references that were coded under program treatment philosophy. In some instances, questionable practices were described in beneficial but somewhat contradictory terms:

> The whole point of the program is to take you away from your support system and all the things that completely take your mind off of what's important in real life (Lawrence, H1145).

> The phrase that the program director would say all the time was "everything we do is therapeutic," and so you know, there was always—they're always finding new ways to poke at you so that you could explore your issues (Ann, H53–54).

> Basically, they would make you feel bad and then they would make you feel really good. So, you would do all these exercises that potentially would elicit negative feelings and negative emotions and then we would do all these exercises that would make you feel positive, but they would come with like, lessons...The intense emotional stuff that they put us

119

through, I think a part of it, or a lot of it, the intention was to revisit the past, hash it out a little bit, have an emotional catharsis about it, and then you can like move on from it and that was kind of my experience (Barry, H735, 784).

This same basic process was described in different terms by others:

They would keep you in the seminar room like super stressed, like your levels, and like the energies were very stressful, and like you are having breakdowns left and right because that was their goal to stress you to the point of having breakdowns and then build you back up (Pat, L1599).

Some described the program philosophy as if it were an unquestionable doctrine:

Donnie: Negative talk of the program was met with a consequence…

Interviewer: Did they explain why that was?

Donnie: It was because we were unhealthy. The program was to get us healthy and if we were like, not working with it then we were working against ourselves and our families (L102–103).

RQ1.5 Learning the Ropes

Table 4-8. Learning the Ropes: Comparison of Code Counts

Topic Number and Heading (Primary Code Categories in Parentheses)	Code Subcategories	Group H (N=15)	Group L (N=15)	Difference	Total
1.5a Learning the Ropes (Structure)	Rules and Consequences: Learning the Ropes	6	5	1	11
1.5b Learning the Ropes (Lived Experience)	Introduction to Program: Learning the Ropes	7	7	0	14
	Internal, Felt: Fairness	7	6	1	13
	Internal, felt: Buy In	2	5	3	7

In the interviews, most were asked about the process of learning the rules and expectations of the program and this process was often described as learning by mistake. In several therapeutic boarding schools, instead of calling rules "rules," they were called "agreements." But contrary to what the term implies, such rules only became apparent after they were accidentally broken and a consequence was applied.

> They tell you there's only three rules here, "no sex, no violence, and no drugs," so those are the only rules, everything else is called an "agreement" and they don't tell you that you're out of agreement until you break the agreement so the first few months are just kind of like, you know, you feel like a puppy waiting to get your nose smacked (Iris H, 1378–1379).

This process of accidentally discovering the boundaries was sharply contrasted by experiences in programs that began the treatment process by requiring new residents to copy word for word, a long, detailed rulebook manual. If you made a single mistake, you had to start again, from the beginning. An exception to the difficulty expressed by others, Lawrence, who scored highest for quality of experience in the questionnaire, reported that the rules made sense and were clearly conveyed by staff.

> There was no rulebook, there were staff members who were explaining it as best as they could and walking you through and getting you changed getting you, you know out of your civilian clothes and getting you prepared with all your physical stuff you're going to need for the program you know. There was a lot of explanation going on there and they were always willing to answer questions and stuff like that at appropriate times (Lawrence, H1142).

Twenty-four participants (80%) described a range of difficulties in the first days adjusting to the program. Yvonne, in group H, and two participants (13%) in group L indicated otherwise: Carmen reported that new arrivals were treated with extra kindness and Pat indicated that she was so relieved to be away from home that at first, the rules were no problem. Three in group H (20%) who reported the period of adjustment in more-neutral terms had also been in worse places (Uriah, Iris, Frank). Greg, also in group H, was transferred from a prior placement but explained that he did not have "too hard" of an adjustment because he tends to go with the flow. "I'm kind of a laid-back kind of person. I kinda go along rather than try to fight it. If you try to fight it, it would just get worse and worse" (1249). Even when the first few days were described in more-neutral terms, the introduction to the rule system was still described as an overwhelming learning curve.

RQ1.6 Program Design

Table 4-9. Program Design: Comparison of Code Counts

Topic Number and Heading (Primary Code Categories in Parentheses)	Code Subcategories	Group H (N=15)	Group L (N=15)	Difference	Total
1.6 Program Design (Structure)	Program Design: Daily Schedule	13	13	0	26
	Program Design: Group Sessions	10	9	1	19
	Settings and Conditions: Control	10	8	2	18
	Program Design: Level System	8	7	1	15
	Settings and Conditions: Location	9	5	4	14
	Rules and Consequences: Means of Recourse	4	7	3	11
	Program Design: Home Visits/ Graduation	7	4	3	11
	Program Design: Seminars/ Intensive Practices	6	5	1	11

Interview participants were asked to describe the program design by responding to questions about the schedule of a typical day. One of the program features operationalizing the concept of totalism was a prescribed level system. The initial levels were characterized by few privileges, low status, and less freedom of movement, communication, and privacy. With advancement to each successive level, the resident was granted more privileges, status, and freedom, along with more expectations to supervise and scrutinize other residents and "lower levels." Depending on the program design, residents could progress through a system based on daily tallies of gained and lost points, or a less formal system of progress based on peer and staff assessments often conveyed during ritualized ceremonies.

On the first level, regardless of program type, newcomers were typically started off on a "black-out" period. During this introductory period, new intakes were forbidden to contact anyone in the outside world or to speak to other newcomers. In some programs, all new initiates were forbidden to speak a single word for several weeks, unless prompted by staff. Along with restrictions on communication, first levels of treatment were characterized by fewer privileges and more deprivations of privacy and autonomy. Lawrence was the only one who reported an exception to this basic design feature saying staff in his outdoor program were more lenient on newcomers and then became increasingly demanding in the final weeks. For him, progress through the phases meant increased scrutiny and intolerance for infractions. His short-term program served as an introductory component preparing youth for entry into a long-term therapeutic boarding school.

In describing program designs, some of the most dramatic elements were the group sessions and intensive seminar practices. As a general finding with some exceptions, in the wilderness programs and in two of the residential treatment facilities, group sessions were less extreme than those described by participants from therapeutic boarding schools, other residential treatment centers, and intensive outpatient programs. Rudi and Mary described notable exceptions to this generalization. In Rudi's wilderness program, she witnessed and participated

124

in group confrontations on a youth who was ill and having trouble keeping pace on the hike to the next water source. After numerous peer-led attacks, this youth was motivated to avoid further confrontation and chose to vomit and defecate in his pants while he kept walking in order to keep pace (Rudi, L338). In Mary's wilderness program, participants may have been pressured to disclose traumatic experiences in a way that was unhealthy.

> How you did in therapy, and how you opened up, related to how you were progressing in the program so there was pressure to disclose certain things…the other girls had experienced sexual assaults and I remember them like, recalling those memories in great detail in these groups and you could just—looking back on it that, it was so not healthy for those girls. Like they were forced into disclosing that in that uncomfortable setting (Mary, L1092–1094).

The programs that incorporated intensive seminar practices were described with a range of positive and negative statements. Intensive seminars involved marathon sessions involving sleep deprivation, arbitrary level setbacks, personal attacks, humiliation and ridicule by staff and peers, and extreme forms of "anger work." Participants in both subgroups reported these secretive group rituals that they described as "culty" or as "brainwashing."

These rituals involved role play, costume performance, "towel work" (where youth bite on towels and/or beat the floor with them for hours on end), written exercises, group challenges, and guided visualizations where they were asked to get in touch with their "magical child."

The lessons were like, literally, phrases written on the wall that they would hang up. Some of them were like, not so outright and they were like, usually they would like have at least one or a number of components that were super emotional. They were like geared to really give you an emotional response. The culture of the school for a large part was based off a large part of this I think. You were like, crying was a good thing, like having like an intense emotional release was regarded as good. They also like, a lot of crying would be happening at these things, screaming and doing crazy weird exercises (Barry, H735–736).

Participants reported that graduation was contingent on successful passage through a series of progressively more intense seminars. Being dropped to a lower level meant repeating any seminars required, regardless of the number of times the seminar had already been "passed" or "graduated." Graduation from the program required the completion of all the seminars and to qualify for each seminar, sufficient points had to be earned through adhering to the daily schedule between seminar sessions. The first seminars were typically one-day-long and increased in length with each level increase, culminating in a multi-day series of intensive rituals.

Programs that did not utilize seminar rituals implemented varying types of group therapy sessions in the daily or weekly schedule. In three of the four intensive outpatient programs represented in the interviews, constant group sessions called "raps" lasted all day, every day, six and a half days each week. In other programs, group therapy occurred every day during scheduled, or unpredictable, times—and often lasted into the night. In two of the residential treatment centers, group therapy occurred a few times a week but with less-intensive objectives, and in one of them, group sessions were combined with daily or frequent individual counseling with a therapist. The typical day's schedule varied across programs, but the schedule for every program was maintained with a similar degree of totalistic design features and conditions.

RQ1.7 Personal Autonomy

Table 4-10. Personal Autonomy: Comparison of Code Counts

Topic Number and Heading (Primary Code Categories in Parentheses)	Code Subcategories	Group H (N=15)	Group L (N=15)	Difference	Total
1.7a Personal Autonomy (Structure)	Rules and Consequences: Walking, eating, bathing, bathroom, sleep	1	8	7	9
	Program Design: Physical Contact	6	4	2	10
1.7b Personal Autonomy (Lived Experience)	Internal, Felt: Autonomy/ Privacy	7	6	1	13
	Internal, Felt: Sexuality	4	4	0	8

There are some striking contrasts when comparing the way group H and group L described their programs' rules and consequences. Participants in group L placed more emphasis and spoke more often about rules governing personal functions such as walking, eating, using the bathroom, bathing, masturbation, and sleep. They described such controls as a dominant aspect of the program or a humiliating experience that extended into some of the most fundamental aspects of life. Intrusive rules and the violation of personal boundaries were emphasized more often by participants in group L.

> I kept notches in my notebook to count the days because I was just like you know, 14 more days, 13 more days, 12 more days of keeping these notches, and they found those notches at the end at the time we had solo and they took my notebook and I couldn't keep my notches anymore (Mary, L1079).

> I'll never forget…when I first went in there I was actually on my period and I just could not stand like people sitting there like looking at me while I had to like take care of that and everything, that was really disturbing for a long time, I think it takes most people a while to get over that (Ziggy, L1906).

> Masturbating was a cat-five self-inflict. You know masturbating. Like one dude, like I staffed all his seminars and the dude, he made it a goal to stop masturbating because you know it's against program policy and he was doing it in secret, like ridiculous, they just, ridiculous. A self-inflict could also be like cutting on yourself, making yourself throw up, stuff like that (Pat, L1591).

RQ1.8 Controlled Communication

Table 4-11. Controlled Communication: Comparison of Code Counts

Topic Number and Heading (Primary Code Categories in Parentheses)	Code Subcategories	Group H (N=15)	Group L (N=15)	Difference	Total
1.8a Controlled Communication (Structure)	Rules and Consequences: Communication, Connection, Content	9	14	5	23
	Settings and Conditions: Parent Knowledge	5	7	2	12
	Rules and Consequences: Isolation	5	6	1	11
1.8b Controlled Communication (Lived Experience)	Connection and Communication: Barriers, Parents, Each other, Outside World	4	7	3	11
	Connection and Communication: Parents and Family	5	5	0	10
	Connection and Communication: Bonding	4	2	2	6
	Connection and Communication: Isolation, Blackout	3	4	1	7

Both subgroups discussed controls over communication, information, and connection with others. However, in sharp contrast to group H, participants in group L spoke much more negatively and more often about these restrictions. Participants in group H more often phrased such restrictions in the positive, referring to the therapeutic benefit of being cut off from the world and forbidden to speak with people outside the program.

In general, participants in group L more often described such restrictions as problematic, painful, or traumatic. Some worried that their friends were concerned about their disappearance and were distressed at being unable to reach them to explain. Five and ten-minute phone calls home, which occurred once a week to once a month, were described as privileges that could be taken away for minor rule infractions. Along with banned books, censored letters, monitored phone calls, and forbidden music and movies, the content of personal discussions was also governed by strict and specific rules.

In describing uniquely intense rules governing communications, participants resorted to program jargon to express the range of ways communication was controlled. Topics not directly related to personal problems were referred to as "fluff talk." When newcomers broke the rules by speaking to each other, the program referred to this as "coalitioning" or "having a contract." Several described states of punishment called "black-out," "yellow zone," or being "put on bans," when other residents were absolutely forbidden to speak or even look at the punished resident. If a forbidden word was spoken and went unreported, the person hearing it could be just as guilty as the rule breaker and both could be accused of insincerity and threatened with a set-back.

Almost all participants described the way communication rule violations were met with swift and extreme punishments. However, participants in group L emphasized that such punishments often seemed unfair, too extreme, or involved humiliation rituals. Others described work punishments such as being forced to dig large stumps up from frozen ground or having to work outside all day in freezing weather while sick with a fever, for a single, minor rule violation. Others described simple punishments for violating communication rules that could last for days, weeks, or longer, such as carrying a bucket of rocks or a progressively larger rock for each subsequent infraction. In such incremental punishments, the smallest indication of communicating disrespect toward staff could result in adding another rock to the bucket or exchanging one's rock for a heavier rock.

RQ1.9 Deprivation of Basic Needs and Harm

Table 4-12. Deprivation of Basic Needs and Harm: Comparison of Code Counts

Topic Number and Heading (Primary Code Categories in Parentheses)	Code Subcategories	Group H (N=15)	Group L (N=15)	Difference	Total
1.9a Deprivation/ Harm (Structure)	Settings and Conditions: Deprivations	1	6	5	7
1.9b Deprivation/ Harm (Lived Experience)	Harm, Punishment Contexts: Medical Neglect/ Abuse	2	8	6	10
	Harm, Punishment Contexts: Punishment Contexts	6	3	3	9

Participants in group L were much more focused on program conditions characterized by deprivations of adequate water, sleep, food, and being subject or witness to extreme forms of abuse, medical neglect, and risk of harm.

> I remember getting really, really, sick and I was in the dorm and I was throwing up, but I was throwing up and had the shits at the same time, like literally at the same time, and that's never happened to me before and it's not happened since. But everyone had that nasty illness and I was like so sick I could barely walk and the staff member wanted me to go, you

know like younger students had to be watched by older students and I was an older student at the time, the staff member wanted me to be in the dorm with a much younger student so I could supervise them (Kam, L2096).

Some deprivations, like the deprivation of privacy, communication, and access to information, were enforced by design. Other deprivations were intensified because the staff assumed youth were lying or exaggerating.

I was really ill and they didn't believe me so for about three weeks I just kept getting sicker and sicker and sicker and then finally my fever was so bad that like I was cold and shivering and it was really hot, but then they still couldn't get a horse in there or anything so I still had to hike for two days to get out. Looking at it now I understand that I could've died, but at the time I didn't understand that they didn't believe that I was sick (Rudi, L285, 287).

RQ1.10 Emotional Intensity

Table 4-13. Emotional Intensity: Comparison of Code Counts

Topic Number and Heading (Primary Code Categories in Parentheses)	Code Subcategories	Group H (N=15)	Group L (N=15)	Difference	Total
1.10 Emotional Intensity (Lived Experience)	Internal, Felt: Overwhelm, Devastation	4	6	2	10
	Internal, Felt: Disorientation, Shock	4	6	2	10
	Internal, Felt: Fear	6	4	2	10

The emotional intensity of daily life was often described as an important feature of the lived experience. "It was stressful, it was nonstop stress, all I could think about was how to get out of there, you know?" (Aaron, H1997). The experience of being overloaded with the amount of information and emotion in part because of the nonstop stress of "being poked at" and the terrifying experience of being publicly confronted, led to a daily experience of overwhelming, if not traumatizing intensity. Dee Dee described how the intense demand for compliance was made more uncomfortable when the expectations were unclear. She knew that "fluff talk" was forbidden but how it was defined was unclear.

> It made no sense to me, like it wasn't logical, and I have always been someone, been like "tell me why!" And so, none of it made sense to me and I wanted to question but questioning it was its own—was against the rules you know. So it was difficult, and I found that being held against me, kind of in its own cycle— well, you questioning it is against the rules. So, some things are very easy, you only have three minutes in the bathroom or you're late, you get a consequence, and other things like, like wondering about what is "fluff," right? And defining that was very rough because you know, it could be birds or something that I could not talk about, it was insane (Dee Dee, L387–389).

Participants described an environment where there was tremendous pressure to respond correctly to all expectations at all times, but some reported that the acceptable way to comply with these expectations was often unclear and ambiguous.

I don't remember them explaining it, I just remember being in shock, but I do remember pretty much the entire time I was there never really understanding what I was supposed to be doing, it was this huge mystery, nothing was really clear (Tony, L944).

Nathan described the constant pressure and threat of unpredictable punishments as a sense of oppression. "It felt like all the moments that I was happy there were a reprieve from the constant, like, oppression" (H1791–1792). He explained that his favorite time of day was when he was finally allowed to go to sleep and was left alone, and his least favorite time of day was waking up in the morning. However, he also reported benefiting from the extremely intimate bonding that occurred in the group sessions.

It's hard to sometimes to think of it that way, the way that it's helped me. I think that primarily a lot of the ways that it helped me is the individual connections I made with certain staff members and my peers there. I think that's where most of—now to its credit [the program] is "therapy through peers in connection" and all that—but I'd like to think that a lot of what helped me was the initiative of the people rather than the facility. I don't really think that they deserve all the credit for the kindness and the emotional labor that people put into understanding me and listening to me, as well as sharing themselves with me (Nathan, H1782–1783).

RQ1.11 Witnessing

Table 4-14. Witnessing: Comparison of Code Counts

Topic Number and Heading (Primary Code Category in Parentheses)	Code Subcategory	Group H (N=15)	Group L (N=15)	Differ- ence	Total
1.11 Witnessing (Lived Experience)	Connection and Communication: Witnessing	8	9	1	17

Another important aspect of the program experience for both subgroups was the learning and visceral impact that occurred through witnessing the experiences of others' in the program. The most positive aspects of witnessing were described in terms of seeing others grow or make themselves vulnerable by disclosing secrets about the past and receiving acceptance in group sessions.

> I saw for example a teammate with an incredible display of vulnerability, in great difficulty, talking about having had as a young man or as a kid having an incestuous relationship with his brothers and the acceptance of everyone in the room and the encouragement and support was really remarkable (Nathan, H1772).

Other's mentioned witnessing shocking behavior by residents or terrifying behavior by staff as one of their strongest current memories or as one of the first things they remember about their introduction to the program culture. One of the most prevalent ways that the witnessing experience was described was in terms of shocking and harmful behavior. In one program, staff members placed chronic misbehavers in a boxing ring and while the rest of the group watched, the misbehaver was beaten up by a larger resident in order to teach them humility. One participant in this study witnessed a peer's death caused by medical complications brought on by this method of punishment. In other programs, participants witnessed brutal and unfair punishments and described their memories as if haunted by them. For some, what lingers is the feeling of helplessness when their conscience compelled them to intervene, but they chose not to out of fear of being punished themselves. Higher and lower scoring participants in both subgroups witnessed questionable forms of treatment.

> We had a kid, a lot of kids who were on the [autism] spectrum, but you know that wasn't something we said about kids back in the late 80s, early 90s, they were just weirdos, but to have that kind of noise and sensory overload to those kids, I think about it every day, it's like giving me chills right now how terrifying it must've been. It was just, it's so abusive it turns my stomach to this day (Iris, H1405, 1407).

> I was never restrained but I did see lots of other girls get restrained and it wasn't necessarily, you know it's a really specific process the restraint, they would push some kind of button and staff would come running from the other buildings or whatever and they would all come in and hold someone down and it, it wasn't necessarily because the person was being violent, in fact I saw where someone didn't want to come to group therapy in the center of the room and she just wanted to stay on her bed and they said "come on you have to come, you get to go to group therapy" and she said "No, I'm not going" and they said "Okay, well we're going to help you up" and she said "No" and they started to help her up, she kind of resisted and so then they came in and restrained her for resisting, so it was really crazy (Ann, H30).

RQ1.12 Ultimate Terms and Frames of Reference

Table 4-15. Ultimate Terms and Frames of Reference: Comparison of Code Counts

Topic Number and Heading (Primary Code Categories in Parentheses)	Code Subcategories	Group H (N=15)	Group L (N=15)	Differ- ence	Total
1.12 Ultimate Terms/ Compara- tive References (Lived Experience)	Meaning Making: How Challenging	6	4	2	10
	Meaning Making: Frames of Comparative Reference	4	2	2	6

One of the ways the two subgroups are similar is in the way participants in each group described the program experience in ultimate terms. Their time in the program, regardless of their opinions about the structure or the way it affected them, was almost always described in ultimate terms: the hardest, the worst, the most miserable, the most challenging, or the most rewarding.

> I hated being awakened at 6 o'clock every morning and this, like it's brutal you know, "Everybody get up!" you know, like every—what's the song they play in the military with the bugle you know? It was-n't, it wasn't quite like that, but it was almost like that. And then it was just hard, every day, and so to say that I adapted to it, I mean don't get me wrong—I can like, I feel like it was probably the most valuable ex-perience of my life and I'm so grateful that I did it and if my daughter were to start acting up the way I was acting up and that program was still available I would send her in a heartbeat, but it was awful (Ann, H51–52).

137

Participants in both groups framed the experience in terms of other programs they had been in or compared the rules and dynamics to what they were accustomed to. Those without a point of reference or without a "worse" place to compare it to, were perhaps disadvantaged in that way.

> I was in juvenile and the prior program was a pretty secure facility so the transition to something that's out in the middle of the woods, and I mean we slept in these tents that were made out of pine trees. And these people that were our counselors, so to speak, were not dressed in uniform, and basically were regular people. My first impressions, without actually getting to know anybody, was to say, "I'm glad to be here, this is a lot different than where I've been (Uriah, H500–501).

> Some of it was weird, like you can't touch people's hair or talk in the bathroom, like those are things you just don't get used to, wearing socks all the time, stuff like that, but a lot of the basic rules, they were more harsh at my mom's house, my mom's punishment was like 5 million times harsher than any punishment, at least at the beginning (Pat, L1564).

RQ1.13 Escape

Table 4-16. Escape: Comparison of Code Counts

Topic Number and Heading (Primary Code Categories in Parentheses)	Code Subcategories	Group H (N=15)	Group L (N=15)	Difference	Total
1.13 Escape (Lived Experience)	Harm, Punishment Contexts: Escape/Resistance	8	6	2	14

Almost all participants explicitly indicated that they were unable to leave the program. Some programs were located in wilderness areas of the Rocky Mountains, other wilderness areas, or remote desert settings. The remoteness of the facility was a primary barrier to escape and another was the likelihood of being physically stopped by staff. Bobbi reported that they were afraid to escape because they were told stories of locals shooting at runaways. Lawrence reported that there was no use trying because private agents called "bounty hunters," routinely picked up any escapees and returned them to the program. Iris and Greg (group H) did manage to escape but were brought back after weeks or months, and subsequently completed treatment. Aaron (group H) made up lies about an actual medical condition he did have, in order to be taken to the hospital and privately speak with his parents to convince them to take him home. Cee Cee (group H) lied about being pregnant, and Quill (group L) made up lies about engaging in sexual activities—both hoped that it would lead to their release. For Ozzie, leaving without permission was the only action she could take to experience any sense of control over her life.

> I did not feel like I had any personal agency or control over my circumstances, the only means of exerting control would be to leave the building when you weren't supposed to (Ozzie, L1691).

Five in the higher scoring group (Iris, Greg, Cee Cee, Xander, Howard) had escaped or tried to.

> I specifically remember trying to leave the program, to leave the building when I realized where I was, when I was told where I was. And as I tried to bolt out of the door and run away, a female staff member stood in my way and I came out of the door swinging

139

and she said "You wouldn't hit a girl would you?" and I said "No, I won't," she said "Good"—she thumped me in the chest and pushed me back in the room and then five or six people came in behind to make sure that I wasn't running away (Howard, H2043–2044).

Others did not try to escape because they knew they would be unsuccessful.

Staff were actually required to wear running shoes because we would have girls that would try to run away all the time. Like all the time we had run drills where someone who was a higher level like five or six, staff would come get them and tell them to go hide somewhere and then tell everybody like "this girl ran away" and everybody was like on lockdown when that happened. And so that happened so often where girls would try to run but staff would actually be able to tackle them in the parking lot and take them down and bring them back into the house and then of course we would be put back on safety for as long as they deemed necessary, so we absolutely had no choice of leaving (Sebrina, L684).

RQ1.14 Program Fit

Table 4-17. Program Fit: Comparison of Code Counts

Topic Number and Heading (Primary Code Categories in Parentheses)	Code Subcategories	Group H (N=15)	Group L (N=15)	Difference	Total
1.14a Program/Social Fit (Structure)	Rules and Consequences: Physical and Crazy Punishments, Rules	3	8	5	11
1.14b Program/Social Fit (Lived Experience)	Introduction to Program: Goodness of Fit	9	8	1	17

When comparing subgroups, another striking difference in lived experience is that more of the higher scoring participants indicated that they felt well-matched with features of the program but lower scoring participants described numerous ways the program was a poor fit. The highest scoring participant, Lawrence, felt scared at first but quickly came to relish his time in the woods and the team building activities. He was placed there against his will but quickly felt a strong sense of empowerment and increased self-confidence.

> I remember being scared and nervous and then by the time I was ready to leave I didn't want to because I had really found something in myself that I didn't know existed....I mean, so in nine weeks it went from "I'm nervous about what the activity is gonna be tomorrow" to when I was ready to leave, to "I can't wait to find out what the activity is because I'm gonna knock it out of the park" you know? (Lawrence, H1158, 1162).

Lawrence was in his late teens when he was placed in the program and his experience is essentially opposite to what Mary reported: "From the very beginning of the program—when I said one of the biggest emotions for me was pure confusion, fear and confusion, well I was tricked into going, my parents told me we were having brunch with a family member out of town" (Mary, L1049). At 14, taken to a house in the woods, she learned that she would be spending several weeks on a hike with strangers, walking all day, every day, in silence. She was taken to the basement, strip searched and put into a windowless van. "They took one of us at a time into the back room and did a strip search, which at the time I had no idea what was happening, I didn't know who these people were, where my parents were, anything" (1058). She was forbidden to speak or ask questions on the drive through the night.

> They put us in a van that had no windows, so we didn't see where we were going. They didn't explain much. One of the things that they said over and over and over was "no questions, no questions," so obviously a lot of us were asking a lot of questions, were trying to. I wasn't necessarily, I was just kind of stunned at this time, but yeah it was a pretty quiet ride for about a 10-hour drive (1059–1060).

The van stopped around 4:00 A.M., she was given a backpack that she could not lift. Unlike Lawrence, Mary was physically unprepared for the program, weighing 105 pounds, her daily life consisted of walking with a 65-pound backpack, eating beans and rice, and drinking small amounts of collected water, sometimes muddy—always treated with iodine. Her hike was three weeks long and she still experiences physical pain where the backpack straps cut into her shoulders.

> Every day you would pack your stuff up, eat, and keep hiking in a straight, single file line, staff at the front, staff at the middle, staff at the back, no talking. And then they had like interval bathroom breaks and water consumption breaks. They would monitor how much water you drink (1069).

Lawrence and Mary were both sent to treatment for marijuana use. Lawrence reports that he had a substance abuse problem and was out of control, but Mary had only experimented with it a few times. Before placement, she was mildly depressed, struggling with puberty, and her best friend had recently moved away. She was sent to her program after being caught smoking marijuana in a public park.

In addition to basic physical competence, participants in both subgroups described program fit in social terms. The highest scoring participants reported feeling like they fit somewhere in the middle in terms of the intensity of their lives prior to the program, or they felt matched with others who had similar personality traits.

> The intake process, I felt very at home with the residents, I wasn't so sure about the staff members. The first couple of weeks were really hard. It was something that was only partially voluntary but after a couple of weeks, after things evened out a little bit, I did feel much more welcome, especially by the people I was living with (Yvonne, H609–611).

In contrast, lower scoring participants reported that they were placed with youth with much worse problems, disagreed with the program philosophy, questioned the arbitrary rules, the one-size-fits-all approach, or the reason for the seminar rituals.

> They definitely didn't help me with any of my actual non-imaginary problems and I remember thinking when I was there "Why have they not adjusted the therapy program to account for like more than one type of kid?" and I remember saying that to staff and them telling me I was wrong because everybody has to do the "insights," like the "Propheets" they called them (Quill, L1500–1502).

For some, the feeling of fitting-in well with others and with the program could vary with the cabin or the team they were placed with. Ann reported feeling glad she was placed in "the cabin for

143

extroverts" and Nathan reported how vastly different the quality of his experience was in the orange team compared to time with the green team.

> The difference between my time on orange team and my time on green team, I think that on one side of the culture they understood that the spirit of the law was more important than the letter and I would not say that was true in terms of the other team (Nathan, H1795).

Nathan was one of the highest scoring participants in the sample and although he describes his experiences as a complicated mix of receiving valuable help and also being traumatized and harmed, he remains unsure about the way an institutional setting can provide truly individualized, genuinely therapeutic care.

> It's a weird mix and it really is one of those things I try to keep in mind is how complex my experience is there in terms of harm and benefit even though my initial reaction is always to think that it did more harm, and it certainly left its marks in ways. That wasn't true for everyone else. I'm a bit of an obstinate stubborn person and so is much of my family, and I think for other people who are a bit more easygoing and were finer with being told what to do, that their experience was different than mine if they were less impulsive and better at following structure and rules. I'm very often very absent-minded which is perhaps another qualm with the program. As much as they, I think tried at times, the difficulty to fully adapt—I mean how do you create uniform rules and implement those when you're treating people who have differing mental disorders and have different

capabilities of that, in terms of empathizing or being aware of their actions or being able to stay organized, so it's—you may be uniformly applying them but then ironically enough not fairly applying them (Nathan, H1790, 1793–1794).

Subgroup Comparisons

The results reported in the previous sections showed that, in some ways, the High and Low subgroups described the program structure in similar ways. The strict system of rules, the social environment, controlled communications, and the level system of progressing through the program were described in highly similar, if not the same ways. The lived experience, or how it felt to experience the program structure, was also comparable in several ways. Table 4-18 summarizes the main commonalities between groups.

Table 4-18. General Similarities in Pre-Program Context, Structure, and Lived Experience (RQ1)

Topic	Commonality Between Groups
Parents and Home Life	Conflicts with parents; Parents' mental health issues.
Reason for Placement	Depression; Childhood abuse, early trauma, externalizing behavior; Experimentation with alcohol and pot; Acting out, rebellion.
Prior Placements	Wilderness programs as prelude to intake; Short-term residential.
Daily Schedule	Everything governed by rules, planned and timed; Little time for fun; Strict enforcement of schedule but group and individual punishments trumped other activities; Frequent written confessions/personal moral reflections.
Social Environment	Emotional Arousal; Peer policing; Special lingo; High level of scrutiny, demand for performance.
Program Philosophy	Focus on your authentic self; Tear down, build back up; Clear out the past; Pressure and punishment result in health.

145

Table 4-18. Continued.

Control	No option to leave; Content of communications restricted, censored; Threat of worse punishments; Petty compliance; Minute infractions = big consequences.
Level System	All levels had to be completed; Very few privileges on first levels; Higher levels had more freedom and responsibility to control lower-level peers; Progress required perfect compliance, genuine willingness, and emotional openness.
Intake and First Few Days	Disorienting; Shocking; Scary; Betrayed; Few, but similar exceptions in both: i.e., unusually nice for first few days then demanding after grace period.
Witnessing	Helpless or motivated to get in line when seeing others treated harshly; Scared of punishments others received; Disgust, crazy, sad when seeing others suffer.
Emotional Intensity	Constant Pressure; Anger at power imbalances; Hopelessness and depression; Periods of extreme catharsis, exhaustion, and emotional breakdowns.
Learning the Ropes	Learn by mistake; Rules not explained and vague, OR, had to copy rule book in excruciating detail; Pressure to catch on fast because of harsh punishments.
Fairness	Illogical rules; unfair punishments; unclear expectations; arbitrary set-backs; few but similar exceptions.

One of the most striking differences between higher and lower scoring participants is that participants in the lower scoring group often described intense, lingering concerns about medical neglect and abuse. Participants in the higher scoring group rarely discussed medical or physical maltreatment. Among the higher scoring participants, those who spoke of negative experiences, or mentioned instances of institutional or psychological abuse (Appendix L), emphasized they are grateful for the overall experience and few named these explicitly as abusive. Among the lower scoring participants, these same, or similar, examples were more often explicitly labeled as maltreatment or abuse. Some of the general differences between group H and group L are summarized in Table 4-19.

Table 4-19. General Differences in Pre-program Context, Structure, and Lived Experience (RQ1)

Topic	Group H	Group L
Forcible Transport or Deceptive Method of Intake	Five participants.	Ten participants.
Staff	Three participants spoke in general, positive terms. Wide range, of positive and negative experiences. Reports that there was one staff member who made all the difference.	Participants reported that some, or one staff member, was kind, especially at first. More emphasis on inept, inappropriate and abusive staff members.
Goodness of Fit	"It was scary at first," "It was hard, somethings didn't make sense, but I do well in those settings." Or "I fit in with the other kids. It was a challenge, but I enjoyed it, or could do it."	Adjusting to structure was painful: couldn't figure out what they wanted; kept getting set back; not prepared for it. It was stupid and made no sense at all; didn't fit in with the others.
Boundaries/ Personal Autonomy	Fewer emphasized intrusion. "Structure and controls were good for me." Five emphasized sense of personal violation.	Almost all emphasized intrusion and boundary violations. No privacy, unreasonable control of bathing, eating, bathroom use, clothes, movement, and control over content of discussions.
Communication	More reported that intensive control, censorship, insularity, made sense.	Almost all reported these restrictions as painful, traumatizing, devastating, frustrating, and/or crazy.
Deprivations	Less emphasis on deprivations of basic needs.	Strong emphasis on derivations such as: lack of privacy, lack of sleep, low-quality food, inadequate education, exposure to severe risk, three-minute showers.

147

Table 4-19.	Continued.	
Psychological Abuse	Wider range, roughly 3 subgroups. About a third reported "therapeutic" incidents using positive/neutral language to describe what many professionals would consider unethical treatment. A third described harm from psychological maltreatment. A third did not describe obvious cases of psychological abuse.	All reported experiencing or witnessing psychologically harmful practices carried out or directed by staff.
Medical Neglect/ Physical Harm	Less emphasis on physical harm or neglect.	Strong emphasis on medical neglect, exposure to dangerous, painful, and physically harmful conditions and practices.
Generalizations	Much wider range of experiences: Ten framed negative experiences as challenges, not as harm. Five reported complex perceptions of harm, trauma and years of healing from trauma. Thirteen (not Lawrence or Yvonne) reported overwhelming pressure to comply with unpleasant, harsh, or questionable demands.	Narrower range of reported experiences: All 15 reported some amount of harm, trauma, and difficulty healing from trauma. They emphasized overwhelming pressure to comply with unreasonable demands.

RQ2: How Do Participants Describe the Immediate Effects of the Program?

In answering Research Question 2, Immediate Effect was defined as personal changes that participants went through while in the program. Participants were explicitly asked about changes in their family relationships and changes they may have noticed within themselves. This concept is intertwined with Lived Experience but is distinguished by whether the participant was emphasizing a change process that occurred in the program. Many statements about changes that occurred in the program were coded as Impact because the participant was emphasizing something about their current perspective on changes they went through in the program without being aware of them, or without understanding them, or while understanding them in a different way now, compared to then. This is especially true when coding statements about trauma, as noted in Table 4-25.

Interview questions in this section of the interview were meant to transition from talking about the program structure to talking about the personal change process. To shift the focus, the lead-in question was specific and narrow: When you were in the program, what did your [parents or guardian] know about your daily life there? This question was followed with: Did your family relationship change while you were in the program? If so, how? And follow up questions, if needed, were: Did you have to earn the privilege of speaking with your parents? What was it like to talk to them while you were in the program? Then, to funnel in toward the research question more directly, participants were asked: Can you give some examples of how the program did or did not help you with the things you may have needed help with? Do you remember noticing changes in yourself? If so, what were they?

Research Question Two Topic Headings

Table 4-20. RQ2 Topic Headings

1. Changing relationships with parents
2. Personal Growth
3. Practical benefits
4. Negative changes
5. Making Progress: A slippery slope

When summarizing codes in the category of Immediate Effect, many differences between subgroups are quite distinct. Participants in group H focused on improved relationships with parents, personal growth, and better social skills. In group L, participants focused more on worsened parental relationships, the exacerbation of psychological issues, and physical complications. Participants in both groups brought up topics of "faking it," "putting their heads down" to get through, "brainwashing," trauma, physical improvements such as getting stronger, tougher, or gaining practical skills such as construction or camping skills.

Table 4-21. RQ2 Code Subcategories Under Each Topic Heading

RQ2 Topic Headings	Code Subcategories
1. Changing Relationships with Parents	Improved Worsened
2. Personal Growth	Self-Discovery, Growth Better Social Skills Broadened Horizons
3. Practical Benefits	Improvements in School/ Practical Skills/ Physical Improvements Toughened
4. Negative Changes	Exacerbation, Maladaptation Indoctrination brainwashed School or Physical Complications Resisted, Misbehaved, Ran Away, Trauma
5. Making Progress: A Slippery Slope	Normalized It, Adapted, "Faked it" "Put head down to get through"

Unlike the results for Context and Structure, in the category of Immediate Effect, there are more differences than similarities between the high and low groups. A count comparison of code subcategories under Immediate Effect is shown as an introduction to each topic heading section below. A full review of the codes and counts that each topic heading is based on can be seen in Appendix H. A list of the immediate effect code subcategories each topic heading is based on is provided in Table 4-21.

Because the contrasting differences between subgroups are more prominent than similarities, the immediate effects are reported primarily in terms of how the subgroups compare. Although the changes participants described do fall roughly into positive and negative categories, an effort is made to avoid simple dichotomous terms and to present the full range of complex findings. Some exceptional cases that do not fit with generalities are given more attention to demonstrate this range.

RQ2.1 Changing Relationships with Parents

Table 4-22. Changing Relationships with Parents: Comparison of Code Counts

Topic Number and Heading	Code Subcategories	Group H (N=15)	Group L (N=15)	Difference	Total
2.1 Changing Relationships with Family	Improved	8	1	7	9
	Worsened	5	9	4	14

Participants in both groups emphasized important ways the first level or phase of treatment was marked with fewer privileges and more restrictions. One of the most interesting restrictions described was the way communication with parents was controlled. Incoming letters were redacted, and outgoing letters were revised or changed by staff so that the content of emails and handwritten communications were in-line with staff expectations. In general, complaints about the program, or requests to be released were discouraged or punished. In addition to the content of communications, especially during the first stages of treatment, the amount and frequency of communication were also severely restricted until residents progressed to the higher levels. These restrictions were identified as a primary reason for a range of changes in parent relationships.

In comparing subgroups, the majority of higher scoring participants (53%) reported that the program led to positive changes in their parental relationships.

> Lawrence: They took out anything that was inappropriate, and they would also give us letters from our folks wishing us luck and telling us what is going on at home and stuff like that. And when I say blanking out inappropriate stuff, like I was really upset with my parents at that point in my life, I wasn't upset that I was at the program, it was just that I hated my parents, so there was a lot of like you know "Hey, write your parents a letter" and then write "fuck you" on a piece of paper and they'll be like "Well, were not sending it." That's what I mean by censoring, they're not going to let you curse out your parents in a letter, it's not helping or therapeutic it's not good for anybody.

> Interviewer: Did your family relationship improve during that nine weeks?

> Lawrence: So again, it's kind of, I'm gonna say yes but it's kind of hard to tell because I went straight

from there into a year and a half long program and during that year and a half long program, yes, our relationship certainly improved greatly (H1170–1171).

The majority of lower QOE scorers (60%) reported that their relationships with parents and family changed for the worse during their time in the program. Only one lower scoring participant (Joan) reported improved communication with parents while in the program. Five participants (33%) in group H (Frank, Uriah, Valorie, Xander, and Iris) reported that their parental relations were unimproved or became more complicated in some way. However, these numbers are somewhat complicated because these five participants in group H described five distinctly different types of complications, and although Joan's relationship with her mother improved, her relationship with her father worsened.

In group H, Frank reported that his family relationship was complicated because his spiritual growth created a barrier between himself and his family members. While he was in treatment and growing spiritually at a rapid rate, his parents were not working on themselves in the same way.

> It really was difficult for a while, it really was you know. For 18 months I didn't see my house and was provided with 10 minutes to talk to them on the phone each week you know, on speakerphone with my therapist. So you know it was a lot of talking about what had happened that week or what was going on for me but I also held an awareness that I might be here and doing this, but they are not...And I think that had a strong impact for me, feeling like "How can I just go on normal and like, I have to be the one to fix all this while you guys get to sit at home

and not really work on yourselves?" And through time, as I was realizing that was really important to me, it became more and more frustrating that I was going to leave and not be met where I was leaving from, you know? I was gonna be met back from where I left from…So I think you know that was the biggest change that I saw was the, just the lack, the difference in pace that I was experiencing, and they were experiencing in terms of actually working on ourselves (Frank, H1479).

Barry reported that his family relationship improved, although due to multiple program placements, he rarely spoke with or saw his parents since he left home for the first treatment when he was 15 years-old. Iris and Valorie also reported complicated changes in their relationships with parents. Iris reported that her relationship with her parents only improved within the last couple of years and for Valorie, changes with parent relationships were superficial because expressions of anger were forbidden. Iris reported that program staff had encouraged parents to make somewhat inappropriate confessions in therapy sessions with their children.

At [the program] your dirty little secrets are called disclosures because you disclose them to the group. So they would have the parents tell us their disclosures and my dad told me some of his, which are pretty tame but I think he's still embarrassed, and I still wish he had never told me, so, I think that was an overreach of the program (Iris, H1439).

The most positive changes in parent relationships were described as improved language skills, more vulnerability, better honesty, and feeling closer because there was so little interaction and therefore, any contact was more valued.

We were a lot closer and we were also, weren't with each other every day so the little moments that we did have, that we did get to talk, they were nice. So once you're level three you talk to them for 30 minutes every other week on the phone...You had to talk about emotional stuff though, you would make goals with your rep about the things that you would bring up, so the whole point of that was to talk about the issues that you did have at home because obviously you're there for a reason, you obviously had some kind of, you know, parental issues with your parents, so you know the whole point of it was to bond with that relationship, help you guys communicate, hopefully build those skills...That was the whole point of it (Wilma, H1008–1011).

While in an intensive outpatient program, one participant began to empathize with his parents and to appreciate the sacrifices they were making for the program by temporarily housing residents from out of town.

There was a certain charity that I developed over time, so my parents and I communicated better and got along better and obviously they were making sacrifices for us to be there because I'm sure they didn't enjoy having nine kids sleeping in their house every night coming home at 11 and getting up at 5:30 and all the disruptions that go with that (Howard, H2075).

Four (27%) participants in group H (Greg, Cee Cee, Uriah, and Iris) described the program's effects as being just the start of a long process of healing that they were not ready for. Iris reported delayed beneficial effects that manifested many years after exiting the program.

155

It was many, many years until I became a parent myself that we really could connect, but that was definitely the beginning of getting out of the anger and
the ugly disowning back and forth stuff that we were
doing (Iris, H1438).

For participants in group L, negative program experiences coupled with a sense of being abandoned to inept or abusive staff members led to disrupted relationships with parents
and broken trust. The sense of betrayal was made complicated
by the restricted and censored communications.

My mom was in denial and did not want to know, she
just wanted me to be safe and alive kind of thing. So
they knew that it was outdoors, they came to visit on
the parent visit days, but everything changes on those
days, of course. So, they didn't know that much
about the day-to-day stuff and all, and if you did call,
they gave you 10 minutes to talk on the phone to your
family and if you started to say like this place is ter-
rible, this place is a prison, you know, they would
hang up the phone because you're manipulating
(Bobbi, L1335–1337).

Some participants in group L reported that their parents
told them that even if they had to stay past the age of 18, they
would never speak to them again if they failed to graduate from
the program. Donnie was 19 at the time of the interview and
prefers pronouns of "they/them/their." Donnie was placed in the
program at age 13 and while in the program, was forced to sit
in stress positions for three days at a time, in silence, in a very
small isolation room, while motivational tapes were played over
a loudspeaker for 16 hours a day. Donnie was made to sleep on
a concrete floor without a mattress because the staff said they
might use a mattress to commit suicide. There was dried semen

on the walls of the cell and it smelled of blood, urine and feces. After several months of being forced to sleep in this cell, and after 72-hour-long stretches of this type of "in school suspension," Donnie earned more opportunity to speak with their parents but was still unable to tell them everything.

> The stuff that they didn't know, that I've told them since, was stuff that I had tried to tell them or stuff that I hadn't been able to tell them through letters. But you like had family reps, they would read through your letters. Your family rep was usually your case manager for lack of a better term. They would kind of facilitate all the communication between you and your family because you only have to write home once a week. You had to like write an email and then they would edit it before you would send it home to your parents and they would edit your parents emails coming in so it was like whatever my family rep wanted me to receive from my parents (L215–219).

Elsa's relationship with her parents became worse after she was able to tell them in person, how bad the conditions were. She was placed in treatment very soon after she started showing signs of depression during her parent's separation. She started avoiding her parents because of their constant conflicts but this urge to be away from them changed soon after she entered the program. During the first part of her stay in the program, she was desperately lonely for them.

> I just wanted to be home, I wanted to be with my family. My communication with them was very limited and so it changed in one way to where I'm almost you know, like clinging to them like, desperately in any way I can. Like any communication with

157

them is just so important and all I want is just to get home, right, it becomes this kind of huge focus in your life but at the same time there was also a lot of trust lost as far as you know feeling like I just kind of got dumped there because I was too much trouble (Elsa, L2321).

After six months, her parents came for one of the parent/child seminars and she tried to communicate with them about some of the negative aspects of her experience. Her parents' disbelief, and then their decision to leave her there after she told them about the place, added another dimension to her sense of betrayal and abandonment.

I had been there maybe six months and they got to come to the facility and we did a seminar together, and you know the intention is that we kind of start working on our relationship... and I kind of just dumped everything on them like you know, this is scary, and this and that, whatever, you know, just kind of dumping all of this stuff on them and of course they are kind of like "wait.... What?"

Her parents went to the director to ask if Elsa's claims were true and the director said "No, she's manipulating you, she just wants you to take her home, nothing she said is true." When her parents sided with the director and left her there, one of Elsa's last possible sources of comfort, that her parents were simply unaware, was gone. At that point, her sense of abandonment and betrayal was amplified.

That was honestly, probably one of the most traumatic things that happened, because they left, I mean they just left me there again. So, I think before that it was like, they don't know what's happening here,

like how am I supposed to tell them? How do I communicate this to them when all of my letters are being
read? And anyway, when I told them that, they just
left anyway, and so it was like okay, this is a whole
new different level (Elsa, L2322).

RQ2.2 Personal Growth

Table 4-23. Personal Growth: Comparison of Code Counts

Topic Number and Heading	Code Subcategories	Group H (N=15)	Group L (N=15)	Difference	Total
2.2 Personal Growth	Self-Discovery, Growth	11	3	8	14
	Better Social Skills	8	3	5	11
	Broadened Horizons	4	3	1	7

Eleven higher scoring participants (73%) described beneficial
program effects related to personal, inner growth. In describing
these changes, some pointed to a single crystalizing event that
triggered a life-changing realization. Others spoke in more general terms or described how the program's effects were delayed,
and only beneficial after many years of increased substance
abuse following their release from treatment. Six participants in
group H (40%) (Greg, Cee Cee, Xander, Uriah, Iris, and Aaron)
reported increased substance use after exiting the program.

For Iris, the main source of personal growth was the realization that her anger came from being hurt and that her sensitivity, which made her vulnerable to feeling hurt, could be a
source of strength and connection rather than a weakness.

159

That's been a core that changed my entire life, because I was an angry kid, it was me against the world and I thought that my innate sensitivity was a weakness and through my friendships and my relationship especially with one staff member at [the program] I came to understand that as a strength and that is something I carry with me now. I'm able to be the caring sensitive person that I really am instead of like a little angry guarded kid and I credit a lot of that towards work that was done there (Iris, H1440).

For Ann, there was a sudden flash of insight in the humbling realization that her mother could refuse to take her back. She experienced this as a point of connection as she realized she was deeply connected with all the people in her life. She described this as a process of becoming more authentic, which required more than just talking about childhood abuses and following rules. She reported having "a big internal change" after many months of adhering to the program's strict regimen.

I talked about all the hard stuff with my stepdad and I talked about all that, but I think that ultimately the big change hadn't happened within me. Like I've done all the external stuff you know, but see, I had started going to therapy when I was seven years old, so at that point I knew all the words to say, I knew how to participate, I knew how to not get in trouble, I knew how to do the stuff, but the big internal change hadn't really happened as far as being myself for who I am I guess, and so, and I think that, I think that that's just a long process. I guess maybe some people it could happen more quickly but for me it didn't (Ann, H97).

She reported a long process leading up to the big change, but the moment of change was a sudden flash of insight that taught her humility.

> Somehow, I learned humility and that was my big lesson, that was my biggest lesson from my whole experience there...it was a huge turning point. And I think that if it all hadn't happened exactly the way it did, if I hadn't been isolated for a month...I mean this packet they gave us to do, the fourth step, was so in-depth where we just describe everything about our families and everything about experiences in our lives in a huge packet and so I just dug through all of this and I think if all of those things hadn't happened exactly the way they had I don't know that I would've had such an experience (Ann, H75–76).

This month-long period of isolation was an unexpected setback for her. She had been in the program for 10 months by then and was progressing well when the staff decided she was just "skating through" and needed to be placed on a lower level.

> I'd been there for about 10 months and I thought that I was you know progressing really well through the program, and then at the last minute, right as I was about to move up to the new level in the program they turned around and took it away from me and ac-tually put me on kind of like, this isolated thing. It was a really wild kind of moment because they actu-ally decided that the way that I'd been interacting with my mother and the way that I'd been interacting with the rest of the group was really controlling and you know that I was just kind of like skating through and that it wouldn't really be right for me to move up. And so, here I thought that I was about to get to move

up to the next level and actually they drop me down to like below the first level (Ann, H71).

This setback meant she lost privileges and would have to spend her time in isolation, called "blackout."

> When the whole group was all eating together, I was sitting over in the corner, if they were all standing around, I was off to the side facing the wall. I didn't have to participate in chores, I didn't have to participate in work. If everybody else was chopping wood, I was sitting over next to a tree facing the tree all day (Ann, H72).

But after spending a month with fewer privileges, in "blackout," her family therapist told her that her mother could refuse to take her back and she experienced a big turning point and learned humility.

> So I was really kind of confronted with that possibility and then the next day I did my fifth step which is where you kind of, in recovery you don't necessarily read your fourth step to the person but you kind of talk about what you, what you found out about yourself in your fourth step, and that was really illuminating for me and that was really the big turning point that weekend (Ann, H68, 70).

Other changes described in positive terms by participants in group H were described as simply growing up, learning self-control, and learning to accept injustices in life.

> Probably the biggest thing that I gained when I was in there was self-control. And I don't know if that was just a matter of the fact that I matured as I turned

from a 16-year-old into an adult...I definitely learned that I had more self-control than I knew that I had because if I didn't use it, it was very painful in there and I definitely saw the consequence for people that didn't have it or didn't use it. That's probably the biggest thing. Before I went in there, I had temper tantrums and stuff where I would break things and scream at my parents and that kind of thing. I never got real violent... but I did destroy things and I pretty much got over that. And they had things in there they would call "injustices." You know, hey, you got blamed for this or you got—somebody put this sign on you and it wasn't right, and maybe somebody else knows it wasn't right, and then say, "Okay well that's just an injustice and life is full of injustices and if you can deal with injustices in here then it's going to be easier for you when you get out there." And it's true, I mean I definitely learned from that (Greg, H1251–1254).

In a similar way, Ann told herself that there was merit in learning to obey rules that did not make sense because of how easy it would then be to follow rules that do make sense, once she graduated. Others reported that they received the important "reality check" that they could not continue doing whatever they wanted and that there are real consequences in life. Some learned to be less stubborn, to explore spiritual beliefs, or gained a better understanding and awareness of hidden motives.

Four participants in group H (27%) (Valorie, Nathan, Xander, Aaron) scored high on the questionnaire but in interviews reported that the benefits of the program came through recovering from trauma experienced in a program that they now judge to be unethical. For Aaron, the awareness and ability to assess hidden motives were gained from his experiences in the program but he describes a complex mix of insights into the program's iatrogenic effects.

> When I arrived, I was a very good manipulator. I was very coercive and had a very good command of the English language. I could get people to do what I wanted them to do through using my words, but I didn't know how that worked. I learned a tremendous amount while I was at [the program] about insights into people's behavior and what makes them tick. That enabled me to organize my loose skills into something a little bit more efficient, I guess is a good word, I became a master manipulator and more importantly I got a pretty good understanding of what makes people tick and a better understanding of the big picture versus the minutia. In that respect—it was beneficial in that respect (Aaron, H2005–2007).

In order to help counter potential negativity biases, some participants in group L were asked specifically about the ways the program may have helped them. Bobbi, a special education instructor who currently works with at-risk youth responded to such a question by listing off a range of "good" things.

> I think it made me more responsible...you have to take responsibility for yourself and your reaction because who else really is to blame, which is good. And understanding other people, like having to be in that group setting, for some, and trying to help the people in my group, I mean we were the therapists, for better or worse, so we were the ones you know just having people from all walks of life with all kinds of serious trauma. And working with those people, being around those people in different dynamics of that

group type of environment is all good for careers…I
don't know what to attribute to there necessarily, but
it did give me experience that a lot of other people
never had (Bobbi, L1346–1348).

The experience of being exposed to a diverse group of
people with a range of mental health issues was described as a
positive by some, but as a negative by others who were shocked
at details that emerged in group sessions or by others' bizarre
behavior. Some described a broadened perspective as a positive
long-term impact that was the result of processing, over many
years, the pain and trauma they experienced in treatment. This
type of effect overlaps with the concept of Impact and will be
reported on in the next section.

RQ2.3 Practical Benefits

Table 4-24. Practical Benefits: Comparison of Code Counts

Topic Number and Heading	Code Subcategories	Group H (N=15)	Group L (N=15)	Differ- ence	Total
2.3 Practical Benefits	Improvements in School/ Practical Skills and Physical Improvements	6	5	1	11
	Toughened	3	2	1	5

Participants in group H were unique in the way they described
positive effects in terms of personal, inner growth but a few in
both subgroups described a range of positive effects such as becoming physically stronger or developing outdoor or survival
skills. One-third of participants, five in both subgroups, described practical improvements like better grades, learning how

to cook, build a fire, or how to crochet and macramé. Uriah reported that learning how to fish and how to take care of his basic needs came in handy, but it was not until he was in his 20s and 30s that he put them into practice. One reported that a physical, tangible improvement was that although her eating disorder became worse in the program, she no longer cut herself because of the constant lack of privacy. Toughening was described as the learned ability to "get through shit" and "keep pushing forward" while in the program.

RQ2.4 Negative Changes

Table 4-25. Negative Changes: Comparison of Code Counts

Topic Number and Heading	Code Subcategories	Group H (N=15)	Group L (N=15)	Differ- ence	Total
2.4 Negative Changes	Exacerbation, Maladaptation	4	10	6	14
	Indoctrinated, Brainwashed	3	6	3	9
	School or Physical Complications	2	7	5	9
	Resisted, Misbehaved, Ran Away	1	4	3	5
	Trauma*	2(5)	3(10)	1(5)	5(15)

Note. Numbers in parentheses are total number of participants who described trauma, traumatic effects, traumatizing experiences, or re-traumatization in the program but did so from a current perspective (coded as Impact) rather than emphasizing explicit changes they went through as a result of trauma responses or traumatic stress symptoms. Code counts not in parentheses are numbers of participants who described changes in the program due to trauma as an immediate effect.

The range of negative immediate effects reported by group L is as diverse and complex as the range of positive effects reported by group H. Higher scoring participants emphasized personal growth, but lower scoring participants emphasized maladaptive learning, unhealthy thinking habits, psychological trauma, and exacerbation of pre-existing negative traits and tendencies. Descriptions of personal growth were mostly emphasized by participants in group H but participants in both groups described a range of "negative" immediate effects.

Impaired social development was one of the most common negative changes reported. Participants attributed these changes to the structure and intensity of the program. Negative changes were described as survival mechanisms in response to life lived in a high-control, insular setting where emotional arousal was commanded at certain times but not allowed at others. Paradoxically, the experience of personal emotional regulation was externally commanded, even when the staff instructed residents to lose control.

> I sort of learned to express anger there but not in any appropriate way. We were not allowed to express anger except when they wanted us to express anger. And when we were supposed to express anger it was all out of proportion, like it would happen like, shredding things, and rolling and screaming, doing all kinds of stuff, so I sort of learned how to explode and lash out but I had no anger management. It was just like, "Now it's time to express your anger and it's okay to do anything you want." And even if you don't want to, there was a saying about feelings there, they really wanted to us to "control our feelings." Like if you're in a group or in a workshop they're like "Okay, now it's time to cry, you need to cry." And if you're not crying then you're not doing what you're supposed to do," or, " Now it's time to be angry, so you need to be angry." And if you're not angry you're doing something wrong. So it's like the normal course of the day, like if you're at school or

your cleaning and you start being angry or crying they're like "You're not supposed to be feeling right now, you're supposed to be working on school work." So, it's this weird way of learning like to get in touch my feelings but having no way, no sense of proportion or direction on them (Tony, L930).

Others reported negative changes such as a reduced ability to cope with stress, learning how to channel anger toward peers they disliked, and learning to overshare in group sessions. Participants in group L described discovering these changes after they got out of the program and began to interact with people in the outside world. It was then that they noticed their boundaries, mannerisms, tendencies, and ways of communicating had changed for the worse. Since their awareness of these changes occurred after exiting the program, such changes are reported in the next section on Impact.

Some reported change as harm that occurred through medical neglect, inappropriate punishments, or forced exposure to environmental extremes. These reports included prolonged overmedication, being denied needed medications, more disordered eating, and physical harm due to not being provided with needed medical care. Physical complications and negative changes also included weight gain, becoming pale with the lack of sunlight, or becoming hairy because girls were not allowed to shave. Xander, Valorie and Cee Cee, (20%) in the higher scoring group reported some negative physical changes and nine participants (60%) in group L experienced physical problems as immediate effects. In total, 12 out of 30 (40%) reported physical harm or negative physical personal changes.

In describing changes that occurred through psychological trauma and persistent stress, 14 participants (93%) in group

L and four participants (27%) in group H (Xander, Valorie, Nathan & Aaron) reported frequent or extreme discomfort with the daily routine and negative changes in their psychological well-being. Some reported that although they knew some of the practices were abusive they learned to believe such treatment was deserved—either as recipients or as the ones delivering it. Tony described group disclosures and anger work as a re-traumatization by being forced to witness others' explosive outbursts of anger.

RQ2.5 Making Progress

Table 4-26. Making Progress: Comparison of Code Counts

Topic Number and Heading	Code Subcategories	Group H (N=15)	Group L (N=15)	Difference	Total
2.5 Making Progress: A slippery slope	Normalized it, Adapted, Faked it	5	10	5	15
	Put Head Down to Get Through	3	3	0	6

All participants in group L and 11 in group H (73%) described something about the process of adapting, "putting their heads down," or "faking it" in order to make progress. Such statements were coded as "Normalized it, Adapted, Faked it, "Put head down to get through." In group L this process was framed as a slippery slope, or as a negative change attributed to indoctrination or "brainwashing," and some commented that performing a role can lead to a loss of self. Eight participants (53%) in group H described this in the positive, something that led to real growth. This topic was reported on by 26 (87%) participants and not all code categories related to this topic are reported here because when it was referred to as indoctrination or "brainwashing" it was organized under the previous topic heading, Negative Changes.

Ziggy was raped before being placed in an intensive outpatient drug rehabilitation center. In group sessions, she was told that her rape and resulting medical complications were essentially her fault. She reported that she had only experimented with marijuana and alcohol a few times prior to entering treatment and she now believes that she learned to blame herself and a drug addiction she did not have.

> You go through this big traumatic experience and then I guess your therapy is people telling you, well that basically it wouldn't have happened if you weren't, you know, doing drugs…It's pretty harsh to tell someone, like anyone that went through something like that, but especially someone who's 15 years old. That was definitely hard, but yes, it did work, they definitely brainwashed me for a while, that's what I believed, that all these bad things happened to me in my life because I was doing the wrong thing (Ziggy, L1950–1951).

Quill reported that one of the main problems with the program was the way pressure in group sessions could encourage or pressure youth to make false confessions that could be used against them.

> I mean number one is that they intentionally—part of their manipulation is intentionally causing problems or creating issues that did not exist in order to treat them for their own entertainment or to manipulate, like make them up. Like we knew that we were making false confessions, obviously, and just creating problems that don't exist and then treating them and being able to do whatever they want to them, I don't

170

know if that kind of makes sense, like they were creating problems that didn't exist to be able to treat them. I mean that is weird (Quill, L1520–1521).

Donnie, who prefers the pronouns "they, them, their," described a learning process that involved self-betrayal. Once they gained a substantial amount of level-status and had more at stake, their willingness to "hold others accountable" was driven by a desire to be released from treatment. But Donnie's performance had to be sincere, and any indication that it was just a performance, could be reported to staff at any time.

> I just had to put on this show, like "I'm just doing this because it's the right thing."...I think it was easier to just give into it for a little bit...I think I kinda got into the Stockholm mindset at level four which is when you get upper levels...when I got to the upper levels I was like okay I need to get my shit together because I need to get out of here and I need to go home because this is horrible. So, I just tried to get into that rhythm as a level four, like I can't mess this up because if I mess this up I am not going to have enough motivation to pick myself back up to do this all over again. So, it took months of holding up others. Like I want to hold my peers accountable for things they didn't do and punish them for things that aren't fair. And I would say I snapped out of things at about level five but I was so emotionally invested in doing whatever the fuck I had to do to get home that like, I don't know, it was worth it (Donnie, L134–137, 226–229).

For Quill, the slippery slope was a process of learning to fake it and then feeling as if some more authentic part of herself had been lost or confused with thoughts that had been "put into her mind."

> I remember towards the end of being there, I was like not even sure if I had any personality left or if they had like—I couldn't differentiate what thoughts were going through my head like which ones were mine and which ones were trained from the workshops, so I feel like they had definitely replaced my personality, which, they do it in such a systematic way you know, which is similar to, if you read about like cult behavior it's like you stress them enough to having a mental breakdown but they disguise it as an epiphany so you can put things into their mind and replace the old thing, so it's basically you know, disguising a breakdown as epiphanies and then replace information in their mind (Quill, L1512–1513).

Group H described a different perspective on the process. Higher scorers indicated that this process was an opportunity "to put our heads down" that led to beneficial effects. For Frank, one of the highest scoring participants, although there was "brainwashing" in the program, it was difficult or impossible to know what caused what. At the time of the interview, he had only been out of the program a few years and just being better-off and happier is what really mattered to him.

> While I appreciate things I gained from that experience I think there was a level of brainwashing that happened in that space. Like your life becomes this bubble and your life becomes "how do I get out?" and you start kind of like performing for the system... I do think it's influenced me you know...[but]

172

it's so hard to tease apart what actually influenced what, because it all just kind of like happened...I like who I am now...so sure I think it was good. I know I couldn't have necessarily have gotten exactly where I am, I wouldn't be exactly where I am without that experience. And the path that I was on was not a healthy path and I probably would've continued it in a more unhealthy way. Not to say that I don't still struggle with smoking too much pot, or whatever, but you know, wasn't it was pretty clear that I was headed down a path that was not going to look anything like this? So, I'm happy where I'm at today, is the best answer (Frank, H487, 490–492).

Subgroup Comparisons of Immediate Effects

In reviewing the experience and effects of totalistic treatment methods there was a wide range of responses in most of the categories identified here. Some of the overarching themes that began to emerge had to do with induction, boundaries, containment, and release. The process of changing, creating and dissolving personal boundaries seems to be close to the heart of the core differences between the subgroups. In group H, Lawrence, Ann, Frank, Barry and Wilma provided examples of how intensive program structures ultimately led to a sense of greater integrity. For Yvonne, this led to the ability to manage healthy boundaries in a way that allowed for healthy intimate relationships. Greg and Uriah described a similar process of finding strength through humility. But for all in group L, and for five (33%) in group H (Aaron, Iris, Nathan, Valorie, & Xander) the dissolution of boundaries, and lack of personal agency, were described also in terms of unethical methods or harm, as if personal boundaries were punctured and violated.

Comparing the two groups on immediate effects, both High and Low subgroups were most similar in two ways. Similar numbers in each group discussed ways they gained practical skills and got physically stronger, and similar numbers in each group described a positive change that occurred by being exposed to a wider range of types of people and issues they faced, which in turn broadened their perspective. Table 4-27 summarizes these similarities between the two groups.

Table 4-27. Major Similarities in Immediate Effect (RQ2)

Topic	Commonality Between Groups
Physical Improvements /Toughened	Participants in both groups mentioned becoming physically stronger from participating in program activities. Several reported improved practical skills such as camping, cooking, wilderness survival techniques, and macramé and crocheting skills.
Broadened Horizons	In both groups, participants reported that exposure to a wider range of mental health issues and to people from all over the country introduced them to new ideas and to the realization that life, and the world, were bigger than they had realized.

The groups were similar on their perceptions of these two immediate effects, but they differed in six general ways. The differences were largely a matter of positive vs. negative effects, although sometimes the differences emerged because many in one group reported on a topic while only one or a few reported it in the other group. Table 4-28 summarizes six contrasting general differences between the two.

Table 4-28. Major Differences in Immediate Effect (RQ2)

Topic	Group H	Group L
Self-Discovery and Growth	Strong emphasis: they matured, learned to feel empowered and connected, learned to accept injustices.	Less emphasis: along with negative effects, there were some valuable lessons learned about themselves.
Family Relationships Improved	Strong emphasis: more family relationships improved as a result of participating in the program, but some reports were complicated.	One reported immediate benefits and this was mixed: a benefit with one parent but worsening with another.
Family Relationships Worsened	Some reported that family relationships were only worsened temporarily. A few reported worsened or unimproved negative relationships.	Almost all reported that their family relationships worsened because of program practices and conditions.
Psychological Exacerbation or Maladaptation	Five reported experiencing or witnessing worsening of mental health issues.	Strong emphasis: their mental state was negatively impacted or worsened while in the program.
Physical Complications	One male participant reported that he did not eat for the first 10 days after his intake. One injury due to punishment. One sexual assault while on permission away due to staff failure to protect.	Nine reported worsened or new health/physical complications such as sudden weight gain, physical injury, worsened eating disorders, and physical harm from medical neglect.

Table 4-28. Continued.

Topic	Group H	Group L
Better Social Skills	Strong emphasis: better communication skills, becoming more humble, more empathetic, better able to connect with others, more honesty.	Very few reported improvements while in the program.
"Faked It" to Progress, Normalization, Indoctrination	Participants used positive framework to describe "being able to put heads down," able to get with the program, able to hold tongue and fake their way through. A few reflected on this negatively. It was what they had to do, and none described having to betray themselves.	Strong emphasis: being torn down and having to "suck it up," lie to themselves, make false confessions, punish or hurt peers in order to make progress. They bought in after seeing they had no choice and described this as self-betrayal.
Generalizations	A wider range of immediate effects. A) For seven: the program facilitated immediate genuine growth and ability to connect with others. B) For four: the immediate effects were beneficial but short-lasting, or ineffective in the short-term. C) For four: the immediate effects were traumatizing, but not entirely negative.	For all: the effects were described as problematic, traumatic, harmful and/or requiring self-betrayal in order to survive and progress out.

RQ3: How Do Participants Describe the Long-Term Impacts of the Program?

Research Question 3 encompasses the widest range of topics and the longest stretches of time. Participants' beliefs about how the course of their lives has been influenced by their program experience involves personal, familial, social, practical, physical, emotional, and spiritual trajectories. Their knowledge about their respective programs, cohorts, and the topic of teen programs in general were all considered as Impact. Even their participation in this study is an example of how the program has impacted their lives. Even after 20 or 30 years, their months or years spent in a teen treatment program are prominent factors in their development today and Impact is a current event that continues to unfold in new ways.

Interview Questions

To collect data about program impacts, several interview questions were designed to allow participants freedom to identify and explain what was most important to them while also inviting a wide range of responses that would invite discussion related to several dimensions or domains of life. The main question was open-ended but direct: When you think about the way your life has played out, has your program experience impacted your life? If so, in what ways? Additional interview questions invited some contextual information and asked about any relevant comparisons between their perspective and others': Do you know people from your program who have a really different perspective? If so, why do you think your perspective is different from theirs? Then, to ask about any significant shifts in perspective, or ways the impact of the program has changed over time, they were asked: If we'd had this discussion right after you got out of the program, would you answer my questions in the same way? If not, how would they compare? In some interviews, a follow up question asked: Are there any other ways the program has influenced the person you've become? If so, in what ways? In order to better understand the ways they value their program experience and their relationship to the program's impact, they were asked: Why were you interested or willing to participate in this interview? And the closing question was meant to understand how they identify or label themselves in relation to the experience: Are you an alumnus, a former student, former resident—how would you like to be identified?

Research Question Three Topic Headings

Table 4-29. RQ3 Topics

1. Memories
2. Social Impact
3. Trajectory
4. Personal Impact
5. Social Skills: Improved and Impaired
6. Knowledge
7. Perspective

In this section, the impacts of totalistic programs are organized under seven different topics. These topics were distilled from nine code subcategories and 29 code sub-subcategories under the primary category of Impact (Appendix F). In reporting the findings in this section, the tables list the code sub-subcategories that contribute to each topic but in the text, these code sub-subcategories are not the section's outline, they are meant to provide a glimpse of what went into the topic's development.

Some of these code subcategories, for example, "memories," were driven by the interview protocol as participants were asked about their strongest memories at the beginning of each interview. The subcategory, "family," was closely linked to descriptions of Immediate Effects and when participants described the way their family relationships changed they often extended their explanations to describe how it has changed over the years after exiting the program and these statements were therefore coded under Impact. Some subcategories, like "trajectory," include descriptions about life decisions related to work, education, and substance use.

When participants described multiple causal factors related to the program experience that impacted their lives, these statements were coded as "pathways" because they demonstrate a flow of logic and the participant's understanding of how causal factors flow and lead into one another. Occasionally, statements that were unique in how they articulate a difficult-to-describe aspect of life were coded as "pearls." Additional subcategories under the heading of impact were personal, knowledge, perspective, and social.

Table 4-30. RQ3: Impact; Introductory Summary of Topic Headings and Sub Headings

Topic Number and Heading (3=RQ3)	Code Subcategories
3.1 Memories	Reflections on Memories "Bad" "Good" Strong but Neutral Polemic
3.2 Social Impact	Family Intimate Relationships Friends Suicides and ODs
3.3 Trajectory	Reentry Substance Use School/Career Advocacy
3.4 Personal Impact	Tangible/ Physical Trauma Healing Complicated Mix
3.5 Social Skills Improved and Impaired	Interpersonal Barriers to Jargon/Habits
3.6 Knowledge	About Program About Self
3.7 Perspective	On Program On Others Changes In Meaning/Value of Program

Table 4-30 summarizes topic headings in the order they are presented in this section. The code subcategories under each topic represent the code subcategories that were deemed most important through counting and qualitative analyses. The code counting comparison tables are presented as an introduction to each topic heading.

RQ3.1 Memories

Table 4-31. Memories: Comparison of Code Counts

Topic Number and Heading	Code Subcategories	Group H (N=15)	Group L (N=15)	Difference	Total
3.1 Memories					
	Reflections On	5	11	6	16
	Bad	9	11	2	20
	Good	9	5	4	14
	Strong & Neutral, Polemic	9	7	2	16

The first interview question invited participants to share in a general way: When you think back and remember your time in the program, what are some of your strongest memories? The results presented in Table 4-31 reflect two main types of memories described by both groups, "really good" memories related to human connection and "really bad" memories related to program structure. Joan, a younger, lower scoring participant, was 19 at the time of her interview and had recently exited her program. She reported psychological trauma in her experiences with group sessions and started the interview by acknowledging that there are gaps in her memories: "I have a lot of blank spots from my time there so my memories are either really good or really bad" (L531). Participants in group H reported a similar dichotomy of two types: "unfairness and friends" or "friends

181

and WTF?" A general trend in the interviews made explicit by one participant, was that while the strongest memories were most often about the strong bonds forged in the program, the most prevalent type were often less positive memories about the program design. Because this is a retrospective study that is based on participants' memories, it might be important to provide examples of the wide range and yet similar trends that were mentioned when asked about their strongest memories.

> Most of the memories are very negative but the strongest memories are actually the positive ones. Like the few positive memories that I have there, most of them, it mostly had to do with the relationships that I built there, you know? We would have to go to transport at the end of the night where the whole facility would go into the gym and we would sit down in a line by our group and we would get snack. So usually what happened, was some type of fruit. So one girl would take them and pass them all down the line and it's like one or two people would clean up the cores and put them in the garbage. But we would take the stickers off the apples because you know we weren't allowed to write notes to each other or anything like that we would take the stickers off of the apples and call them love stickers stick them on like friends, or you know the people in our group, and that's one of the best memories I have now. It's the only thing I've carried with me from the program and I do it with my son now like this little secret between us you know, I take the sticker off my apple and I'll be like "Love sticker!" and I'll put it on him (Pat, L1550–1552).

One of the most surprising findings is that even participants who experienced extreme forms of institutional abuse also described some positive things that grew out of the experience. This mix of positive and negative ways that participants were impacted is reflected in the mix of current strongest memories.

> I have a lot of memories. I think about the people a lot. Like the other kids that were in there mostly, not so much the adults. It was a pretty, probably the worst time in my life but there was also some good things, mostly not great. I think there was a lot of pretty dark things too (Carmen, L1820–1822).

It was common to hear that memories of close friendships and memories of the structure were strongest but lower scoring participants seemed to refer to these as two distinct domains. For participants in group H, it was more common to hear that they were intertwined in positive, and perhaps complicated, ways.

> My strongest memories would definitely be the levels, the system in general, and family representatives, the structure of the buddy system, and just how you had to work your way up. I personally saw it as a game just so I could go home. Sort of fake your way to do what you need to do. And people around you who are going to look after you not snitching on you or something, or who's gonna be a good buddy or who you can trust basically. You just kind of observe your surroundings. My friendships that I made there are very close. I talked to maybe a couple people there, I think that's what really made me go through the program was the close friendships there and just having someone there for you (Wilma, H951, 953–955).

For lower scoring participants, the negative effects of the structure seem more separated from and contrasted with the positive memories of close bonds.

> Group therapy is definitely one and just in general, coercive treatment, kind of, and discipline, like timed bathroom, like being like timed in the bathroom you know, three minutes to go, to go crap in the morning, or you know, timed eating, which for somebody who had disordered eating to begin with is really problematic. And really fond friendship. Some of the memories with some of the people I grew closest to for sure, for sure, and you know those definitely are awesome (Dee Dee, L365–367).

Valorie's strongest memories, although negative, were shared with some amount of humor.

> Sitting in group therapy feeling like it was a witch hunt and they were just trying to figure out what was wrong with you so they can just publicly crucify you and put you into a feeling of such intense shame that you can't help but break open in front of the entire, like staff and student population so that they can then fix you, somehow you're broken. And shoveling horse shit every morning. What else, let's see, and there were cats, and that was probably the best part, in my opinion (Valorie, H2215).

And for Ann, who experienced a great deal of gratitude for the program, memories of the rigid structure elicit warm, fuzzy feelings.

> So, it was planned to the minute and every moment of the day was planned and this is actually one of the

184

things about the program…when I look back on
that…I get like a warm fuzzy feeling about it because
it provided so much structure for a person like myself
who maybe lacks the internal structure a little bit.
That was amazing for me (Ann, H43–44).

RQ3.2 Social Impact

Table 4-32. Social Impact: Comparison of Code Counts

Topic Number and Heading	Code Subcategories	Group H (N=15)	Group L (N=15)	Difference	Total
3.2 Social Impact					
	Social: Family	10	10	0	20
	Personal: Understanding/ Self-Perception/ Sexuality/Intimate Relationships	11	10	1	21
	Knowledge: Cohort	12	8	4	20
	Social: Cohort Friends and Relations	10	4	6	14
	Social: Suicides and ODs	3	7	4	10

Family relationships

Participants in both groups described a difficult, years-long process of reconciling their program experience with their parent's
understanding of what happened. Some indicated that they are
still unsure of what their parents currently know or do not know
about the more negative things that occurred. Those who reported that the program deceived their parents or gave them a

superficial description of their daily schedule, explained how this continues to be a source of angst or conflict.

For those who had a more negative experience, this incongruence between what parents imagine and what actually happened has been a barrier to healing and reconciliation. Participants in both groups indicated that they believe the program deliberately deceived their parents.

> Earlier this summer I started talking about it to my mother and she was stunned, I thought she knew [and that] my father didn't know. The [program] was very good from a marketing standpoint keeping you and your parents kind of separated. You have group therapy once every other week that lasts like half an hour with your therapist but they don't get to see the daily parts of your life. And again, your phone calls are monitored. And I remember I once complained about a whole bunch of things saying "Hey, I think this is unfair." And in hindsight the really awful policy is to tell parents that "Your kids are being manipulative to avoid facing their problems and you need to just trust us." And that seems to have, by and large, been a very effective strategy to everyone that I've talked to. All of their parents are kind of hoodwinked and left in the dark, kind of were like "Well, my child has these horrible problems and I want so much for them to be healthy and this place is saying that we need to trust them and there really isn't much of a way, or any way, for me to independently figure out what is going on there." And I think my father was upset about that because he is, he was worried (Nathan, H1777–1778).

Where the program design encouraged false confessions by rewarding participants for sharing such disclosures, participants reported that these exaggerations could then be communicated to parents in a way that confirmed parents' worst fears while increasing their loyalty to the program. For some, this impacted the image parents had of their children and impacted their approach to parenting. Kam, who was 17 years old at her intake, describes how her own exaggerated confessions impacted her parents' approach to parenting for many years.

> The program basically made us super-exaggerate everything that we had done so if you did something like, you know, met up with your boyfriend and got stoned and had sex, they would make you say to your parents that you had prostituted yourself for drugs. So, I think my parents, I think that their view of me changed drastically because according to the program I was a junkie prostitute. And so when I was there and after I graduated I think that they felt that they needed to be more, that they needed to like monitor me, if that makes sense, and continue to be unreasonable and overprotective like when I was in my early 20s as well. I mean they said things like, "We didn't realize how bad this actually was, thank God for [the program]" (Kam, L2131–2133).

For others, one of the main impacts was in the negative effects of broken trust and the resentment that came with feeling abandoned. But for some of the higher scoring participants, parental alienation occurred even though the program was beneficial overall. Due to subsequent placements in other programs or other events after exiting, at least six in group H (40%) (for example, Frank, Barry, Lawrence, Iris, Cee Cee, & Uriah) did not live at home again or spend much time with their parents after

187

the program. Greg reports that since he signed himself out of the program when he turned 18 and did not formally graduate, he distanced himself from his parents, but for a relatively short period of time.

> They definitely didn't want me to leave. They wanted me to go through reentry and graduate and all that, and that was a big falling out when I left there. I had a big falling out when I left there and kind of cut ties with them for a number of years. We got over it after a while. Both my parents have died since then but we did reestablish connections and I was actually very close with my parents by the time they died, so you know that was just a short, relatively short, I mean a couple years when you're talking about a lifelong relationship, was a relatively short period of time that I was distant from them (Greg, H1260–1262).

For some, sibling relationships and friendships at school were also impaired.

> My siblings and I used to be very close, like best friends, kind of close and you know they lived their lives, they did what they did without me there and that changed our dynamic. When I came home I was different, we weren't friends anymore, they had their own things going on, which was fine, I understand that, but our relationships definitely suffered because of that...And also, the dynamic with my friends from high school, that all changed. Everyone graduated but I had already graduated early because the educational system there was so far behind where we were in my high school. So I went and my brother had my same class and I watched him graduate with my class

and you know I couldn't be there and it was, that was tough, that was a really tough (Sebrina, L701–704).

For others, the program impacted the way they talked about the program because parents were instructed that complaints about the program were a red flag. If Donnie had been interviewed right after graduating, things would have been different because of an absolute black and white prediction.

> I would have been forced, or lied—I would've like, talked up the program like "my relationship with my parents is so much better," things like, "this really helped me learn how to communicate my feelings more and take accountability for my actions," because I had to praise the program or else my parents thought that I was gonna kill myself. Like that was, it was like "Program, or my kid dies." That was their mindset because that's what the program had fed them (Donnie, L243).

Intimate relationships

Two participants described details about genuinely therapeutic relationships with a staff member. One was described by Yvonne (pronouns "they, them, their"), whose therapist allowed them to explore an intimate, but not necessarily sexual, relationship with a female resident while in the program. This experience allowed Yvonne to decide what the healthiest way to interact might be. They ended up breaking off the relationship but the growth that occurred enabled Yvonne to feel more confident about connecting deeply and intimately with others as an adult in healthy relationships.

It really helped me learn how to not always be with somebody else but to be comfortable sitting with myself for certain periods of time because I would really have a tendency to try and use other people to try to fill that hole in myself, not necessarily that I was uncomfortable with my identity, but just that I was uncomfortable being alone. And that is something that I've gotten a lot better hold of. I'm not necessarily extroverted or introverted and so it's been nice to be able to find a real comfortable balance between socializing with people who are platonic friends and balancing that with intimate relationships, as well as having my own time (Yvonne, H651).

Yvonne's description about the way the program experience improved their ability for healthy sexual relationships is unique. The majority who mentioned that their sexuality was impacted described negative ways their intimate relationships have been affected. Quill was 24 at the time of her interview and had been in treatment for two years. She completed her program approximately six years ago and believes the program negatively impacted her ability for healthy sexual relationships.

The staff at [the program] had an extreme, really extreme, disturbing fascination with anything sexual related to the children. Like they would force us to like, tell our disclosures, which you know they had these special groups where if there was a girl that has been raped, they get male students to act it out and hold her down and you have to walk through with the therapy with the girl who's been raped. They would tell students who had like been abused sexually or had done things, they would tell them, "Okay, here's your special notebook, you have to write everything out in detail and it's only allowed to be read by one staff member." Which looking back on that, that's very disturbing, like they're just, that's just them getting you know, like, custom child porn literature (Quill, L1515–1516).

Participants who reported negative impact in sexual relationships say their difficulties were caused by the program's exclusively negative dialogue pertaining to sex, the total lack of frank discussion about sex, and forced snuggling, called "smooshing."

> I was a fat kid too, so like I don't want anyone touching my belly, this is just horrific. Anytime someone was touching my belly I was like in my body like going "Please, help me get the hell out of here!" Or touching me at all, like gross, like I still have an aversion to being touched by people who aren't my real core group of people because of that smooshing (Iris, H1414).

In the interview, Iris laughed when describing how gross it was to smoosh with teenagers who had been in seminar activities for 24 hours without bathing. Others, like Quill, who described inappropriate professional practices, are more bitter if not outraged because she knows how such treatment has affected some in her cohort.

> That is honestly one of the number one problems. Like the rate of [program] students that are able to be in relationship is pretty much zero. And to be messing around with that in a kid in their formative years causes a lot of problems, I'm sure you can imagine, so that's really the number one thing that makes me angry (Quill, L1518).

191

Friendships

Participants described disrupted friendships, being cut-off from old friends, and denied contact with anyone other than immediate family for long periods of time. But on the positive side, friendships built in the program tended to be long-lasting and strong. Seven participants (23%) from both groups (Ann, H; Elsa, L; Carmen, L; Xander, H; Iris, H; Howard, H; and Mary, L) reported that they thought of this bond, or described the experience, in military-like terms. Some explained that they did so because it conveys the intensity of connections formed in such extreme environments.

> I have other friends that when I did leave we all kind of pulled together and helped ourselves out of it and so we also have that as well. We used to call that like "war buddies" you know we have been through like a war together and so that was, I don't know when you go through something really awful with somebody or group of people then it's always different I think (Carmen, L1876–1877).

But when interacting with people outside of the program, some of their learned ways of communicating tended to alienate them.

> I did feel pretty good about the program when I left because there were a lot of good things to take away from it. So also you know they set you up for like, "if you take your light into the world you can light dark places," and I remember like meeting kids and trying to indict them: " I feel like you seem really hurt do you want to talk about it?"—just being like blown off, and it took a lot of years of that you know

to find a group again. I think that's why we all hud-
dled together because we had that vocabulary that
normal teenagers wouldn't, you know. That was not
in their realm of experience so that was hard (Iris,
H1459–1461).

Greg reported that he found himself going into confrontation
mode with friends who had never been in the program.

It's happened to me where I've gone into that mode
you know like encounter group, or I just all of a sudden boom, started to get my feelings off on one of
my roommates, "HEY!" you know, and they kind of
look at you like "what is wrong with you?" (Greg,
H1276).

And for Pat, the lack of boundaries translated into a general lack
of social skills such as oversharing in ways that were unusual
in the outside world.

When I came out of the program I was talking about
like super personal things you would never tell pretty
much anyone unless you had to, right? Like rape or
incest—and I was talking about them like it's fuck-
ing talking about the weather. It's what you did in the
program. And you know—it was a weird transition
coming into real life, like how do I talk to boys, like
what do I say? I don't know, it's socially stunted me
for sure (Pat, L1619–1620).

One of the most alarming findings in this study was that
three participants in group H (20%) and seven participants in
group L (47%) reported that many of their friends from the program had committed suicide or died by overdose. Often stated
as a simple fact, or even with dark humor, they reported that

193

hearing another friend has committed suicide is not only emotionally impactful, it can be embarrassing.

> I think a few years ago, between 2014 and 2015 I had three friends from the program commit suicide within an eight-month timeframe... It is what it is. It's really common for people who've been in programs and I think that if I hadn't gone I wouldn't know so many people who have committed suicide. So that has definitely impacted me. It was interesting because like I went to a funeral service with another program survivor and it was basically, he was saying he was embarrassed to ask for time off from work because there have been so many suicides and he kept taking time off to go to these services. And so, I think about that, like yeah, and how that like impacts you. Like at work now, I'm going to be like, "yeah, so, taking time out for another service," you know? (Kam, L2152).

Iris emphasized that it's not possible to confidently blame or assume suicides were directly related to negative program experiences.

> We all made decisions what to do with it and everyone went different paths. I was lucky that when I went so bad for so long that I was able to make better choices at some point and had support at some point to turn my life around because a lot of kids didn't. A lot of them aren't here anymore, they're dead. A lot of them are dead. My best friend as a matter of fact; we were close in the program but we met up a few years after the program and she was my best friend for 10 years and she never finished the program and I hesitate to even think that's causative in any way,

she ended up OD'ing and dying, and a lot of the kids did end up OD'ing and dying but I don't know what a normal high school death rate is so I don't know if we are more than the average or if that's just getting old and all your friends die. There's no way to know. I know people that didn't go to any programs and they still have tons of people OD or commit suicide and so did we, and we were a vulnerable population anyway, so I can't blame [the program] but who's to say? (Iris, H1463–1464).

Regardless of where to assign blame, the large number of overdoses and suicides known to participants were described as a way to convey the intensity of the experience. And the impact of having so many friends commit suicide has been an important program-related factor shaping the life course.

Many of the people that I went through that school with, a lot of them have overdosed on drugs or committed suicide. It's just been, it's a huge part of my life and it happened at such a young fundamental part of my life that it's you know—I've spent my entire life since I've gotten out trying to process and come to terms with it (Tony, L942–943).

RQ3.3 Trajectory

Table 4-33. Trajectory: Comparison of Code Counts

Topic Number and Heading	Code Subcategories	Group H (N=15)	Group L (N=15)	Difference	Total
3.3 Trajectory	Reentry	6	9	3	15
	Substance Use	6	3	3	9
	School/Subsequent Placements	6	10	4	16
	Career	4	9	5	13
	Advocacy	6	8	2	14

Reentry

It is tempting to simplify post-program trajectories in some dichotomous, good/bad, type of summary. Some participants, in group H especially, were placed in other programs that were worse than the one they reported on in this study. For them, exiting meant another intake and another cycle of disruption, reorientation and slowly learning the ropes. However, the majority of participants exited their programs and reentered the outside world. This reentry process was often initiated with some sort of aftercare, or "home internship"—a probationary period where rule violations at home could trigger placement back in the program. Surprisingly, participants did not describe the reentry process as a celebratory regaining of freedom. It was more common to hear that exiting the program and reentry into the outside world was a shock they were ill-prepared for.

In the most positive cases, when the participant did not go directly into another program, reentry was described as an emotional, bittersweet transition of being separated from close friendships formed in the program. Participants in both subgroups described a difficult adjustment and Frank framed this as a transition into the "real world." He was in his program for two years, from 15 to 17 years-old, and was 23 at the time of his interview.

> The biggest changes were realizing what I wanted for myself. It wasn't until years later that I would really be able to define and like, provide a voice to this concept, but I definitely started the path, like I want to live a life of self-growth, and you know of pushing myself and living uncomfortably in moments where definitely—it was starting to realize satisfaction, you know the satisfaction that came with experiencing myself as a—experiencing my life as playful, you know trying to have a relationship to myself and to life itself….and to be totally honest that was not something that I could have voiced in this way five years ago or six years ago but I think it was the biggest, you know catalytic thing that I got from that experience…you know you can like learn all the stuff about yourself within that space and when you leave it kind of all goes out the window you just have to learn it again within the context of "the real world" (Frank, H476–477).

Three in group H (20%) (Frank, Iris and Uriah) described having to relearn program lessons in "the real world." Four others (27%) (Greg, Cee Cee, Iris and Uriah) described delayed program benefits, saying that "seeds that were sown" in the program took many years to unfold.

> I would say it has [impacted my life]. It didn't immediately because I wasn't ready, or at least not in any major way. But the things that I learned there that, the ideals so to speak, the teamwork and problem solving you know, everything down to how to cook and clean and maintain your personal health, those

are all things that I probably used my whole life, and more importantly when I was in my mid-to late 20s when I finally decided to pull my head out of my ass you know some of the things, some of the things that they, some of the behavioral things they did, there are things that I thought back on and reflected upon (Uriah, H520).

Participants in group L spoke more in terms of devastation and disruption. They described the unique experience of realizing not only that they no longer fit in with old friends, they were surprised to learn that they had changed in ways they were unaware of in the program. Several reported that they were isolated or alone with such discoveries while also feeling like an alien.

You want to have an explanation for people, what it was like, but how the fuck do you explain this to anybody?... I was just so socially behind. I missed out on like two years of learning how to be a teenager, like going through puberty, which is probably like the worst time of your life anyway, and I didn't really know how to interact with people. I didn't have any context of pop culture...I hadn't listened to music in two years...I didn't have anything to talk about with these people other than like this weird program jargon that nobody else knew. And I couldn't talk to anybody else about it because I wasn't allowed to keep in contact with anybody else but this program (Donnie, L235, 237–238).

Along with the sense of alienation, some reported being embarrassed for not understanding social conventions that are generally taken for granted. Pat spent much of her adolescence in a program, missed her high-school years and went right into

198

college. In one class she asked for clarification about the rules: "Do we have to raise our hands to go to the bathroom?" She was embarrassed for not knowing: "Everyone laughed at me, like, I didn't know in college you could just get up and go to the bathroom, like I had no idea, you know?"

The freedom of the outside world and the lack of structure were described as barriers and hurdles to be overcome. Participants had difficulty adjusting to the lack of consistent structure they had become accustomed to. "When I first left, I was still very much, I don't want to say brainwashed, but in the sense I still had very internalized a lot of the rules and boundaries and acceptable behaviors of the program" (Dee Dee, L424). Joan reports something similar, "I didn't know how to handle inconsistency, like if anything changed I didn't know how to handle it because I was so used to everything happening at a certain time in a certain way" (Joan, L579). She recently graduated from her program and said that for the first few days she was really upset about leaving because she was certain that it was the best place for her to be.

> I got out in 13 months which was super-fast, normally it's 18 to 24. Mainly because they really thought they had me, and I didn't do anything wrong, because like I'm not happy to say it, like I really did have to lie and manipulate my way out...otherwise you'd be there forever. One girl had really bad Asperger's and she was there for almost 3 years because they couldn't change her to the point that she was socially acceptable to their standards (Joan, L581).

Even though she admits to lying and manipulating her way through the levels to graduation, at first, she was unhappy about leaving. But as she was reminded of her life before the

199

program, she apparently became disillusioned and began to become conscious of the lies she had internalized.

> A couple of days later, I saw my mom and my dog and I think—I wasn't like an imagey kid before I left, I'm not now, but they really couldn't find anything to object to in my wardrobe, and like who I was, just like my stuff is pretty similar. I came home and I just like saw, kind of, I guess like who I was, and I kind of realized like, this is right, this is the truth, like I don't have to be like that anymore. I don't have to lie anymore (Joan, L580).

Substance use

Six participants (40%) in the higher scoring group and four (27%) in the lower scoring group reported that their substance use escalated after their graduation or release from the program. For four participants (27%) in group H and one (7%) in group L, problematic substance use began after they completed treatment. The one participant (Howard) who reported that he has remained absolutely chemical-free since exiting the program does attribute his sobriety directly to the program experience. Two participants (7%) described their relationships with psychedelics, and similar to the way others reported that exposure to confessions about drugs made them want to try new, "harder" things, Iris reported that it was the program philosophy that made her want to experiment with psychedelics.

> The minute I got out [the program] I got addicted to crystal meth, like I went crazy. I was on drugs for years. I was still functional, but I did all the things I wanted to do when I was locked up that I couldn't do and I was a mess for many years. But I feel like [the

200

program] and its hippie bullshit kind of like made me see it in this Timothy Leary way. Like I did a lot of hallucinogens because I always thought it was like soul growth, that kind of stuff. And I don't want to discount any of it, I mean it looks stupid and juvenile now as I was 20, but there is a real stuff I took away from ecstasy, from mushrooms. That part of my life is long over but I think [the program] put me on that path with basically the Propheet and that kind of stuff (Iris, H1445).

For Valorie, psychedelic insights led to gratitude for the experience overall. She was sent to a drug rehab before she had actually used drugs and was cruelly targeted by the program owner in group sessions. Additionally, she experienced physically painful punishments such as being forced to carry a bucket of rocks in spite of her scoliosis. She reports that although the program did not help her in a direct way, it prepared her for helping others. She was one of the highest scoring participants and reports a remarkable sense of gratitude.

After being sent to rehab—after not doing drugs—I went through this period in my life where I was like "Fuck you, universe! I'm gonna do a bunch of drugs." And I did a lot of psychedelics and smoked pot and would run around in the woods thinking about all this stuff, like "Why?", and "How?" I had been through like why and how, it's one of those things where, I don't know if you've done psychedelics, but psychedelics make you ask a lot of questions, so I asked myself a lot of questions about, "Why did I experience this? And what can I gain from it? And is there anything beneficial here? Like filter through the stuff. I did for myself like, what I've always done

201

for other people, and that took a lot of work, digesting what I experienced, and realizing that it was worth it in the long run (Valorie, H2281).

Cee Cee, who is among the ten highest scoring participants in the study, has been sober for 20 years but described an intergenerational effect related to substance abuse. After spending five years in a therapeutic boarding school, which she entered more than 30 years ago, she began using addictive substances. Since then, her adult children have also become involved in substance use. Although two them are no longer using, at the time of the interview, one child had just been arrested for a drug related crime. She describes her life as being centered around recovery and during the interview she described ways her experiences in the program negatively affected her approach to mothering and her children's development.

Ann and Greg mentioned that they currently drink alcohol in moderation and a few described their past or current relationship with marijuana as "self-medication," none indicated that they are currently struggling with addiction and only one (Frank, H) indicated that he currently smokes "too much pot." Considering the large number of participants who were placed in treatment for teenage substance use, it is striking that so little emphasis was placed on the topics of addiction and recovery in treatment. Howard has remained sober since his time in treatment and it is possible or likely that others have also remained free of illicit drug use since exiting the program but did not mention it.

Participants in this study reported a wide range of experiences with drugs after exiting the program. Two (13%) in group H (Cee Cee and Iris) and four (27%) in group L (Tony, Dee Dee, Sebrina, and Donnie) have lost numerous friends from the program to overdose deaths. Three (20%) in group H (Iris,

Valorie & Aaron) reported therapeutic benefits from substance use after exiting the program.

School, career, and advocacy for youth

About one-fourth of interview participants, two in group H and six in group L (27%), emphasized that inadequate schooling and a disruption to their education were important negative aspects of the program. For some, the quality of the education was too remedial and for others, the lack of qualified educators on staff had a negative impact on their learning. Others reported that school learning was of secondary importance, and punishments or other program related functions could routinely take up scheduled classroom time. Kam reported that after she graduated from the program's high school, she later discovered that because the program was unaccredited, her high school diploma was invalid. Only two (7%) participants (Cee Cee & Nathan) emphasized that they had a positive opinion of the classroom education received in the program.

A surprising finding in this study is that seven participants (47%) in group L and four (27%) in group H are currently working, have attempted to work, or are working toward a job in human services, education, or social justice professions. Mary, Joan, and Donnie are currently in college, or have spent most of their adult life in college working toward social work or counseling degrees. Carmen, Ozzie, Sebrina, Dee Dee and Bobbi are currently employed as social workers, special education instructors, and therapists. Lawrence is currently working on a graduate degree so that he can work as a program director.

Among the lower scoring participants, extremely negative program experiences led to a life-changing urge to do everything they can to ensure that others are provided with better options. Additionally, two in group H and two in group L (13%)

(Xander, Iris, Quill and Rudi) have done volunteer or advocacy work directly related to their concern about program impacts. These findings linking negative experiences to efforts to prevent harm and be of service to others are especially interesting because most of the advocates were in group L, which was randomly selected.

The prominence of youth-oriented career choices is contrasted by participants who described a range of ways that the program has impacted their career paths. Some reported that program-related teachings are applicable in the professional setting. Others reported that valuable life lessons taught them how to better accept and communicate with co-workers. On the more negative side of the spectrum, similar to Greg's description of "getting his feelings off" on roommates, Pat reported that her "brutal honesty" and tendency to confront coworkers as if she were still in the program has led to being fired from numerous positions. Xander reported that his tendency to confess personal details led him to disclose his experience in the program on his application and now, because he admitted to substance use as a teenager, his promotion potential is limited. What is striking is that in both groups, participants described personal tendencies that they explicitly or implicitly link to post-traumatic stress disorder symptoms. In both groups, but primarily in group L, despite these barriers, several are currently in college or graduate school; at least six (40%) (Carmen, Tony, Dee Dee, Bobbi, Sebrina, and Ozzie) have earned graduate degrees and are currently succeeding in highly respected professions.

RQ3.4 Personal Impact

Table 4-34. Personal Impact: Comparison of Code Counts

Topic Number and Heading	Code Subcategories	Group H (N=15)	Group L (N=15)	Difference	Total
3.4 Personal Impact					
	Personal: Understanding/ Self-perception: Tangible/ Physical	1	6	5	7
	Personal: Experience of Trauma	4	12	8	16
	Personal: Healing from Trauma	4	4	0	8
	Perspective: Complicated Mix	5	3	2	8

Twelve participants (80%) in group L, and four (27%) in group H, explicitly named symptoms associated with traumatic stress as one of the most impactful aspects of the experience. Panic attacks, debilitating anxiety, flashbacks, triggering reminders, nightmares, mistrust of clinical professionals, difficulties in relationships, social isolation, a sense of loss of self, and a lingering sense of violation, were dominant topics in the interviews. Two noted that although they suffer from post-traumatic stress symptoms, they are unable to afford counseling or have been resistant to seeking professional help.

The onset of traumatic stress symptoms was often delayed and/or worsened during the first few years after exiting the program. For others, especially among those who have been out for many years, it was common to hear that symptoms resulting from exposure to trauma were much worse during the first few years after release. At least nine out of the 16 who reported such symptoms are college educated, currently employed as social workers or counselors, or are educated in the social science fields. One of the key findings in this study is that there seems to be a link between healing from "treatment trauma" and work in the social service professions.

Participants in both groups reported that they have navigated for many years a set of PTSD symptoms that originated in the program. This navigation of long-term effects was described as a long-term relationship with healing. One participant, who recently participated as a research subject in a university project studying the treatment of PTSD, found that meditation practices and psychoeducational aspects of the therapy were helpful. Others described an important piece of healing that occurred through "discovering" their trauma and learning about the way trauma affected them throughout their lives.

They emphasized the importance of working as advocates and how they have gained from their traumatic experiences by applying themselves with determination to work in care-providing fields. They described this as one way to put the experience of trauma to a constructive purpose so that others do not have to go through the same types of experiences. Some explicitly indicated that they have learned to turn their resentment into a passion for prevention.

At least six (40%) (Iris in group H, and Dee Dee, Quill, Ozzie, Donnie, and Rudi in group L) have worked to raise awareness or have worked with other former members of their programs to obtain state records or provide information to journalists. Those who work as advocates see their education and career choices as part of their long-term effort to prevent harm in institutional settings. Even five in the higher scoring group emphasized that the program design from which they directly or indirectly benefitted, was an unethical way to treat youth.

Others were more direct, stating that they have been actively involved in closing down abusive programs.

At least three (20%) in group H (for example, Valorie, Iris, and Xander) had more-negative treatment experiences but have found gratitude in their healing, have found meaning through connecting with others in fields other than youth services. Xander reported that until he began to identify and heal from trauma, he compulsively brought up his teen treatment experience when introducing himself to new acquaintances, even decades after his release from the program. When his wife pointed this out, he made an effort to stop talking about it, but in that process, became more isolated in general. But he was unaware of this until he began doing prison ministry. When relating to prisoners and sharing about his own experiences with institutional abuse, he discovered an appropriate context for sharing his personal details.

Part of his healing was in discovering that his traumatic experiences can be a source of connection, and as a connecting point, a new meaning and new dimension of healing gave him new perspectives on the experience. After three decades of being driven by traumatic stress symptoms, he has found a new relationship with his trauma and a complex mix of gratitude, insight, and spiritual acceptance in the ability to embrace his past. This embracing of the past as the past has afforded him space and a healthy distance from the experience. He says that his life was impaired by trauma and he wished he could just cut off that part of his self and bury his disturbing memories. Only in recent years has he gained a perspective on the experience that has allowed him space, but not total freedom, from the program's negative impact. This type of "healing journey" was described at length by Rudi and was mentioned or alluded to by others in group L.

Those who experienced harm and a long-term process of healing described a life course marked by stages of reconciliation. Rudi described a noteworthy example of reconciliation with a former staff member who denied her medical care. Rudi was in a wilderness program more than 20 years ago and in recent years she went to visit the staff member, "Bob," who did not believe she needed medical attention during a long hike in the desert. Bob thought she was faking it and denied her requests for care. Her kidney infection and dehydration had become life threatening when she was finally allowed to see a doctor. After Rudi graduated she learned a similar but even more tragic story of a boy under Bob's care who died because he was denied medical attention. She felt compelled to go and confront him face-to-face and ended up buying him breakfast, and then lunch, so they could keep talking.

> That's part of what I'm trying to swallow. Bob didn't intend to hurt anyone, but he did. People died under his care. But when I met him for breakfast there was remorse, he didn't do it on purpose he just, you know he wanted to help. I hugged him, that's the first thing I did when I saw him. He denied me the hospital, denied me food, denied me everything. I bought him breakfast and water and coffee, we sat down we talked for hours and then I bought him lunch, you know? And that was like huge, and I really think it was important for both him and for me, and I don't hold any anger towards him because he was, he just was, ignorant you know? (Rudi, L328).

Rudi went to see him before she had forgiven him, and part of her struggle was that if Bob had "learned his lesson" with her, perhaps a death could have been prevented. After going and facing him, as she reflected on Bob's own childhood and his current struggles, she found the ability to forgive herself also.

> He has his own struggles in life. Imagine being responsible for the death of a teenager because you didn't believe that they were sick. And like part of me is thinking like, he didn't believe me when I was sick, and when he found out I really was he didn't learn his lesson. And then I'm thinking you know I can't hold everyone to the same [standard] not everyone's going to behave right, make the right decision, do the right thing, you know. I don't do the right thing every time either (Rudi, L329).

Rudi explained that this ability to forgive and empathize allows her to forgive herself for how she treated others in the program. The conditions in her program were extreme and the culture was abusive at times. She engaged in group confrontation sessions as part of the therapy, and for Rudi, empathy for Bob enabled empathy for her own participation in abuse.

> So, it's like, I think trying to forgive [staff] and have compassion for them is giving me more of an opportunity to forgive myself. Forgive myself for being an asshole to "Cathy," you know. You know acting in a certain way towards "Glenn," or you know, like the times in the program where I wasn't very compassionate (Rudi, L329).

Rudi's understanding of healing from trauma also informs her understanding of the social dynamics among her cohort. She believes that some former residents from her program continue to engage in abusive behaviors in their current lives. Based on her own experience, she believes this is partly due to their inability to perceive and understand the intensity of the abuse and neglect they were exposed to.

> I think it's tragic, and you can see how they maintain that abusive relationship throughout their life. On Facebook we have a survivors group we also have a [program name] group and there's people who defend some of the [staff]. I will defend Bob, he didn't intend to hurt anyone but he did, you know, so there are these other people who think he's a great man who, you know think he saved them from their destructive lives at home, blah blah blah, which I think is like they're telling themselves that story because they can't swallow the reality of what happened, you know they can't see the human behavior for what it is (Rudi, L337–338).

One of the surprising findings in this study is that in general, participants who praised their programs did not seem to minimize the harm that they or others experienced. Similarly, lower scoring participants emphasized or mentioned that it "wasn't all bad" and that they had managed to get some good out of an overwhelmingly negative experience. Participants described a complicated mix in the range of impact and responses to treatment. For example, Howard, who has been sober for 35 years since his intake into a program, said that one of the main benefits is a mindset and source of strength he gained there. After exiting the program, he found that even in the harshest military trainings, he found comfort in knowing that no matter what he had to go through, it would not be worse than his time in treatment. "I haven't found a thing yet, that, you know, was worse than being stuck in a rehab for 18 months as a teenager with 400 other kids, 300 kids that were there at the time" (Howard, H2079).

A similarly complicated mix of impacts is described by Mary, who gained empathy and sympathy for others but now experiences chronic pain in her shoulders where her backpack straps cut into them.

> I have such a great interest in working with teens in similar situations so that's really what I've done with my life until recently is work towards that. And I believe that going through something like that really helps you develop a great sympathy and empathy for others. And I've used that trait of mine in deciding what career I want to choose for myself. But it's also, obviously the chronic pain is something that affects every aspect of my life so that's been something huge that I would say came from this program (Mary, L1113–1114).

RQ3.5 Social Skills: Improved and Impaired

Table 4-35. Social Skills: Improved and Impaired: Comparison of Code Counts

Topic Number and Heading	Code Subcategories	Group H (N=15)	Group L (N=15)	Difference	Total
3.5 Social Skills	Social: Improving Skills	5	4	1	9
	Social: Impaired Skills	3	10	7	13
	Personal: Understanding/ Self-perception: Jargon, Habits	3	2	1	5

In describing the way program experiences impacted their social skills, the two subgroups were clearly divided, but in an interesting way. Participants in both groups identified ways that

211

their social skills were improved but the emphasis on impaired social skills was more prevalent in group L. In the code subcategory for impaired social skills, ten participants (67%) in group L were counted. This count does not include the statements that only mention impaired social skills in passing or those coded to other subcategories. Three participants (20%) in group H discussed program impact in terms of impaired social skills directly linked to their program experiences.

Improved social skills included better use of language, communication and conflict resolution skills. Also, more ease in disclosing personal information, more interests and appreciation for loved ones, learning to accept and deal with disliked people, healthier boundaries, enhanced ability for self-expression, and ability to understand a wider range of mental illnesses. The participants who attributed these improved social skills to treatment, attributed their development directly to growth and learning within the program.

In the same way, negative social impairment was also described as being a direct result of adapting to demands within the program environment. Participants reported that the impairment of social skills resulted from or was identified as they navigated the disruption of lost friendships. Statements coded as negative impairments identified by participants included such things as the tendency for oversharing and overstepping personal boundaries, not being understood when talking about the program, yelling too much, experiences of shame and stigma over being sent away, a general sense of alienation, rigid or black and white thinking, becoming more confrontational, blunt honesty, difficulty trusting or letting others in, and when forming new relationships feeling as it is necessary to disclose the full extent of a dark experience.

RQ3.6 Knowledge

Table 4-36. Knowledge: Comparison of Code Counts

Topic Number and Heading	Code Subcategories	Group H (N=15)	Group L (N=15)	Difference	Total
3.6 Knowledge					
	Knowledge: About program	8	12	4	20
	Knowledge: About larger related issues	4	13	9	17
	Personal: Understanding/ Self-perception: Compared to Others	9	1	8	10
	Trajectory: Internal Processes	9	10	1	19

Three participants (20%) in group H (Nathan, Iris and Aaron) and 13 (87%) in group L, said they participated in the interview because they wanted others to know these places exist and they want to help prevent harm; they want to raise awareness and for parents to know how harmful such programs can be. Participants who had more-positive experiences reported a different sort of advocacy: that they want others to know their side of the story. They want the world to know that these programs are not all bad and do help people to lead healthier, empowered lives. Whether concerned about how harmful programs can be or concerned about how negatively others speak about them, all are impacted in various ways by their knowledge. All participants in this study have been impacted by their knowledge of the program, knowledge about their cohort and staff members, and/or the larger issue of "the troubled teen industry."

Knowledge about their programs

All participants discussed at least one topic related to program history, current events, and program closures but not all such statements were coded as knowledge. Six participants (40%) in group H (Lawrence, Ann, Cee Cee, Frank, Barry, Wilma) reported being sad, uncomfortable, or concerned that their programs had closed, or they indicated concern that teen treatment programs in general seem to have a bad reputation. In explaining the reason their program had closed, they mentioned civil or criminal lawsuits and insurance reasons. Lawrence reported this as one of the main reasons he wanted to participate in an interview. "The reason for that is these programs, as I'm sure you know, you've done a lot of interviews, they get a lot of negative attention, they're closing down all over the country and I don't think it's right" (Lawrence, H1190). His positive treatment experience contradicts the negative reports that he hears frequently.

> The thing that people don't talk about when it comes to these programs is yeah, there are a lot of kids that go out there and have a really bad time, don't listen to directions, get hurt or whatever it is, and that's just kind of the nature of the beast. So anyway, I just wanted to have an opportunity to speak my part. It's, I think it's way more beneficial than not...I'm on a couple of different groups on the internet and you know, it's about 50–50—50% of people say that they have PTSD and stuff like that from it, and other people say it was awesome, so it's just a mixed bag. Just like any therapeutic model, it doesn't work for everybody (Lawrence, H1194–1196).

Wilma reported her knowledge about a current criminal case against her program's owner. The program was forced to cease operations in 2016 when the FBI opened an investigation. The owner was recently convicted of assault with intent to commit sexual abuse, sexual exploitation of a child by a counselor, and child endangerment. While the case was being tried, several former residents wrote op-ed articles about the abuses they witnessed there, explaining how the program was designed. Former residents who were critical of the program started a petition to gather signatures among eye-witnesses who experienced abuse in this program. In her interview, Wilma reported that she was disturbed by the way such critics "backlashed" former residents who publicly supported the program owner during the investigation. To Wilma, their actions indicated something negative about their personal character.

> So, it also questions them, kind of who they are as a person. Like if you're against him then you're against him, you know. You're doing your whole petition, do your whole petition, but like the ones who are helping, like, let them help. Like you don't need to backlash. We're not backlashing you, you know. So, it really shows who you are as a person and how you're doing right now, you know. (Wilma, H1401).

Four participants (13%) (Rudi, Nathan, Quill, and Aaron) reported that there have been deaths within their programs. Others (for example, Mary, Cee Cee, and Bobbi) learned about near death experiences while in the program or soon after release. Rudi reported that after she left, the same staff member who did not believe her when she became seriously ill, was responsible for the death of a youth who was denied medical care for a perforated ulcer. She reported that the year before this death, a young girl had overheated and died in the same program.

Knowledge about systemic issues

Participants discussed their knowledge about historical and political research as well state policy issues related to totalistic programs. Others reported that their knowledge came from reading news reports about civil court cases brought against their program after they had exited. One participant had recently learned that the day after a youth was found dead, the owner of her program filed for bankruptcy. This had occurred just a few months before her interview and although she had graduated years ago, the news impacted her deeply.

Joan and Quill reported that they were impacted emotionally and in practical ways when they learned that their records had been destroyed right after their graduation. They learned that the state where their program was located did not require therapeutic boarding schools to adhere to ethical and professional record keeping standards. Others mentioned the status of the program, whether their program was closed, that it was still open, that it had changed names, or that it had become less abusive over the years.

Knowledge, identity, and cohort

In the most positive cases, participants reported that their program experiences led to very positive changes in self-identity and how they know themselves.

> I was the guy who would yell at strangers for no reason because I thought it was funny and now I am

known by everyone that's ever known me as like the sweetest person on the planet...I was a really broken person for a really long time and now I'm one of the most powerful people you'll ever meet (Lawrence, H1186, 1207).

As mentioned earlier, when among other former residents they have referred to themselves as something similar to war veterans and one reported that although he does not identify himself that way, he believes that his treatment experience "had this sort of intensity of war" and reports that one veteran of America's war in Vietnam recognized something within him.

They would all identify with me. At some point a guy at a bar I was at was asking you know, we were talking about stuff, he was asking me if, if I had seen action, you know. And I was like "Dude I've never been in a uniform of any kind." And he was like "Man you just, the way you seem to understand this," and I was like well, you know, I said I went through some stuff, that's all I can say. I didn't really even know how to explain that to somebody. But it was like, no, but it was like being a war veteran (Xander, H2183).

Five participants (17%) identified themselves as "survivors" (Mary, L; Kam, L; Sebrina, L; Aaron, H; Nathan, H). Rather than identifying specifically as survivors of abuse, they implied or explicitly stated that they were program survivors, survivors of treatment. As mentioned above, several are working as professionals in care-related fields, but not all referred to themselves as advocates and none identified as an activist. At the end of the interview, when asked how they would like to be identified, six (40%) in each group indicated that they think of themselves as, alumni, graduates, or former residents.

217

RQ3.7 Perspective

Table 4-37. Perspective: Comparison of Code Counts

Topic Number and Heading	Code Subcategories	Group H (N=15)	Group L (N=15)	Difference	Total
3.7 Perspective					
	On Program	7	9	2	16
	On Other People	8	8	0	16
	Changes In	4	9	5	13
	Meaning and Value of Program	11	4	7	15

Some of the most interesting findings are those that reveal participant perspectives on the topic of totalistic teen treatment. Almost all of those interviewed have been interested in this subject for many years. They are experts in the way their program worked, its history, and the way their cohort thinks and feels about the experience. The informed judgements of participants in this study help to demonstrate some profound insights and areas of needed research.

Participants explained how a short-term outdoor program that is experienced with a sense of empowerment and comradery can have as many long-lasting benefits as a long-term program. When there is good fit with the program design and when placed with other youth who are similar, simply working together on fun projects can be a pivotal turning point.

> [The outdoor program] had as much impact in eight weeks that [the therapeutic boarding school] had in a year and a half...There's something about coming together with 10 strangers who all have similar issues and similar thought processes and you know, working together and trying to complete a task every day was really awesome (Lawrence, H1125, 1127).

The way Lawrence described program closures indicates something unique among those who have a more positive perspective on their own experience. Participants in group H seem more aware of how negative bias affects perspective and that this has unfairly affected the status of their programs.

> People who are negative about it are way more likely to talk about it. You know, my friends that went through [the outdoor program], I'm still close with almost everyone in my peer group but we don't talk about [the program] you know what I mean? Because there's nothing to talk about. We went through it, everything was good and fine and dandy, it's just nine weeks of our lives and we moved forward. But if it was a really negative experience, that's all they would talk about (Lawrence, H1197–1199).

Cee Cee explained that several women who were in her program currently blame some of their problems on the years they spent in their facility. But she believes that it is family connection and the reason for placement that determines the outcome a program will have. She was raped repeatedly by her father and then rejected by her mother who placed her in a program for many years "to get rid of her." In Cee Cee's perspective, after speaking with women from her program, she was convinced that it is not the program that determines outcomes, but family support. She explained that if a parent cares enough to place their child in a program, they must be a nurturing parent who will also be there after treatment. In her experience, she has come to believe that the girls who were placed by concerned parents had stronger connections with family after the program and this made all the difference for them.

Kids that are there for their behavior, I'm sure had a nurturing parent. I'm just giving an example, let's say they skip school, whatever, I'm sure they had a nurturing parent, let's say, and then they grow up and when they get out they're still close to their parent and had a nurturing parent growing up, and they just chose to act bad and then they put them in there for certain to teach them a lesson or whatever, and when they get out they're still close to their parent, they still have that parent to go to. Well I didn't have that coming out (Cee Cee, H859).

For others in group H, their perspective has deepened as they have reflected on their experience over time. Nathan identified a perplexing paradox where opposites can be true at the same time.

[In the program] was this weird dichotomy of always being afraid of something you could say while also in other regards feeling pretty safe because you know you can't be ridiculed in a certain way for certain topics—you'd be at least taken seriously. So, like on the one hand for example, you do have to worry about your peers reporting you, in a somewhat Orwellian sense now that I think about it, while also, though, however, those same mechanisms prevent anyone from speaking or gossiping about you. Like if someone has a problem with you they can talk, can talk about it with someone else and think about it out loud and talk to them but they then will be expected to confront you in a productive way and to resolve that issue. You can't just talk crap about someone behind their back, that would be punished. So again, this weird dichotomy of never feeling safe while also feeling very safe and feeling that you can be open and emotionally sensitive. It puts you, or, I was put anyway, in this very oddly psychologically vulnerable state which I think by design is meant to help us talk about really personal, troubling things (Nathan, H1742–1744).

Participants in group L emphasized various ways their perspective has changed over the years since exiting the program. Those who graduated with more-positive perspectives described a process of disillusionment. Those who left with an exclusively negative perspective, whether they formally completed the program or not, acknowledged they now see some positive effects mixed in with the negative. They used phrases like, "I know now," or "now that I am an adult," to explain that as teens in treatment, they were unaware of the inappropriateness of certain practices. For others, with education they developed a larger vocabulary and only gained the ability to articulate things about their experience years after the fact. When asked how their responses to interview questions now might compare to when they first got out of the program, some reported that the main difference between now and the time they exited is that the emotional intensity has softened.

I would probably be a lot more emotional about it. I would probably be angrier about it you know. But you know it's been a long time, like almost 10 years now and so you know those things kind of start to heal over time, but I would say my answers would be the same, just with higher intensity (Sebrina, L720).

221

Subgroup Comparisons

Five code subcategories describe the strongest similarities between subgroups: strongest memories, reentry, knowledge about their program, impact on family relationships, and the interview. The strongest memories were of people and close friendships made in the program. Both groups described the reentry process as a challenge they were unprepared for and demonstrated extensive knowledge about their program and teen programs in general. They both described a similar range of long-term impacts on their family relationships. The five main similarities are summarized in Table 4-38.

Table 4-38. Major Similarities in Impact (RQ3)

Topic	Commonality Between Groups
Strongest Memories	The best memories were of close friendships. The most prevalent memories, and/or the majority of strongest ones, were somewhat or extremely negative memories of the program structure. Participants in both groups noted that there were two distinct types of memories: good ones about the people and bad ones about the place.
Reentry	Transitioning to life after the program was difficult for most. Six in group H (G, CC, X, U, I, AA) described escalations in substance use after exiting. Even in some of the most positive cases, "good things" had to be relearned in the real world. Nine in group L and five in group H (G, F, N, I W) described a very challenging or shocking transition out that they were ill prepared for.
Knowledge About Program	Participants in both groups have extensive knowledge about the current state of their program, its history, and details about the staff members, changes the program went through over the years and the program status with state regulations.

Impact on Family	Both described a range that is similar for both groups. Participants in each group reported strained or broken relationships with family that have not yet healed. Some in both groups reported many years of estrangement that have been mostly or completely reconciled recently. Perhaps four in group H reported that the program caused authentic, sustained improvements in parent relationships that have been simply, consistently "good."
The Interview	All participants were highly articulate, insightful, warm and grateful for the chance to talk about their experiences and current perspectives. Most in both groups used program jargon without seeming aware of it, and both slipped into speaking in the present tense at times, as if reliving parts of their experiences.

One of the most interesting contrasts between the two subgroups is in the types of reconciling they seem to be faced with. In group H, there was an emphasis on explaining why they were able to benefit from a program that others found abusive. In group L however, when discussing harm and complex program dynamics, participants brought up the fact that it is impossible to know how their lives would have turned out without the program or that it is hard to know what really caused what. When describing how their lives have unfolded since exiting the program, they brought up their perspective on the program and its influence, and when describing their perspective, they brought up examples about the trajectories of their lives. This reconciling was consistent, but its content varied depending on the different impacts, and the different pathways they described. The ten most striking general differences between the two groups are summarized in Table 4-39.

Table 4-39. Major Differences in Impact (RQ3)

Topic	Group H	Group L
Knowledge About Treatment Industry	Six believe it is unfair that their program has been closed, or that programs in general are closing.	Had extensive knowledge about other programs, books, articles, and movies, about their own program and other programs. They tended to mention political and state level issues that contribute to harm in teen programs.
Self-Perception; Self Compared to Others	When describing benefits of treatment they also acknowledged they are aware of harm others experienced in the same program. Seven (W, F, H, Y, B, L, A) referred to themselves as the "lucky ones," the exception to the rule, the rare example. Four in this group (V, N, X, AA) are actively "redeeming" the experience by continually healing and reflecting on the experience of trauma, and are aware that not everyone is able to do this.	Some emphasized that self-deception was important to overcome, a first step in healing. Many reported that trauma prevents people from perceiving harm visited and perpetrated. They refer to the effects of "brainwashing," denial, and self-deception to explain why others continue to believe such methods are effective.
Trauma	Five (V, N, X, AA, I) experienced or witnessed trauma and have healed or are recovering from the experience. Seven (W, F, H, B, L, A) did not report perceptions of harm.	Eleven reported traumatic experiences and almost all indicated harmful impacts. Healing from trauma was described as a long-term process.
Meaning and Value of Program	Consistently positive meaning or became positive over time. More gratitude. It was a challenge that was uncomfortable, but in a good way, or life-saving.	Increasingly negative or consistently negative meaning. "It taught me how to survive in an abusive environment." More often described as an ongoing trauma or as a long-term process of trying to recover from the experience.
Impairment and Barriers	A few reported their social life and education were disrupted with an experience of alienation upon reentry. Some mentioned healing from trauma, healing ruptured boundaries.	School, educational achievement, career, and social relations were often reported as negatively affected. Intimate relationships were impaired.

Table 4-39. Continued.

Topic	Group H	Group L
Internal processes over time	Positive opinions sustained OR increase in substance use and alienation prior to coming back to feeling grateful for program as part of recovery from drugs. (Almost as if they externalized program trauma or acted out a self-fulfilling prophesy (labeling theory) that prevents perception of harm and trauma) OR, a sense that all the pieces fit just perfectly.	Afraid to criticize the program; positive opinions sustained a short time. Disillusionment, still readjusting to life, discovering trauma, opening eyes and gaining empathy for others as part of healing process.
Changing Perspective	Has changed little. For five (V, N, X, AA, I) opinion may have changed but gratitude informs overall perspective.	With realization and perception of harm comes a sense of self betrayal and resentment for being exposed to such pressure to change. As if learning they were deceived continues to hit them in increasingly profound ways.
Perspective on Other People/ Cohort	More often reported that others are critical of their program.	More focused on amount of harm done to cohort, concern over suicides, overdose deaths, broken relationships.
Reason for Participating in Interview	More often reported they want their side told. Aware they are the counter narrative. Want "good" effects and good programs to be known. Five want to help prevent harm and promote better practices.	Want parents to know that harmful programs exist and want to do what they can to help prevent harm to others. Nine are currently in school or working with troubled youth, advocates for improved options.
Summative Generalizations	The benefits have been consistently positive OR (for four: G, CC, U, I) delayed in appearance. When delayed, if no perception of harm, benefits came after years of substance abuse. If perception of harm, the same, but with descriptions of trauma and healing from trauma.	The impact is still unfolding, the program effects are not in the past. Its negative effects and challenges are still occurring and still being discovered. The most positive effect is the empathy that comes through devoting oneself to advocacy, a career in the human services, or to working to prevent harm.

225

5

❀ CONCLUSIONS ❀

Overview

Chapter 5 is divided into four main sections. In the first, the categorical, comparative, and topical analyses are built upon and interpreted as themes. In the second section, some of the key findings are applied to proposed federal policy for the prevention of institutional abuse. The third section reviews the study's limitations, weaknesses, and recommendations for future research. Finally, a summary of the project concludes with a call to action. Since the researcher is a primary instrument in any qualitative study (Cresswell & Poth, 2018; Yin, 2016), the thematic analysis is introduced with a note about reflexivity as a means of improving the quality of research.

Reflexive Practice in Qualitative Analysis

The researcher's lens always shapes the emergence of themes (Yin, 2016) and in this analysis, the researcher's lens is informed by insider and outsider perspectives (Eppley, 2006; Matthews & Salazar, 2014). The researcher's insider perspective is informed by personal experience in a totalistic teen program during the 1980s and by adult learning experiences spanning three decades. The outsider's perspective has been intentionally developed in personal ways and in undergraduate and graduate studies of scientific literature relevant to the topic and the methods for exploring it. The qualitative researcher who consciously shifts between insider and outsider perspectives is not fully "in" or "out," but on a continuum of subjective inquiry that can result in richer and more rigorous analysis if that subjectivity is actively examined (Eppley, 2006; Roulston & Shelton, 2015). In this project, the researcher actively engaged with the data by examining personal assumptions in light of multiple perspectives at all stages of the project (Charmaz, 2017). Rather than attempting to become more disinterested and objective, the researcher attempted to be sensitive to his "inquirer posture" and how easy it is to misunderstand and misrepresent participant statements (Roulston & Shelton, 2015, p. 335). A first-person narrative essay describing some of these reflections is included in Appendix I.

One of the dangers is that the researcher's personal perspective may be mistaken for the participants'. Without the reflexive capacity to distinguish between the two there is more chance the researcher's thumb will wind up in every picture, influencing the way data are understood. In all stages of this project, an attempt was made to remain aware and extra careful when participants' reports were uncanny in their resemblance to the researcher's personal experience. In coding decisions and in analysis, the researcher worked hard to develop personal skills and practices to remain true to the data. This involved frequently double-checking and self-checking; double-checking the transcripts to examine the data repeatedly from the participants' perspectives and self-checking to distinguish between personal experience and the evidence. Hopefully, the design of this study is rigorous enough to ensure the interpretation does not extend beyond the data. And hopefully, enough detail and transparency are provided to allow readers to judge the researcher's trustworthiness and "methodicness" in developing this thematic analysis (Yin, 2016, p. 14).

227

Themes

This section describes three themes in the data that help to explain the differences and similarities in experiences, effects and impacts described by participants. These themes were informed by the explicit topics and code subcategories most-often mentioned by both group H and group L, or those showing greatest the most contrast between the two. Themes are one of many possible ways to express some of the implicit meanings in the data and to summarize large amounts of data in an abstract and meaningful way. These themes were identified through the development of codes, categories, and topics and were refined through journaling about dominant patterns and processes found throughout the stages of this project.

The goal of thematic analysis is "to identify patterns in the data that are important or interesting, and use these themes to address the research or say something about an issue" (Maguire & Delahunt, 2017, p. 3353). Themes are abstractions, "ideas that run through" the data (Harding, 2013, p. 6). Saldaña (2016) emphasizes that topics and code categories are explicit labels and a theme reflects more implicit patterns and processes (p. 16). The thematic analysis presented here distills the explicit categories and topics presented in Chapter 4, condensing their implicit essence in three themes that answer the research questions.

Table 5-1 helps to provide examples of the way the themes answer the research questions and relate to the topics presented in Chapter 4. This introduction briefly describes the themes and concepts that are explained at length in this section. In answer to Research Question 1, totalistic teen treatment methods are experienced as a process of induction/abduction and of being contained. In answer to Research Question 2, the immediate effects are described as a process of containment/release. The experience leads to changes, and these changes were described as learning to become part of the program. In this sense, containment involves becoming part of the container—an active member and an integral part of the containment structure. Release is the short-term experience of congruence and the long-term goal of graduation. In answer to Research Question 3, the impacts are described in terms of trajectory and perspective across the adult life span. Each theme refers to two concepts that are expressed in different ways. These concepts are informed by sets of topics that were based on prominent code subcategories.

Table 5-1. How Themes, Research Questions and Topics are Related

RQ	Theme	Concept	Topic Numbers	Most Relevant Topics
RQ1	Induction Abduction	Induction (led toward: induct, induce)	C3; C5; 1.1; 1.2; 1.3; 1.5; 1.10; 1.11;	Prior Placements; Attitude Toward Placement; Intake and Introduction; The Staff; Social Environment *; Learning the Ropes; Emotional Intensity; Witnessing
RQ1	Induction Abduction	Abduction (led away from: the past, the outside world, the old-self)	C1; C2; 1.8; 1.12; 1.3	Reasons for Placement; Parents and Home Life; Controlled Communication; Frames of Reference: Social Environment *

Table 5-1. Continued.

RQ1	Containment Release	Containment (being contained)	C4; 1.4; 1.6; 1.7; 1.9; 1.13; 1.14	Educational Consultant, Forcible Transport, Deceptive Intake; Program Philosophy; Program Design; Personal Autonomy; Deprivation of Basic Needs; Escape; Program Fit
RQ2	Containment Release	Containment (becoming the container)	2.1; 2.2; 2.4	Changing Relationships with Parents; Personal Growth*; Negative Changes
RQ2	Containment Release	Release (short-term relief within the program and long-term release from the program)	2.2; 2.3; 2.5	Personal Growth*; Practical Benefits; Making Progress
RQ3	Trajectory Perspective	Trajectory	3.2; 3.3; 3.4; 3.5	Social Impact; Trajectory; Personal Impact; Social Skills
RQ3	Trajectory Perspective	Perspective	3.1; 3.6; 3.7	Memories; Knowledge; Perspective

Note. * indicates topics of social environment and personal growth appear twice.

The first theme, induction/abduction, describes a simultaneous "toward and away" motion expressing placement in the program and removal from the world. This experience of being "led toward" treatment and "led away from" the past was described as one overwhelming phenomenon. Personal boundaries within the milieu were reduced while boundaries blocking access to communication with the outside world were increased.

The second theme, containment/release, has two parts. This theme highlights the act of containing the individual as well as the process individuals go through as they become part of the containment structure. Interactions within the program environment create a milieu of transformation where youth actively participate in their own containment and the containment of others. The process of containment is driven by a long-term and short-term desire for release. In the short-term, the experience of release was described as relief from constant pressures and the sense of making daily progress. The long-term goal of actual release from the program was described as a realization that the easiest way is to "put one's head down" or to "do whatever it takes to get through the levels." Containment and release are conceptualized here as two opposing forces that are inseparable and driving each other.

The third theme, trajectory and perspective, reflects the complex relationship between life events and how one views and reflects on them after exiting the program. In this study, participants provided a cross section of 30 different lives at various stages of the life course—windows into different stages and different relationships with the program experience. Four distinct types of impact pathways were identified in this analysis, helping to demonstrate the range of trajectories and perspectives expressed by this theme.

These three themes are presented as a framework for a multidisciplinary literature review of selected theories that help contextualize some of the different ways patterns in the data are woven and expressed. The interpretation presented here is certainly not the only way these findings could be organized and explained. Qualitative data do not speak for themselves, themes do not emerge as ready-made objects, and they are not assumed to have been there just waiting to be picked up by any researcher "who happens to pass by" (Pidgeon & Henwood, 2006, p. 627). Each passerby would certainly identify other ways to make abstractions about the data collected here. The qualitative researcher is the primary research instrument and this thematic analysis is filtered through several decades of personal experience and learning. Although this framework is subjective, it is grounded in empirical findings and stays as close to this "ground" as possible, using just enough abstraction to make a meaningful generalization with minimal distortion.

Induction/Abduction

> It was like stepping into Alice in Wonderland you know, it was a very unusual living environment. It was designed to make you uncomfortable all the time. It was a nightmare. It was a horrible, it was nuts. It was absolutely nuts. There's no way to imagine what it was like. Alice in Wonderland is the closest thing, although, if the rabbit had fangs (Aaron, H1968, 2003).

The origins of the word "induction" trace back to at least the 1300s when it was first translated as "induccioun," from the Latin, *inducere*, meaning "introduction to the grace of God" (Barnhart & Steinmetz, 2000). The Latin root, *ducere,* means "to lead," and the original meaning of induction was "lead into," and abduction, "lead away from." Since 1934, in American English, "induction" has also described enrollment into the military (p. 523). As a thematic pattern in this study, induction and abduction are conceptualized together, as a paradoxical motion because they occur simultaneously—toward and away at the same time.

Close to the meaning of induction, the Latin stem of *inducere*, *induc*, means "to induce." In describing their introduction to the program as an overwhelming disorientation, it is as if participants are describing the inducement of a process that began with a surprising or overwhelming shock. The theme of induction describes the challenging process of learning the ropes while experiencing intense or overwhelming emotions. For example, in Chapter 4, participants reported how rules and "agreements" could be broken, and harsh punishments prescribed, before any warning was given. New arrivals learned, that like the entry threshold they crossed unawares, they soon broke "agreements" they never made.

Participants described a double bind where resisting or questioning the program's fairness or logic could invite more punishments or restrictions. But in accepting this logic there is an implicit turning point—led away from predictable and conventional understandings of cause and effect and toward compliance and desire for progress through a new set of values and beliefs. As the structure's power was induced, the outside world, old habits, and the old self, became farther away. This turning was described on a continuum: in positive terms as being led away from all the negative influences of the outside world, and in negative terms as going down a rabbit hole, led away from the common sense and predictability of the outside world.

Participants referred to the induction process as a frustrating experience that taught them there was no choice and only one way out: to make progress through the levels of the program. Program staff might refer to such teaching moments as "institutionalized turning points" (Hitlin & Kramer, 2014, p. 17) or as inducing therapeutic surrender. However, some participants experienced this frustration as a lack of self-agency, reporting that those in authority acted in unpredictable and unethical ways. Regardless of how distressing it might feel to the initiate, the induction/abduction process is always officially "therapeutic" in the same way "treatment" is always something inherently good (Jöhncke, 2009). Initiates were led into the treatment process while being taken away from the past; led toward a new self, away from the old, presumably for their own good.

The transition from the outside world into the program milieu is a liminal experience. Anthropologists describe such initiatory moments as the exiting of one social realm while crossing into another. In pubescent initiation rites, the liminal experience is marked by statuslessness and dependency where the neophyte is "ground down" (Turner, 1987, p. 11) to a blank slate so they can be built back up (Turner, 1969, p. 103). In classic theories of change, the theme of induction/abduction describes an unfreezing process, a loosening of unwanted beliefs, attitudes, and identities (Lewin, 1947; Schein et al., 1961). This ancient process of total transformation is found throughout history in religious and military settings as well as modern day treatment facilities of many types (De Leon, 2000; Salter, 1998).

This ancient process is also expressed in some unusual and distinctly American narratives that help to situate this theme in a historical context while providing a rich, perhaps visceral description. In an ethnographic study among Americans who believe they were captured by aliens from outer space, Susan Lepselter (2016) explores the theme of abduction running through the uncanny stories provided to her during years of field research in the American West. She presents these accounts in historical context by honoring them as one of the many "captivity narratives" in American history. Her rich descriptions convey the expression of a unique trauma without focusing on how factual or fictious the source may be. As a group, her respondents described a collective experience of what Jeffery Alexander (2012) might explain as socially constructed cultural trauma, which can impact groups and populations as meaning is created and atrocities are processed in narrative form, regardless of their factual accuracy. Lepselter artfully alludes to alien abduction narratives as if they are emanating from some collective conscience, a social memory that is shared but also haunted by the darkness of genocide and slavery that mark our nation's past.

Many participants in Lepselter's research live in fear of an alien abduction happening again, and in discussing this fear, she describes a creative video (no longer available), featuring a Native American high school student rapping, "I'm not scared [of alien abduction], I went to boarding school" (p.60). In the video, these young artists flipped the narrative about the fear of alien abduction by pointing to UFOs as a way to escape the captivities of earth: "boarding school survivors, you're welcome on this flight!" Lepselter explains that for them, "the real abduction narrative is the boarding school story, and the true captivity is on earth" (Lepselter, 2016, p. 60).

Historically, in Native American boarding schools, youth were subjected to an overtly "benevolent" process of death and rebirth. In the late 1800s, Richard Henry Pratt, founder of the Carlisle Indian School explained his school's mission by saying it was necessary to "kill the Indian" to save the child (Archuleta, Child, & Lomawaima, 2000, p. 16; Dunbar-Ortiz, 2014, p. 151). This method required "tearing down of the old selves and the building of new ones" and these disorienting internal motions were carried out simultaneously (Adams, 1995, p. 101).

Participants in this study described the experience of disorientation and shock as overwhelming processes. These processes have been considered a therapeutic element in "shock incarceration" programs, which have been based on the therapeutic community model at least since the 1970s (Aziz & Clark, 1996). In the 1990s, treatment professionals such as James D. Lovern (1991) advocated for "Erickson-inspired" approaches to treatment in closed settings, reporting that professionals of the time believed "confusion is beautiful" and shock leads to "creative chaos," a necessary program component essential to breaking down treatment resistant residents (Lovern, 1991, p. 137–138).

> One of the primary functions of one treatment program was to induce confusion in both patients and groups, and then resolve the confusion by providing Twelve Step, Alcoholics Anonymous information. Gradually, as the cycle of confusion—restructuring was repeated over and over, patients and groups became more and more accepting of A.A. ideas and principles (Lovern, 1991, p. 136).

Participants in this study indicated that such methods may be in use today. And for youth who are informally incarcerated in private programs, after being tricked by parents or delivered by hired agents, the element of surprise may be especially shocking simply because there is no police or court process to legitimate the transition. Entry into the program was discovered after the door to the outside world had already been closed shut. Some described the pain of not being able to call loved ones to let them know what happened to them. Others described induction/abduction as an experience of being "yanked out" and "disappearing" from circles of friends.

The theme of induction/abduction describes transition in the treatment milieu. If there is a transition between induction/abduction and containment/release, it may be related to the process of becoming familiar with the program's philosophy of containment and accepting that there is only one way to obtain release. This process of adapting to the milieu, of "putting one's head down to get through" is expressed in several ways, revealing multiple dimensions of containment and release as a paradoxical process.

Containment/Release

> The biggest thing, the first thing was just the shock of the reality check that like, life doesn't just keep going as normal. Your whole world gets flipped upside down. I went in with some malice in my heart feeling like I didn't deserve this…so I definitely had moments of feeling resentment and feeling frustrated and feeling like it didn't make sense…feeling like the innocent prison inmate who knows that nothing they can say can get them out of the situation, they just need to put their head down and do their time. There was a lot of that feeling (Frank, H471–473).

> There were people who had bought into the program who were all like, you know, serious about the rules, and then there were like the newer people who were not that way, and who just wanted to be out of there (Bobbi, L1299).

> I didn't change for about nine months there, about half of my stay, and then I tried to run away and when I was trying to run away I was hitchhiking, trying to hitchhike out on the highway and it dawned on me

that as a 17-year-old girl this probably was not a very good idea and I went back. A staff member drove by and picked me up and I went back to the school and at that point I basically totally bought into the program, but it was because I realized that there was, you know, there was no way to escape (Kam, L2128).

If you just have one person who can't get their stuff together it affects the whole group negatively, so my group was able to put our heads down and get our stuff done (Lawrence, H1180–1181).

The theme of containment reflects a paradox: the program structure provided near-absolute boundaries against the outside world while softening, or violating, boundaries within the milieu. Personal boundaries were pierced through demanding and intensive practices in the name of breakthroughs and progress that could lead to release. Participants described these processes in short-term and long-term contexts. In the short-term, personal release came through gaining new insight or making oneself vulnerable, learning trust and being rewarded with progress, status, and privileges. They reported that moments of connection with friends were intensified because they were a moment of reprieve. Even brief moments of escape, like the ability to finally go to sleep, were described as a relief from the constant pressure of the milieu.

In the long-term, release from the program was earned through progress and genuine, sustained openness within the confines of this closed setting. Obedience and sincerity were rewarded, and only by earning these daily rewards could the resident access a formally sanctioned exit. Only by adapting in officially sanctioned ways to the demands and conditions could they gain release from the milieu. The officially sanctioned responses, whether they accompanied therapeutic changes or not, were those which also increased the power of the program. By learning to identify with the program and to enforce its rules by policing peers, containment also implies a process of becoming the container. This process appears to have the potential to help and/or harm, depending on the individual.

At the center of this theme, there is a driving logic that is circular and difficult to challenge. Participants in this study described four interlocking assumptions: a) the only way out is working up through the program levels, b) resistance, lack of compliance, or complaints were seen as a symptom of a personal disorder, never indicative of some larger systemic problem, c) the more resistant or disordered you are, the more treatment you need, and d) progress and graduation are only possible for those who establish a genuine emotional bond with other residents and staff and demonstrate consistent attachment, commitment, and gratitude for the program.

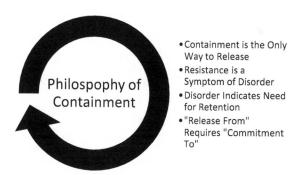

Philospophy of
Containment

- Containment is the Only Way to Release
- Resistance is a Symptom of Disorder
- Disorder Indicates Need for Retention
- "Release From" Requires "Commitment To"

Figure 5-1. The Philosophy of Containment

New arrivals were to be transformed into "upper levels" by learning to enforce the rules of the program; they became part of the structure of the milieu, part of the container. In this sense, containment means becoming a key feature of the vessel, a feature of the environment. In the process of containment each individual is shaped through shaping their peers' containment and transformation processes. By accepting the boundaries that prevent access to the outside and by providing others with access to one's interior space, progress and freedom from the program are gained. This paradox culminates with graduation, when release from the structure of the program has been formally attained through bonding with, and identifying with, the container. In some kind of ultimate paradox, only by becoming part of the program can the individual earn their release from the program.

The process of containment is driven by the experience and hope for release in immediate and long-term contexts. It is as if daily experiences of release from routine pressures are what help to sustain the long-term goal of actual release from the program. Short-term pressure is described as the experience of daily dread, fear of unpredictable confrontations, the exhaustion of the schedule, being "poked at," and by the constant threat of punishment. In cathartic expressions of rage, in channeling anger toward misbehaving peers, frustrated emotional pressure may be released. But a subtle form of release is found in daily rewards, compliance, acceptance, earning points for the day, and by adhering to official explanations and meanings.

Pat provided an example of how intense the desire of release can be and how this intensity can lend power to the container. Participants reported that during the seminars, sleep deprivation and heighted emotional arousal were designed to facilitate the sense of growth and progress, and to amplify the threat of punishment. To break a rule during the seminar could mean a level set back, lengthening one's stay while waiting to re-take the seminar. Participants were desperate to graduate each seminar and make it to the next level. But the smallest infractions were taken to reveal "truths" about one's character that could mean failing, or "choosing out" of the seminar. Pat reported that in the eyes of the staff and group, a smudged mirror was no simple oversight, it meant that one's low self-esteem made a resident unable to look in the mirror. It was safer to confess to the "real" reason and be allowed to stay in the seminar than to point out the facts and risk being set back.

> You agree to the rules to be in the seminar, like "I will obey the facility rules." So, if you get a Category, like let's say a smudged bathroom mirror, there's like a smudge on your mirror, you'd stand up and be accountable over that in front of everyone. And then the facilitator basically decides whether you stay or whether you go because you broke the rules. And you can try again next time, that's the first lesson everyone always learns is about the Category and it like blindsides you. So every day in the beginning you would have to stand, you know be accountable for the night before. I swear to you, like girls would sit in that seminar bawling hysterically because they had a smudge on their mirror. And I swear to you, they totally believed that it was because they thought they were too ugly to look at themselves in the mirror so they didn't clean it properly. Bawling hysterically, girls all the time. Tell you what, it worked every time. They would talk to you for 20 minutes about your self-esteem and your self-esteem problems and then for the rest of the time you're at [the program] you'd be known as a person with low self-esteem... in reality everyone knows we got two hours asleep, we're stressed to the max (Pat, L1603–1604).

Anthony Giddens describes the way human autonomy is corroded in social settings that infringe on basic bodily functions, restrict privacy, and severely limit "ontological security" by preventing any sense of knowing or predicting the immediate future (Giddens, 1984, p. 62–63). In his discussion of the resocialization process, he describes how individuals in such settings are able to reconstruct their own personalities by identifying with the authority figures who have near-total control over them. Janja Lalich's (2004) theory of bounded choice is informed by Gidden's work and describes a similar process in cultic group settings, where personal boundaries are ruptured, privacy and autonomy are absent, and the daily schedule is controlled by those in positions of power.

Lalich describes the way power, beliefs, systems of influence and control can lead to a fusion process, where personal freedom is sought through merging one's personal values and goals with those of the group. In highly totalistic settings, the internalization and identification with the organizational goals and values can enable "the fusion of personal freedom and self-renunciation" (Lalich, 2004, p. 244). This fusion process is similar to what participants described about treatment settings except the goal in teen programs is not life-long retention. Instead of fusion as self-renunciation leading to life-long loyalty and commitment, this fusion is expressed in the process of containment as the individual finds ways to relieve dissonance and experience short-term release as they are transformed into a feature of the program, becoming part of the containment system.

Release in becoming the container

> It could be hours that you are getting screamed at and the best way to avoid a heavy confrontation was to confront other people about things that you saw them do (Kam, L2125–2126).

> The program encouraged us to do things like that and like punish people who didn't hike fast enough, or you know, fall in with the group (Rudi, L300).

> For a while I was a dorm head and I absolutely hated it, so thankful that I never have to do that again, but I was responsible for making sure these other people get their stuff done otherwise I would get in trouble (Joan, L587).

> If you didn't conform to what they expected then you were the object of attention of who was going to get dealt with, you know, so basically everybody was just trying to keep the spotlight off of themselves (Aaron, H1996).

By accepting the program's logic of containment, the individual can begin to work toward release in a process that transforms the individual by establishing a role for them as part of the container. By learning to enforce the rules, to report others for infractions, to confront others in highly-charged encounters, and to model these behaviors to new arrivals, each individual becomes part of the program structure. This process is described by the theory of differential association which posits that the best way to change person "A" is to create a milieu that motivates or requires "A" to change "B" (Clark, 2017; Cressey, 1976, p. 581). One of the best examples of the theory is found in the totalistic treatment model (Volkman & Cressey, 1963).

To maintain personal integrity, the meaning of one's performance shifts from merely "acting as if," to something that can be claimed with authenticity. And as the meaning shifts, identity and the "whole self" are changed in the process (De Leon, 2000).

By actively engaging in one's own containment, the individual enables a process of personal closure within a self-sealing system (Lalich, 2004). By establishing congruence between the demands of the container and one's perception of life within it, a daily process of pressure building and release, and incremental signs of progress, sustain the hope of eventual, actual release from the program. The experience of relief in small daily events, and the sustained longing for actual release, are inherent parts of the containment process.

In containment, the individual is contained and changed into an active part of the container. By adapting to the milieu, by working toward release, by responding in appropriate ways and finding acceptable ways to perform in each new situation, the interiority is brought into congruence with the environmental demands. This sense of congruence is experienced with a relief that is sometimes tinged with inner conflict as well as hope that release from the program is closer.

Containment and release also describe a process of reframing the past: participants reported that they learned to assume responsibility for negative experiences whether they initially agreed or not. Old self images, old friends, and for one participant, even her favorite color, had to be cut off, changed, and let go of. In adapting and complying with rules, agreements, and expectations, questionable practices became normalized. Power imbalances, severe restrictions, and unethical deprivations were reframed as justified, necessary and helpful. For some, actual release in graduation was somewhat bittersweet or confusing and disorienting. For all, the experience of containment and release seems to have affected trajectory across the life course and perspective on the treatment experience.

Trajectory and Perspective

> I only relied on myself for years you know, and I didn't reach out or connect with other people. I really didn't have any coping mechanisms to kind of deal with the things that had affected me, and I kind of shut down in a lot of ways, and I actually got to a point where I realized like, I didn't even know what I was feeling because I was shutting it down so much, like I was so numb that I was just kind of in this overall numb state of life in general. It was really bad especially the first couple years after I got out. I started doing therapy about a year ago and did some trauma therapy and honestly it really wasn't until then that I totally realized what was going on and I mean that's a long time, I mean that's like 12 years that I would honestly say like that's probably about how long it took for me to really come out of it in like a real impactful way (Elsa, L2317–2319).

> I've seen people [online] who've done different years say they had a great experience. [It's] kind of like, "You have that post [program] glow, give it another five months and come back to us, we'll see what you're gonna say you know, once, you know, that kind of, brainwashing wears off and your perspective changes and you really start thinking about everything you went through (Nathan, H1800–1801).

I know what it's like not to have family, so it does teach you stuff, what you've been through, it will teach you, it will show you, you know, when you don't have anything it will make you open up and want to give back. That's what I've learned from it (Cee Cee, H855).

The origin of the word "trajectory" helps to explain some of the nuances of this theme. The Latin, *trajectus*, means "thrown over or across" and in early translations, the word "trajectorie" was first used to describe a funneling effect (Barnhart & Steinmetz, 2000, p. 1158). The theme of trajectory implies a changing arc after exiting: funneled into the container and then out, into a course of life. This theme is informed by life course theories that view adult development as a continual series of changes as the individual is "produced, sustained, and changed by their social context" (Elder & Shanahan, 2006, p. 670).

The participants in this study emphasized a relationship between the way their program experiences affected them and the way they view those long-term effects. Regardless of how good or bad their experiences were, or how long they had been out at the time of the interview, each narrative contained an arc of life and a view of its curve. In this analysis, perspective is conceptualized as an accumulation of influential experiences and outcomes that inform multiple simultaneous viewpoints as understanding and connections unfold over a span of years and decades. Figure 5-1 illustrates how themes are conceptualized to inform perspective.

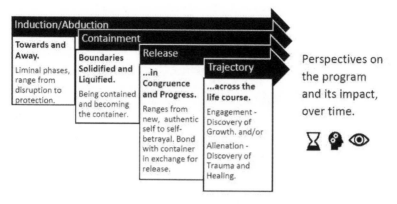

Themes accumulate and inform multiple simultaneous perspectives as understanding and connections unfold over years and decades.

Figure 5-2. Perspective as the Accumulation of Thematic Concepts

For some, their program experience inspired them to go to college and study psychology or social work. As their life course introduced them to new concepts and vocabulary, their ability to articulate and identify their experience changed. With these new abilities came the ability to reflect and look back from new vantage points. With the ability to talk about the experience came new abilities to repair parental relationships and form new connections with others from their cohort.

Especially compelling were the professional perspectives of those who are currently employed in the social service fields. These participants stated with confidence that they understand now that the therapeutic treatment they experienced was neither therapy nor treatment, that it was unethical, abusive, and/or harmful. The one exception, Lawrence, reported that although he had a very positive experience in his 9-week wilderness program, when he was in military-type programs he experienced destructive treatment methods. His time in a wilderness program was a transformative experience and he wants to work so that others may benefit in the same way.

For Bobbi and Elsa, motherhood placed them in a new role and provided a new perspective on what they and their parents went through. For Bobbi, the birth of a child and taking the parent role helped to put the treatment experience in the past and initiated a new process of healing and reconciliation. For Elsa, it was more complex. Her panic attacks and fears that her children would be kidnapped in the night prompted her to seek counseling.

> I have kids and my husband travels a lot for work. I was realizing that when he traveled, I would have panic attacks that my kids were going to be kidnapped…and I just this year realized that it's stemming from like, program stuff…it felt good to kind of figure that out and know when it comes up I recognize where it's coming from and I can kind of handle it, but when you don't know where that's coming from it's just really overwhelming I guess (Elsa, L2330).

Elsa sought treatment for panic and anxiety but was diagnosed and treated for PTSD. Until then, her life had been impacted by unidentified trauma symptoms. Demonstrating how complex the impact of totalistic programs can be, she reported that the effects of PTSD and the disruption to her social life were interrelated.

> A lot of time that I was dealing with things like that and it affected a lot of my relationships. I mean, as far as all my family and friends were concerned I just disappeared for a year and came back. My parents were really the only ones who really knew where I was, and so coming back was hard in that not only was I unsure of how to deal with what I had just been

through, I really didn't have tools for coming back into normal life, so being alone felt weird, talking to people felt weird, I kind of became a hermit, as far as I didn't know how to hang out with people or talk to people. I mean I wasn't allowed to for so long (Elsa, L2331).

Almost half in the higher scoring group (40%) reported years of increased substance use after release. Ironically, these participants now have more positive things to say about their programs and express more gratitude for what the program was trying to do. Although they spoke frankly, sometimes in very negative terms, it is as if they now see what the program staff were trying to prevent. After hearing about the horrors of drug addiction, or coming to believe that they were drug addicts, it's as if they pursued the experience just to confirm that it was not for them. And having done so, they confirmed for themselves that the program was right. Aaron spoke directly to what labeling theory predicts about the link between self-image and behavioral trajectories and how messages in the environment are internalized (Terry, 2003).

They say you're a druggie, gonna end up homeless or in jail, and I was none of those when I went into the program, and then when I got out there was the distinct possibility that I was going to end up that way. It's almost like they know that if you went through this program that's how you're going to end up (Aaron, H2026).

Regardless of how they "ended up," perspective is tied to trajectory but not caused by it. The lenses that participants look through inform a trajectory across the life course as view, attitude, and perceived options affect life choices. Trajectory across the life span also informs perspective of the program experience. Whether or not they perceived harm, the degree to which they were traumatized, and the resources available to them in healing, all work together to express the theme of trajectory and perspective.

Theories of resiliency, trauma, and the life course

Three social theories relevant to studying totalistic programs help to contextualize the theme of trajectory and perspective and help to demonstrate some challenges to interpreting the findings in this study. For the majority in group H, it may be that program experiences enhanced their resiliency, but it is surprising that six out of the 15 escalated their use of illicit substances immediately after exiting the program. It is difficult to interpret reported delays to the benefits of treatment, especially when the reported benefits of the program's influence were attributed to many years or decades of recovering from negative program experiences or treatment trauma. Group L seems to be unanimous in describing program environments that limited their access to psychosocial resources, but it is not clear why, within the same program, among the same cohort, some responded positively to these restrictions while others experienced long-term harm from the same set of methods. These three theories provide some context for these challenging questions.

Resiliency

Resiliency theories explain how access to social resources can help youth develop personal skills and the ability to thrive despite living with adverse conditions and living environments

(Shean, 2015). Healthy development is marked by the strength and resilience youth gain through experiencing human attachment, achievement, autonomy, and altruism (Brendtro & Longhurst, 2005). Healthy levels of stress can bring out the best in youth and in ideal conditions, resilience is demonstrated as youth encounter manageable levels of environmental stress that enhance the ability to adjust and grow as they learn to problem solve in response to life-affirming challenges (Garmezy, Masten, & Tellegen, 1984; Ungar, 2013). Perhaps in the best-case scenario, when the intensity of a totalistic treatment program presents a healthy challenge, resiliency enables a youth to adapt, grow, progress and graduate from the program without harm. Perhaps this same resiliency contributes toward the long-lasting perspective of meaning and benevolence seen in the analogy Ann shared.

> The analogy that I often use is of a sapling, and you'll often see a sapling with like a stake in the ground and it's tied to the sapling and I kind of feel like that's what the [program] did for me. I was kind of like bending and leaning over and it, you know, tied me to this thing to keep me straight for a little while until I was strong enough to grow without needing that kind of help (Ann, H87).

Resiliency is typically identified as the ability to function well under stressful and adverse living conditions, but it can also be used to explain why some youth are impacted by trauma symptoms while others, also exposed to potentially traumatic events, are less-negatively impacted. Although resiliency is typically conceptualized as a way to explain why some youth learn to function well under stress and adversity, and others do not, resiliency does not equate to quality of life. Luthar (1991) found that more-resilient youth may experience stress as depression, and that successful coping is not necessarily positive. Luthar found that resilient youth in high stress environments were high-functioning but significantly more depressed and anxious than resilient youth in low-stress environments. Luthar's finding seems to contradict one of the basic premises of totalistic treatment, indicating that successful functioning is not equivalent to mental health.

This finding might also help explain why successful program completion does not automatically translate to positive perspectives on the treatment experience. In this study, each group had an equal number of graduates and in group L, 11 successfully completed treatment and two more, Carmen and Ziggy, left just before formally graduating. It is surprising that there are so many graduates (73%) among those who now believe they were harmed by their participation in the program. Resiliency is typically used to explain human function, such as achievement in school and successful employment, but its use in explaining quality of life among adults who have experienced a totalistic teen treatment program environment is complicated.

In a totalistic program, resilient youth might be those who do not resist or experience distress over the totality of conditions limiting personal autonomy, communication, and access to the outside world. At the same time, for those who experience these controls with discomfort, the resilient youth might be those who put their heads down quickly and learned to comply with demands. Resiliency might help them to quickly adapt and make progress by learning to report and confront their peers for rule violations or lack of sincerity in group sessions. Upon release, resiliency would enable youth to adapt more quickly to life upon reentry, and not be impaired by physiological symptoms of trauma or any alienating tendencies learned in the program.

Ungar (2013) identifies some of the mechanisms that protect against the negative impact of trauma over the life course and he concluded that resiliency is not so much a personal attribute, but more the result of environmental factors: "nurture trumps nature" (Ungar, 2013, p. 258). It is the way in which youth are treated and it is their ability to access psychosocial resources within culturally specific contexts, that counter the potentially negative effects of adversity (Masten et al., 1999). The capacity to respond with resilience is not a reflection of what is in the youth, it is located in "the processes by which environments provide resources for use by the child" (Ungar, 2011, p. 6). However, the psychosocial resources of youth could be limited by treatment practices that restrict contact with the outside world, require participation in confrontational and demeaning group sessions, enforce control over the content of conversations, severely limit personal autonomy and decision making, and govern personal functions of eating, bathing, and bathroom use.

Totalistic environments may limit the capacity for resiliency even as program staff claim to enhance it with slogans such as "everything we do is therapeutic." Resiliency theories that do not focus on qualities of the environment might be most appropriate in describing the best-case scenarios, the experience of "the lucky ones," as they call themselves, but not apply very well to those who were unable to access needed psychosocial resources in the program. At the same time, Ungar's conceptualizations of resiliency may help to explain some of distinctly different trajectories and perspectives reported in this study. In addition to resiliency, theories of complex trauma and developmental trauma can help to describe the impact of totalistic treatment as it was reported by two-thirds of participants in this study.

Trauma

> It helped me understand people better. I mean really, peoples' wounding because that's really who people are. As much as we try to pretend that we're not, we are the amalgam of our pain because we tend to act out of that place until we become conscious of that response…we're just kind of reacting to our experience because that's really all we have is to respond to the culture of what we've already seen. And it helped me have compassion for the fact that usually, the people that we would deem the nastiest and the most awful are the people in the most pain (Valorie, H2279).

For participants who perceived harmful effects, the impact of treatment was described in ways that closely resemble the experience and impact of complex trauma and developmental trauma, described by Judith Herman (1997) and Bessel van der Kolk (2005). The widespread professional acceptance of complex forms of trauma symptoms and the theories explaining them is taken as evidence of their validity and usefulness as a conceptual framework here (Ebert & Dyck, 2004; Kerig et al., 2011; Najavitz, 2017; Smith & Freyd, 2013; Teague, 2013; Terr, 1991). The exposure to prolonged, repeated, or multiple forms of physical and/or psychological trauma is often accompanied by a uniquely impactful set of interacting effects, or symptoms. When trauma exposure interferes with developmental processes during a child's life, their subsequent development in learning, emotional regulation, attachment, identity, and physical health can be impacted (Teague, 2013). The experience of complex psychological trauma overwhelms an individual's access to resources that would provide some sense of control, their ability to establish human connections, and their ability to experience meaningful daily life (Herman, 1997, p. 33). In cases where there are extreme power imbalances and severe restrictions on personal autonomy, especially where multiple forms of stress and deprivations occur simultaneously, the result can be "mental death," a lost sense of self (Ebert & Dyck, 2004). Participants in this study who described traumatic experiences linked them to the ways that they learned to adapt to the environment and learned to label these adaptations as part of a treatment process.

When considering the way such experiences can impact learning, development, and later stages of adult development, all aspects of life can be affected because trauma of this nature impairs brain functioning and social learning over time (van der Kolk, 2005). Emotional bonds, cognitive function, affect regulation, self-concept, behavior regulation, tendency toward dissociation, and physical maturation processes all can be impacted over the life span when complex forms of trauma impair critical processes in youth development (Teague, 2013; van Der Kolk, 2005). Several participants described ways they have been impacted by trauma and some reported that it was only after 10 or more years that they identified their symptoms and received a professional diagnosis and treatment.

Participants reported life events and perspectives that seem to reflect different stages of recovery from trauma that correspond with Herman's (1997) model of healing that included naming the trauma, establishing safety, remembering and mourning, and reconnection, as steps on a long-term path of recovery that is never fully completed. Elements of this process were described by participants and those who have come to find gratitude for "the journey" do emphasize reconnection as a fundamental part of healing and positive change. Xander,

Donnie, Bobbi, Elsa, Cee Cee, Nathan, Rudi and others emphasized these stages of recovery and the way their healing has transformed the experience of trauma into a point of connection and community building. Advocacy was another important aspect of healing. The large number of participants who became actively engaged in advocating for youth or professional careers related to human services expresses part of the healing trajectory found in the literature (Herman, 1996; Herman, 1997).

Life course theory

> Some people are claiming they have nightmares over this…I'm one of the lucky ones…one of the things I used to say was that out of the hottest fire comes the strongest steel…I'm not telling you this stuff just to upset you, I'm trying to show you how I used the good I could take out of that program for my benefit and made myself a better person. Not a lot of those kids had that ability (Aaron, H2018–2022).

> It was not the perfect place, it was traumatizing. I mean there's many traumatizing things that happened there, but you know, I survived, and I survived the place, and I survived those years of my life, and I think I can be grateful for anything like, that that makes you stronger in whatever way (Bobbi, L1363).

The way individuals are contained, released, and launched across their lives, affects the way decisions are shaped by their own sense of control and the ability to decide for themselves what path to take. For those whose lives were shaped by unidentified symptoms of traumatic stress, it's as if their lives were not their own until they began to understand the ways they were harmed. For those who had more-positive experiences, gratitude and awareness of the good timing of treatment that "saved them" before they did irreparable damage to themselves or others has sustained them. All of the "paradigmatic principles" of life course theory seem relevant to the theme of trajectory and perspective: a life span of developmental stages, the importance of human agency, the timing of events with developmental stages, the role of connection and community, and historical context (Elder, 2006, p. 691).

By surviving the milieu, youth are changed (Schein, 1962), and the mix of ways these changes affect the arc of life is complex. The experience of trauma, resiliency, growth, and alienation are some of the wildly different factors affecting access to resources and the tools with which life decisions are made. Early life transitions affect the way subsequent life stages are traversed, and over time, with each life decision and the passage of time, a cumulative effect of advantage and disadvantage interacts with decisions and perspectives on the past and visions of the future (Elder & Shanahan, 2006).

The theme of trajectory and perspective includes the concept of resocialization, especially for those who fully adapted to life within the program and then experienced culture shock upon release. Some participants identified the way the program benefits were delayed and described a type of adult resocialization (Settersten, 2002) as a process of relearning to develop life skills "all over again" in the context of the "real world," as Barry described it. This process of resocialization after release was described with a range of perspectives that became apparent when interacting with people in the outside world. It was then that they began to realize that in the program, the ability to legitimate oneself was limited to the prescribed, therapeutic ways that authenticity could be achieved, and one's goodness would be validated (Cook, 2000). In the program,

257

these social resources were shaped and limited by the program structure, but in the outside world, participants reported a range of experiences in learning to meet these needs outside of the totalistic milieu.

Four types of impact pathways

The participants in this study described four distinct types of program impacts as differing pathways. These four types help to demonstrate the range of program impact as well as the relationship between trajectory and perspective on the treatment experience. The four types of impact pathways could be divided into two main groups: those who described negative experiences in terms of physical or psychological injury, and those who described negative experiences without referring to them in terms of harm. "The Advocates" and "The Equipoised" were two distinct types of perspectives held by those who perceived short-term and/or long-term injury. At least 14 "Advocates" described their experiences in terms of unethical harm. They referred to abusive practices and emphasized in the interview that they want to help prevent harm in teen programs. Their quality of experience (QOE) index scores ranged from 1.00 to 1.80.

Six participants emphasized a degree of balance when describing how their program experience was both helpful and harmful. They are "The Equipoised" because they perceived a mix of ethical and unethical practices; experienced a range of traumas and a range of benefits from healing from trauma. They did not minimize their injuries or the injuries they witnessed, but they emphasized that the good they gained directly, and their healing from program abuses, have ultimately served them and shaped their lives in ways that they have some amount of gratitude for. They emphasized a balance of positives and negatives in a way that focused less moral judgement and more on where the journey brought them. Their QOE scores ranged from 1.73 to 3.20.

Those who described negative experiences as challenging, rather than harmful, described two distinct types of trajectories and perspectives: "The Lucky Ones" and "The Late Bloomers." Seven participants reported immediately-positive experiences, effects, and impacts. They emphasized that they were "one of the few," they were "rare," or used the term, "lucky one." They described overwhelming or emotionally painful experiences as difficult challenges but not as injurious. Five of "The Lucky Ones" described multiple treatment methods that some experts have defined as institutional abuse, maltreatment, or psychological abuse (Appendix J), but they did not label them as harmful. They attributed beneficial responses to practices many would judge as unethical, including: staff ridicule, arbitrary set-backs, public humiliation, extreme restrictions on communication, prolonged social isolation techniques, and unreasonable punishments. They mentioned such practices in passing but emphasized the positive connections they made with staff, the empowerment they felt in opening up to others, and the sense of becoming more mature and authentic. Their perspectives have remained consistently positive over time and their QOE scores ranged from 2.67 to 4.60.

Three "Late Bloomers" described a delayed response to treatment and a trajectory and perspective that were distinct for two reasons: 1) their substance use escalated to dangerous or problematic levels after their release from the program, and 2) they attribute delayed therapeutic effects to their program without referring to long-term harm. Three participants counted among "The Equipoised" also reported escalating substance use problems after release but they described their treatment as a mix of injurious and ethical practices. One of the "Late Bloomers" described short-term harm resulting directly from the program experience. She spoke frankly about sexual assault that occurred while on a permission away from the program because of staff's failure to protect her from a known predator. Despite the short-term harm she described as devastating, her perspective on the program was very positive at the time of the interview. Emotionally painful, shocking, and miserable experiences were reported by all "Late Bloomers" but they described those experiences as "really hard" without referring to long-term harm. In their perspective, the program helped them, but the help was delayed until they were ready to receive it. Their QOE scores ranged from 2.67 to 3.93.

Summary of Thematic Key Points

The experience of induction/abduction, containment/release, and trajectory across the stages of life all affect the way participants perceive, understand, view, and describe the experience, effects and impact of totalistic teen treatment programs. They describe these phenomena with humor, open hearts, and razor-sharp wit. It's as if they have been to "a place of many extremes," as Nathan described his program, and came back determined to love more deeply and to let others know: where there are many extremes there are many impacts. There are seven key points summarizing the thematic analysis conducted here.

- Participants were introduced to the program through a process of induction/abduction that ranged from extremely negative to somewhat positive experiences.

260

- The containment/release process was initiated by induction/abduction—led away from the world, into a structure that maximized pressure to respond while minimizing response options.

- Participants reported a wide range of positive and negative responses and personal changes: the lived experience of the structure shaped a wide range of immediate effects.

- The context, structure, lived experience and immediate effects all affected the program's impact.

- Impact was described in terms of trajectory and perspective: as a series of processes and events unfolding over the life course and as an unfolding view, shaped by their understanding of the program's long-term effects.

- For those who reported extremely negative experiences, healing seemed to result in complex understanding, humor, and generosity.

- Those who exited in a more intact state seem to have maintained a more contained narrative that was more positive, concise, and described in simpler, equally meaningful and deep terms.

Applying Key Findings to Policy and Practice

In this section, a list of key findings from Chapter 4 is bulleted and then used to inform a brief analysis of recently proposed federal legislation, the "Stop Child Abuse in Residential Programs for Teens Act of 2017" (H.R. 3024, 2017). To provide context for this federal legislation, a few relevant points are listed to demonstrate international perspectives described in the United Nation's Convention on the Rights of the Child. To provide state-level context, some relevant conflicts of interest that partially explain some political barriers to researching and preventing harm in residential programs are also briefly discussed.

This study presents new information about totalistic teen programs and some of the lesser-known experiences of maltreatment and harm. Applying these findings to policy and practice will be an important task for future researchers, policy experts, and treatment providers. This discussion is meant to introduce some of the key findings that warrant further study for their relevance to public and program policies.

Key Findings

- *Program Types.* There are a wide variety of totalistic teen programs and these different types can be considered on a continuums of totalistic intensities and ethical standards.

- *Unethical Practices.* Some programs may utilize unethical methods of recruitment, retention, and treatment, by design.

- *Intensive Methods.* The intensity of the milieu and the insular nature of these programs seems to be related to the experience of harm.

- *Unpredictable Responses.* The immediate effects of totalistic program experiences are unpredictable and may be potentially harmful.

- *Undefined Concepts.* In totalistic settings, as psychological pressures increase and the options to leave decrease, there may be little difference between therapy and coercive persuasion.

- *Long-term Impact.* All participants reported that totalistic teen treatment affected their adult development. Long-term impacts vary widely and must be considered over the life course.

- *Complicated Benefits.* Ten participants reported therapeutic benefits from totalistic methods. Six reported a mix of beneficial and harmful effects. Seven participants reported positive responses to programming but attributed them to practices many professionals might consider unethical.

- *Potential Harm to Adult Development.* Totalistic teen programs appear to have a wide range of complex effects on adult development. For some, these may include serious, long-lasting experiences of harm.

- *Knowledge is Healing.* For those who experienced harm, healing was facilitated by gaining the ability to articulate and validate the experience, to identify and name trauma symptoms, and by working to help prevent harm to others.

Applying Findings to Policy

The findings reported here and in Chapter 4 are relevant to the wellbeing of youth currently residing in out-of-home treatment settings and to the wellbeing of adults who as youth, experienced life within such programs. The participants in this study described institutional dynamics that are relevant to public and program policies. When considering quality of care and the potential for harm, three systemic levels can be considered separately and together: federal, state, and program. Federal and state level factors shape the role and function of the "teen treatment industry" and the safety of each individual program.

Federal

According to the US Government Accountability Office (GAO), "the federal government does not have oversight authority for private facilities that serve only youth placed and funded by parents or other private entities" (GAO-08-346, 2008, p. 1). Licensing and regulation of public and private teen programs is the responsibility of a widely varying "patchwork" of state and regional agencies (Cases of Abuse, 2008, p. 51, 57). Federal investigations in 2008 found that there are no uniform definitions of program types, however, "juvenile justice facilities and boarding schools are often exempt from licensing requirements by law or regulation" (GAO-08-346, 2008, i). Figure 5-3 indicates the number of states reporting that they exempt program facilities, by program type. Collected by the GAO in 2008, this information appears to be the most recent available. The GAO found that 42 states exempted certain types of residential schools and academies, and other types of facilities were exempted by one to eleven different states.

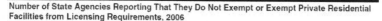

Number of State Agencies Reporting That They Do Not Exempt or Exempt Private Residential Facilities from Licensing Requirements, 2006

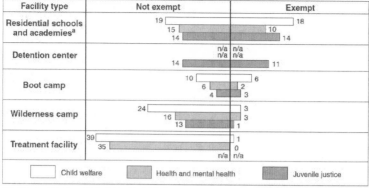

Source: GAO analysis of state agencies' responses to survey.

Note: Other agency responses included no such facility in the state, don't know, and no response.

[a]Residential schools and academies includes both government and private facilities.

Figure 5-3. Status of State Licensing Exemptions in 2006 (GAO-08-346, 2008, i).

At the federal level, there are no uniform safety standards or regulations for privately-funded teen treatment or behavior modification facilities, and at the state level, oversight is provided differently within each locale (Behar et al., 2007; Friedman et al., 2006). In some states, there are few regulatory requirements, a lack of licensing requirements, or licensing exemptions for faith-based programs (Behar et al., 2007; Friedman et al., 2006). Proposed federal legislation that would create such federal standards and regulations is a bill introduced to the House of Representatives, H. R. 3024, the "Stop Child Abuse in Residential Programs for Teens Act of 2017" (H.R. 3024, 2017). If passed, this bill would create uniform safety guidelines for practitioners in all states and would specify new data reporting procedures that would be useful to researchers and to those interested in prosecuting cases of institutional abuse. Currently, in many states officials do not have authority under state law to even obtain information on private programs that do not receive federal funding (Cases of Abuse, 2008, p. 27). The passage of this bill as written would certainly be a historic event. However, the findings in this study suggest additional ways to improve public policies aimed at preventing harm.

If passed, H. R. 3024 would not apply to state-licensed hospitals or foster family settings. It would establish clinical safety standards, administrative training and data collection requirements for four types of programs: behavior modification, therapeutic boarding schools, boot camps, and wilderness/outdoor programs. How such programs would be defined is unclear, and whether intensive outpatient, therapeutic community, and residential treatment programs would be affected is not stated. Religious and faith-based exemptions granted at the state level are not specifically addressed.

The bill states that "child abuse and neglect shall be prohibited" (p. 4) and refers to the most recent, 2010 amendment of the Child Abuse Prevention and Treatment Act (CAPTA). According to CAPTA, abuse is "any recent act or failure to act on the part of a parent or caretaker, which results in death, serious physical or emotional harm, sexual abuse or exploitation, or an act or failure to act which presents an imminent risk of serious harm" (USDHHS, 2010, p. 6). The use of this definition in the prevention of institutional abuse is problematic because abuse in the home is different from abuse dynamics in out-of-home settings (Gil, 1982; Nunno, 2009; Rabb & Rindfleisch, 1985; Penhale, 1999; Thomas, 1982). These cited experts emphasize that the occurrences are different and the considerations for assessment are also different. By failing to address these differences at the definitional level, the ability to define and prevent "serious harm" is limited because the multiple dimensions of institutional abuse are ignored (Burns, Hyde, & Killet, 2013; Gil, 1982; Rittel, 1973). The ability to foresee the risk of institutional abuse and the ability to improve program designs will require definitions, research, and theories that have yet to be fully developed (James, 2015; Nunno, 2009).

Another problem is that although new Federal standards under H.R. 3024 would prohibit the withholding of food, water, clothing, shelter, and medical care as disciplinary measures, the bill does not acknowledge that these deprivations are sometimes applied by design as elements in the milieu meant to facilitate the "goals of treatment," not as arbitrary or intentional abuse or neglect. Similarly, although the bill would prohibit "acts of physical or mental abuse designed to humiliate, degrade, or undermine a child's self-respect" (p. 5), this wording is potentially problematic. From this perspective, in the context of treatment, there is effectively no possibility of abuse because nothing is "designed" to humiliate, degrade or undermine a child's self-respect. Participants in this study reported that complaints of such negative experiences were dismissed or described in therapeutic terms by staff as methods designed to facilitate growth.

For example, Barry reported practices that were designed to make youth feel bad so that they would then feel "really good." His understanding is that negative emotions were part of what he found to be a beneficial design.

> They would make you feel bad and then they would make you feel really good, so you would do all these exercises that potentially would elicit negative feelings and negative emotions and then we would do all these exercises that would make you feel positive (Barry, H735).

Barry spent two years in a program and graduated in 2006. He believed that during the seminars the staff intentionally tried to hurt residents' feelings and that these practices ultimately helped him. He also understands why others in his group had a negative experience with such methods.

> Their purpose is to like reject you, to kinda like, wear you down, I mean at least that's my impression, or my interpretation…they'll tell you what they want you to do differently, or better, but they're also like heckling you during it, like being like, kind of mean, like assholes. But these are like staff members that— you've been there for like 16 or 15 months you know, or however long, and they're like your peer group leaders, so it's a very strange thing (Barry, H759, 765).

Experts in institutional abuse emphasize that intentions are irrelevant when assessing institutional maltreatment and the potential for harm. The foreseeable risk of injury or impairment to development is the critical criterion to consider (Nunno, 2009; 1999; Rabb & Rindfleisch, 1985; Thomas, 1982). There seems to be a gulf between expert opinion and political knowledge, and it may be important to address these gaps in proposed legislation and enacted policy.

The Stop Child Abuse in Residential Programs for Teens Act of 2017 does not adequately address the types of seclusion practices that are currently in use. The bill would prohibit "the involuntary confinement of a child alone in a room or area from which the child is physically prevented from leaving" (p. 4). But participants in this study reported seclusion as "black outs," "being slept," "ghost challenge," or "yellow zone" punishments. These methods enforced seclusion through silence and shunning. While staring at a wall or facing a tree or desk, others were around but forbidden to look or speak to them: "an isolation chamber with people all around," as Nathan described it. In some programs, these modified seclusion practices were imposed by design for all first-level residents or used as punishments that could last for weeks and months on-end. These methods would apparently continue in states that currently allow them, even if this legislation were to pass.

The proposed bill is meant to improve communication access, but based on reports by participants in this study, there are dimensions of potentially dangerous or harmful communication controls that are not addressed by this legislation. If passed, youth in American teen treatment programs would be legally entitled to:

> reasonable access to a telephone, and be informed of their right to such access to maintain frequent contact, including making and receiving scheduled and unscheduled calls, unrestricted written correspondence, and electronic communications with as much privacy as possible, and shall have access to existing and appropriate national, State, and local child abuse reporting hotline numbers (p. 5–6).

How terms and phrases such as "reasonable," "unrestricted," "as much privacy as possible," and "access" are defined will determine how likely it will be that youth are able to report maltreatment and able to do so without fear of punishment, worsening conditions, or a set-back in their progress. Participants reported that censored communications prevented the reporting of abuse and led to misunderstandings and disrupted relationships. In H. R. 3024, censorship and the control of communication content are not addressed.

There are several complex dimensions of communication control reported by participants that are relevant to legislation about the safety and well-being of youth in treatment programs. When progress and graduation are contingent on gratitude and zero complaints, youth may be put in a double-bind of needing to weigh the risks of reporting and of not reporting abuses and maltreatment. When youth can be punished for complaining about maltreatment, or where complaints are labeled as an indication of individual pathology and a need for more intensive treatment, it may be that future risks could seem even worse than any current harm. Participants reported that their parents were instructed by staff to watch out for youth complaints, to dismiss them as a manipulation ploy, or that such complaints indicated a need for more restrictions of communication. These are just a few examples of the types of control that program staff can continue to label as "reasonable." If harm is to be prevented, wherever practitioners claim there is a therapeutic rationale for insulating a youth from the outside world, additional specifications and safeguards must be developed in legislation and administrative oversight.

In addition to the weaknesses noted, several basic human rights are not mentioned in this bill. These are especially important for parent-placed youth who do not have the same legal protections as youth involved with the juvenile justice system (GAO-08-346, 2008). The right to challenge extrajudicial decisions for placement, the right to privacy, freedom of thought and religious beliefs, the right to play, and other "rights of the child" as they are defined by the United Nations (United Nations Human Rights, 1989), are not acknowledged. The United States and Somalia are the only two UN member nations choosing not to ratify the International Convention on the Rights of the Child (Heimlich, 2011; Woodhouse, 2002).

A review of some of these rights is worth considering because they provide a way to examine American youth rights and the "troubled teen industry" from a wider perspective. If the internationally recognized rights of the child were honored in the United States, the current civil right of parents to informally imprison their children in totalistic programs indefinitely without due process or a pre-commitment hearing (*Parham v. J. R.*, 1979; Robbins, 2014; Turner, 1989; Woodhouse, 2002) could be questioned. Currently, when parents sign consent giving third-parties parental rights over their children, they may do so without judicial review, and these third-parties are then immune to liability and tort claims (Robbins, 2014). In the Supreme Court case, *Parham v. J.R.,* these parental rights were guaranteed but the court freed itself from setting "standards and guidelines for the constitutional deprivation" of the child's right to liberty (Turner, 1989, p. 266). According to Article 37 (d) in the UN Convention, youth held in restrictive settings should have a legal right to challenge their placement there:

> Every child deprived of his or her liberty shall have the right to prompt access to legal and other appropriate assistance, as well as the right to challenge the legality of the deprivation of his or her liberty before a court or other competent, independent and impartial authority, and to a prompt decision on any such action.

The UN Convention on the Rights of the Child could help to establish an ethical framework for assessing state and federal legislation meant to reduce the number of youth who are harmed by the "troubled teen industry." Such legislation could be especially useful if it aimed to prevent harm also by preventing placement into high-risk settings. The Stop Child Abuse in Residential Programs for Teens Act of 2017 is meant to prevent abuse within this private industry, but it does not define, or prevent placement into, problematic programs. Importantly, the bill does ensure that covered programs will employ "safe, evidence-based practices, and that children are protected against harmful or fraudulent practices" (p. 13) but how these terms will be defined is unclear. Many states have begun providing financial incentives for the implementation of evidence-based practices, but there are unresolved professional debates about the meaning of "evidence-based" and these incentives vary by state. In many states, funding policies do not distinguish between scientifically valid practices and practices that are experimental and untested (Walker et al., 2015).

Deceptive marketing strategies and professional conflicts of interest identified in federal investigations and senate hearings are not mentioned (Cases of Abuse, 2008; GAO-08-713T, 2008). Two participants emphasized their concerns about contracting agents and educational consultants who are paid on a per-head commission for recruiting youth into the programs they work for. The bill does not address the unethical practice of "conversion therapy," which is widely regarded as harmful (SAMHSA, 2015). There is no mention of the parent-arranged transport services legal experts describe as a dangerous and questionable way to initiate the treatment process (Robbins, 2014). The bill does not state whether faith-based programs will be covered or not. Currently, they are exempt from oversight in some states (Behar et al., 2007; Friedman et al., 2006).

State

At the state level, and sometimes at the county level, differing definitions and regulations pertaining to the collection of data about institutional maltreatment vary (Overcamp-Martini & Nutton, 2009). In order to assess the different ways American states approach the prevention and reporting of abuse in out-of-home care facilities, Overcamp-Martini and Nutton (2009) made repeated attempts to collect information from representatives in all 50 states. After extensive efforts, only three states responded with written information and nine responded by phone. Thirty-eight states did not provide any information. The authors' interest in surveying state level procedures for protecting youth in residential care settings was partly driven by their earlier discovery that out of the 28 states that do report abuse statistics annually to the US Department of Health and Human Services, there was "no information provided regarding out-of-home care" (p. 56).

They also identified a federally mandated, state-level conflict of interest that contributes to the misreporting and lack of reporting incidents of abuse. Considering the lack of federal standards for privately operated programs, this conflict of interest at the state level is especially important. The 1997 amendment to CAPTA specifies that for states to remain eligible for federal grants under this act, the proportion of total cases of substantiated, or indicated, maltreatment in out-of-home settings must remain below 0.57% for all reported incidences. This financial incentive to under-report institutional abuse is further compounded by a 1996 amendment to CAPTA that shifted the responsibility for grant eligibility assessments from federal agencies to each individual state. Since then, each state has been responsible for deciding if they are eligible for federal grants. In their self-assessments, states have implanted a wide variety of procedures for reporting and recording incidents of abuse. Accurate reporting of institutional abuse could threaten federal funding to the very agencies responsible for preventing and reporting it. Several states do not have mandatory abuse reporting standards for program staff (Overcamp-Martini & Nutton, 2009) and this is one of important changes that would be implemented by H.R. 3024.

Summary of policy recommendations

The "Stop Child Abuse in Residential Programs for Teens Act of 2017" would create three monumental policy changes. It would establish for the first time minimum staffing requirements and safety standards for privately funded teen treatment programs. It would create state-level data reporting mandates by amending the Child Abuse Prevention and Treatment Act (CAPTA). And it would allocate an additional $80,000,000 per year in CAPTA funding. To fund these changes, it would allocate an additional $5,000,000 per year to the Department of Health and Human Services for five years to implement these changes (H.R. 3024, 2017).

As impressive as these changes would be, a critical analysis based on the data collected in this research indicates that proposed federal policy could be improved. Based on these findings and a review of expert opinion, the following list summarizes some suggestions that might improve future efforts to prevent harm in residential settings. Some of these suggestions might be most relevant to future amendments of CAPTA and others might be goals to consider in future drafts of legislation for the prevention of institutional abuse.

- Distinguish between child abuse and institutional child abuse (Appendix J).

- In some programs, deprivations of basic needs may be applied for reasons other than punishment, therefore, regardless of intent, withholding practices should be addressed.

- Isolating, humiliating, degrading, or undermining practices, should be defined and limited even when such methods are "designed" to be helpful. Research on the subjective nature of such experiences should inform explicit policy definitions.

- Whether designed as punishment, method of control, or as a treatment method, modified seclusion practices should be defined and explicitly addressed.

- Ensure youth are free and able to file complaints to independent investigators without punishment, threat of punishment, or loss of privileges or status.

- Establish due process and regulation for parent-arranged youth transport services.

- Define and address ways to prevent unwarranted parent placements.

- Define and prohibit deceptive marketing practices.

- Address professional conflicts of interest in recruitment and referral systems.

- Prohibit all forms of "conversion therapy" by licensed and unlicensed practitioners.

- Prohibit state-level regulatory exclusions for faith-based programs.

- Address state-level conflicts of interest and remove financial penalties for reported incidences of institutional abuse.

- Allocate funding for research in the prevalence and prevention of institutional child abuse.

- Establish plans to implement independent investigations and local enforcement procedures.

Applying Findings to Practice

Effective out-of-home treatments are those that achieve their goals in an efficient and predictable manner, and the boundary between experimental and therapeutic practices is the degree to which they are effective (London & Klerman, 1978). Walker, Bumbarger, & Phillippi (2015) estimate that only 5% to 11% of court ordered youth receive evidence-based care and in public and private treatment settings, only a handful of evidence-based practices are used within residential care settings (James et al., 2015). Until proven safe and effective, totalistic treatment milieus might be most accurately described as experimental because they are dynamic systems, presenting unpredictable contexts in each moment that are experienced in unique ways according to the individuals who encounter them (Goldiamond, 1978). In order to protect human subjects from harm in experimental procedures, unpredictable methods must be conceptualized and regulated as experiments (London & Klerman, 1978).

In the United States, an unknown number of youth in privately operated programs have been subjected to experimental treatments but the ability to predict who is likely to benefit from such unproven methods is limited (USDHHS, 1999). Where there is greater risk of harm, there is perhaps an even greater need to predict outcomes more accurately. In a global perspective, many children with emotional and behavioral care needs may not be provided with adequate services. In developed countries, there is often a lack of clear referral criteria and there is a widespread failure to use rigorous methods for detecting which type of treatment is needed (Gilligan, 2015). In the United States, deceptive marketing and recruitment techniques in use by privately operated teen treatment programs were documented nationwide by the Government Accountability Office (Child Abuse, 2008; GAO-08-713T, 2008).

Program staff are faced with the challenge of balancing the needs of the organization against the needs of the youth in their charge. In general terms, the safety and effectiveness of residential programs has been questioned by numerous professionals but there is an evidence-based set of practices designed to improve the safety and quality of care in teen treatment settings regardless of their proven efficacy (Holden et al., 2010; Izzo et al., 2016). The Children and Residential Experiences (CARE): Creating Conditions for Change, model, is designed to help organization staff members improve their interactions with youth in order to deescalate violence and prevent accidental injury during restraint procedures. The CARE model relies on extensive staff training in practices based on research in child development, attachment theories, trauma, family involvement and human ecology (Holden et al, 2010; Holden et al., 2015). The authors do not specify whether such practices can help to improve the safety and effectiveness of totalistic teen treatment programs as the concept is defined here but they do claim that their model is effective in "total" programs. A critique by Sigrid James (2015) emphasizes that although their model is theoretically sound the research evidence supporting it is in the early stages, raising questions about the use of terms such as "evidence-based."

Developing hypotheses about risk

Participants in this study attributed a wide range of effects and impacts to their experience of totalistic teen treatment methods. Ten participants emphasized that the effects and impacts of totalistic treatment were beneficial, and although they described intensive practices as extremely challenging, emotionally painful, or as negative experiences, they did not refer to them in terms of long-term injury. Five out of ten of these participants reported unethical program practices such as arbitrary setbacks, ridicule by staff, or extreme and prolonged modified seclusions, but did so while attributing beneficial outcomes to those methods or to the overall experience. Twenty participants reported a range of negative experiences directly related to totalistic treatment methods and described the effects and impacts as short-term and long-term injuries, raising questions about the unpredictable nature of totalistic programming and the risk of harm.

Participants who emphasized the benefits of treatment within highly totalistic settings indicated that their judgements about the ethical standards and the degree of totalistic program characteristics were two distinct and independent concepts. When conceptualizing risk of harm the response to totalistic treatment can be considered on a dual axis that considers the relationship between the perceived amount of psychosocial resources provided by the milieu and the individual's perceived ability to access those resources. The dual axis describes amount and ability on two distinct, subjective continuums perceived by the individual. Figure 5-4 presents a conceptual model that assumes that higher ethical standards within a totalistic program result in greater amounts of perceived psychosocial resources and therefore, enhanced capacity for resilience for each individual (Shean, 2015; Unger, 2013).

In this model, higher ethical standards refer to generally accepted best practices, such as screening for program fit, staff training and supervision, and the fulfillment of an individual's basic physical, educational, and emotional developmental needs. These subjective needs include the felt sense of safety, predictability, agency, and time for play and spontaneity. The amount of resources and the perceived access to them are two distinct concepts reflected in the dual axis model shown in Figure 5-4. Figure 5-5 explains risk in relationship to the amount of resources provided by the milieu and the range of access perceived by the individual.

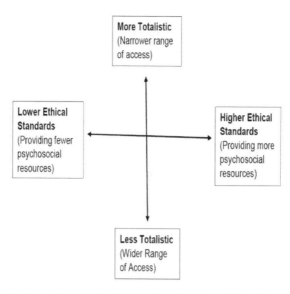

Figure 5-4. Considering Risk on a Dual Axis of Totalism and Ethics.

Range of access refers to the subjective experience of the seven items operationalized in Table 3-2. When stated in the positive, the more totalistic the experience, the narrower the range of perceived access to: 1) information, communication, and the opportunity to freely connect with others within and outside of the program; 2) sensible rules and fair punishments; 3) agency to decline participation in peer policing; 4) agency to decline participation in personal disclosures and group sessions; 5) unrestricted expression and exploration of identity; 6) to status and privileges that are not contingent on bonding with those from whom escape is desired; and 7) ability to leave the program without first completing each level.

In developing a set of hypotheses for future research, totalistic methods and ethical standards may be considered as two distinct sets of factors. Totalistic treatment may be judged more or less ethical and the safety of such methods is assumed to be a subjective concept. There are obviously objective indicators of generally accepted best practices but the amount of resources provided within a milieu and the ability to access them are subjective experiences that must also be considered from individual standpoints. The first proposition is that risk increases with the intensity of totalistic methods as ethical standards decrease. The opposite is also hypothesized—that as the degree of totalism decreases, risk decreases if ethical standards increase.

Figure 5-5. Hypothesizing the Relationship Between Risk and Access to Psychosocial Resources

These hypotheses seem to be supported by Ungar's (2013) social ecological principles of resilience and the findings in this study. Ungar describes the "Environment X Individual" relationship using three principles that conceptualize resilience as a characteristic of the milieu. He emphasizes that the amount of psychosocial resources provided have different impacts within different contexts.

In highly totalistic environments psychosocial resources may be available, but they be available only to those who are able to comply, or willing to believe in the value of complying, with the program. Youth who perceive less access and more degrees of totalism may not have the same access to resources within the milieu or access to people in the outside world who could provide them. Differing responses to totalistic treatment might reflect differences in: a) the amount of resources provided by the milieu, and b) differences in the range of perceived access to psychosocial resources. These two concepts are hypothesized to interact and affect youth well-being within totalistic environments and to impact differing trajectories and perspectives after exiting.

Weaknesses, Limitations and Future Research

The value of any qualitative study can only be assessed by each individual reader. Each reader must judge for themselves how closely the researcher's interpretations adhere to the evidence and whether the generalizations and conclusions are sufficiently grounded (Harding, 2013). Qualitative research is not suited to making conclusive generalizations about a larger population (Small, 2008), but by considering the limitations and strengths together, readers can make "analytic generalizations" and better assess the plausibility of transferring any relevance to other contexts (Yin, 2016, p. 104–107). In reviewing the limitations of this thesis, there are some important weaknesses in the design, data collection, and analysis that should be considered.

Design

The all-inclusive nature of the research questions combined with the number of participants and the open-ended interview questions resulted in an exceptionally large amount of data spanning vast areas of interest. A more realistic approach would have been to limit the research questions to one specific topic, or to limit the amount of data collected using theoretical sampling and a grounded theory approach. Either would have resulted in a more contained set of codes, topics, and themes that could be presented more concisely.

This study simultaneously considered theories of totalism with theories of treatment in a way that is uncommon among youth development researchers. This approach does seem validated by the collected data but there are few examples in the literature to support it. This study assumes that the totalistic nature of teen treatment milieus unifies the experiences of participants in this study. Youths who spent six weeks in a wilderness program and youths who spent two years in a residential treatment facility were asked the same interview questions. The range of responses were similar but there may be no established literature base to justify this design. The concept of "totalistic teen treatment" was explored across 25 different programs attended by a wide range of adults who were treated during four different decades. Readers will have to decide for themselves if the programs and participants represented in this study are too different to be included in the same qualitative study.

The term "totalistic" may be contentious and emotionally charged in a way that biased recruitment and sampling methods. In recruiting participants, the invitation and questionnaire explicitly referred to the term "totalistic." This decision was based on the desire to be fully transparent; however, using a term that may have a negative connotation may have inadvertently discouraged some participants. If the term "intensive" had been used instead, prospective participants might have viewed the study in a more neutral light. To obtain a more balanced sample, programs deemed "totalistic" could be identified and participants from such programs could be invited to participate without the need to label the methods.

The design of this study may have been weakened by a potential for bias toward more-negative scoring participants because of the decision to err on the side of full transparency and use the term "totalistic." Conversely, the term "treatment" may be problematic also because some adults may not consider their experience to be therapeutic and may resent those who assume their program experience was actually "treatment." The term "totalistic treatment" is problematic because it may lead to sampling biases in many directions.

Sampling and Data Collection

Data quality considerations affected by sampling go beyond simply needing a large number of interview participants and a large amount of data. The nature of the sample should be considered also in terms of the project's goals, the depth of data collected, and fit with theory (Roy, Zvonkovic, Goldberg, Sharp, & LaRossa, 2015). The skewed distributions in quality of experience index scores toward more-negative scoring participants is a weakness that limited the number of higher scoring participants to sample from in creating group H. There were too few higher scoring participants in the sampling frame to allow for a random sampling technique. Every higher scoring participant who was willing, was interviewed, but lower scoring participants were randomly sampled from a frame of 154. If a larger number of higher scoring participants had responded to the questionnaire, the data collected from participants in group H may be been quite different. This weakness could be addressed in a larger study with more resources and the ability to advertise and recruit among the general population.

The decision to use a random, rather than a purposive, sampling approach to create group L resulted in an unfortunate imbalance of gender representations. In the full sample of 223, 66% identified as female and in the sampling frame of lower scoring participants (n=154) 70% identified as female. From this frame, two of the randomly selected lower scoring male participants, who had indicated interest in an interview, declined to respond to interview invitations and in the final sample of lower scoring participants, thirteen out of the 15 identified as female. Due to limited resources and other pragmatic considerations, the design of the project was not changed in response to this anomaly in random sampling.

In data collection and analysis, the topic of gender was not placed in a central position. This weakness reflects the decision to stick to the original plan as well as the decision not to seek out data for a comparison of gendered responses to totalistic teen programs. Gendered differences were most apparent in reported reasons for placement, but these were also limited because all but one of the male participants were in group H. By chance of the random draw, the lack of males in group L limited the ability to compare gendered responses between groups. The unique nature of harm experienced by females who reported "slut shaming" and staff focus on sexually explicit disclosures seems to indicate that power over female residents may have been leveraged more often in ways related to sexuality. Male participants also reported unhealthy attitudes toward sexuality and impairment around sexuality but there are uniquely harmful ways females were affected that deserve greater attention in future studies.

The lack of racial diversity in the sample also reflects problems with recruitment. Efforts to recruit among adults who attended publicly-funded programs, reported to be populated by larger proportions of non-white youth (Behrens & Satterfield, 2011), were also unsuccessful. These problems with recruitment limited the range of data and the ability to transfer findings to minority populations. Almost all interview participants were white, and this is an especially important weakness to address in future studies because the experience and long-term impact of totalistic methods may be described quite differently by minority populations, especially if barriers and resources after exiting are not comparable.

The predominance of white participants reflects sampling issues but this may also be a reflection of the population targeted by totalistic programs and the "troubled teen industry." As educational consultants, who are paid on a commission basis, target predominately upper and middle-class parents in white suburban locations, a profit motive translates into a racial difference that warrants research. If privately operated, totalistic programs and educational consultants have targeted white families, perhaps it is because this demographic is more likely to be able to afford to pay treatment costs, but there are probably additional reasons explaining why these families are interested in placing their children in such programs. At the population level, such trends are likely to be directly related federal and state policies that contribute to racial disparities in the juvenile justice system. Statistical probabilities indicate that white families are more likely to be able to afford drastic interventions for their unruly teens, and perhaps they are also more willing to place them in totalistic treatment settings before they are adjudicated or incarcerated by the state (Feld, 1999).

The use of an online questionnaire limited recruitment to those with access to the internet. Since the invitation was shared online through social media and email, potential participants without internet access were less likely to hear about the questionnaire. Another limitation with sampling is that the invitation was shared word of mouth. This type of "snowball sampling" tends to shape response bias by attracting self-selected participants who have similar interests, experiences, and perhaps, perspectives (Small, 2008). If resources had allowed for the creation of a representative sample, a wider range of racial demographics, reasons for placements, and quality of experience, may have led to the creation of a much different interview sampling frame.

The questionnaires in this study were designed by the author and although their Cronbach alpha scores indicated strong internal validity, the skewed distribution of scores indicates that the range of items could be extended. A large number of participants reported the lowest scores possible when reporting quality of experience and even more reported the highest possible when reporting on totalistic program characteristics. The interview participants in this study reported several factors that should be developed into future questionnaires that could extend the range of variables. Factors such as witnessing deaths, witnessing life threatening forms of medical neglect, psychological abuse by staff, and other forms of institutional maltreatment were omitted from the questionnaire, limiting the range of response. The items measuring totalistic program characteristics are also limited in that they fail to measure the most extreme forms of totalism such as physical and psychological torture and unhealthy power hierarchies among staff and residents. For more accurate and even distribution of scores, in future studies, the seven items measuring totalistic characteristics could be treated as domains with multiple items representing each.

Analysis

The creation of higher and lower scoring subgroups based on quality of experience scores was useful, but only up to a point. The neat division between higher and lower scoring participants became messy in qualitative analyses. Among the 15 participants in Group H, five reported traumatic experiences or negative opinions that were not captured by the questionnaire. These five had little respect for the methods used in their respective programs but in spite of this they did benefit and are somewhat grateful for the experience overall. Their higher quality of experience scores may be a reflection of the gratitude these participants have developed as they recovered from the negative impact of institutional abuse visited during treatment, but the interview questions did not address this possibility directly.

This complication could have become the central topic in a formal grounded theory project but because this would have meant a change in plans, the fuzziness was left unresolved. The weakness reflected here is that the relationship between experience, perspective, reported quantitative scores, and the nature of qualitative data collected, is unknown. The findings in the study suggest that the usefulness of quantitative approaches to sampling are complicated because the intuitive assumption that more-positive perspectives indicate more-positive past experiences, is not accurate. A mixed-methods approach with a narrower scope would have allowed for more confidence in transferring findings beyond the sample of 30.

The thematic analysis presented here identifies patterns across the data but the reader will have to judge how relevant these abstract generalizations are to answering the research questions (Braun & Clarke, 2016). Since no formal methodology was strictly followed, the methods used here are unique to the design of this study and are shaped by the researchers understanding of rigorous design and his own subjective biases (Yin, 2016). Almost certainly, additional themes and alternative explanations could be found that were not developed in this report.

Future Research

Future researchers should explore differences and similarities by gender, race, and economic status. They could also compare experiences within evidence-supported totalistic programs to those within experimental program designs. Studies that explore the differences between youth who responded well, and those who did not, may help improve intake screening procedures and enhance the predictability of outcomes. There is a need to know what individual characteristics predict which outcomes in response to totalistic programs. This could be explored by incorporating existing measures of personality or resiliency characteristics into a mixed methods study.

The seven characteristics measuring totalistic programs (Table 3-1) could be tested again in future research designs with different populations. The way these factors relate to each other and why this combination of design features is found in so many types of teen programs seems to indicate something important, yet unknown, about safety and effectiveness. Parents, researchers, and politicians need to know what program features can be combined safely for which individual.

Future studies should examine the subjective experience of the totality of conditions from a developmental systems perspective that can integrate data relevant to multiple disciplines at the personal, social, systemic, and macro levels (Urban, Osgood & Mabry, 2011). In order to test the hypotheses about the negative relationships between risk and ethical standards in totalistic programs, researchers would need to operationalize the concept of ethics specific to totalism. Any research based on the hypotheses described by the models in Figure 5-4 and Figure 5-5 should consider how findings can be applied to policy and practice in light of the macro level factors described in federal studies by the GAO.

When measuring totalistic program outcomes, several factors should be considered: the potential for psychological harm, barriers to reporting harm, the delayed onset of harm, and the ways these factors can influence any selected outcome variables. Researchers should ask about the safe degrees of totalism and attempt to identify the boundaries between reasonable and unreasonable foreseeable risks. The successful recovery from "treatment trauma" and the unique nature of this iatrogenic effect should be studied in gendered, racial, and economic terms within clinical, historical, and political contexts. Future studies could incorporate theory and empirical findings from research on second-generation members who were raised in cultic groups, literature on captive bonding or attachments formed through trauma, domestic violence dynamics, and torture.

At the program and systemic levels, there are two findings that seem most urgent. The participants in this study provide empirical data about foreseeable risks that deserve immediate research. Wherever staff have the option of not believing and not reporting youth claims about medical needs, maltreatment, or psychological harm, there is a need to develop new harm-prevention strategies. At the systemic level, there are potential conflicts of interest wherever educational consultants are paid a commission for referring youth to treatment milieus. Privately funded programs, whether for-profit or non-profit, may rely on recruitment strategies that are unregulated. These professional conflicts of interest should be researched and addressed by the appropriate authorities.

Summary and Final Notes

There are basic challenges to researching totalistic teen programs that may need to be addressed by a multidisciplinary team of well-funded experts. At the heart of the problem is a central conundrum: within a single program, among a single cohort, different youth exposed to the same treatment methods may report wildly different outcomes. In this study, some adults reported their lives were saved while others reported that the same set of methods applied in similar contexts were overwhelming and traumatic. Apparently, there are potential risks but little agreement on how to determine acceptable degrees of risk. Questions about risk lead to unresolvable questions about acceptable casualty rates. To condone the continued use of totalistic methods in teen treatment programs we must assume they can be used ethically. However, some participants in this study challenge that assumption.

Summary

This thesis is among the first to conceptualize multiple types of teen treatment programs together as totalistic environments. The term "totalistic" was operationalized by identifying seven program features (Table 3-1). Three research questions shaped the research design: How are totalistic teen treatment methods experienced? How do participants describe the immediate effects of the program? How do participants describe the long-term impact of the program?

To ensure the inclusion of a wide range of experiences and perspectives, an online questionnaire was designed to collect data from a sampling frame of potential interview participants. Two hundred and twenty-three adults provided information about their experience within the one teen program that had the most impact on their life. Out of these, 212 reported that their program was highly totalistic and 30 interview participants were selected from this frame. The 15 participants who rated their quality of experience the highest, and indicated interest in being interviewed, were designated as group H. Group L was a random sample of 15 selected from the 154 who had low quality of experience scores and were willing to be interviewed.

All 30 participants were asked the same set of open-ended interview questions. Each interview was recorded verbatim and fully transcribed. The transcripts were then coded line by line. First, each codable statement was assigned a primary category and some were also assigned subcategory labels. Five primary categories were based on the three research questions: pre-program context, program structure, lived experience, immediate effects, and long-term impact. In subsequent rounds of coding, additional subcategories and sub-subcategories were developed as codes were applied to participants' statements.

The number of participants counted in each subcategory was tallied and compared between subgroups. Counting and qualitative comparisons led to the creation of 31 topics, organized by research question (Table 4-1). In thematic analysis, these 31 topics were condensed into six concepts and three themes (Table 5-1).

The experience of totalistic teen treatment methods was described as an induction/abduction process that led to containment. Participants were simultaneously led toward the changes required by the program while also being drawn away from the outside world and the past. The immediate effects were defined as personal changes they went through while in the program. These changes were described as a containment process where they became a part of the program structure, or part of the container, as they worked toward short-term and long-term experiences of release. The long-term impact was described in terms of trajectory and perspective. Participants described ways they see the program experience now, and ways the program has affected the course of their lives.

The programs they attended were highly totalistic but the two groups described totalistic program features in different ways. Ten participants in group H reported primarily positive program effects. For them, the treatment experience was challenging but meaningful, or even life-saving. The remaining 20 reported a range of mixed, or primarily negative, effects. All of group L and five in group H reported some degree of harm resulting from their program experiences. Serious psychological and physical harm was reported but some of those who were injured emphasized that there was some "good" mixed in, even when the negative side effects were long-lasting. For others, it was "all bad" and they are interested in working to make sure others do not experience what they did. Four participants in group H and nine in group L have devoted much of their adult lives to becoming educated in the social sciences or currently have graduate degrees and are working with troubled youth as social workers or as counselors.

The wide range of responses to totalistic treatment, and the extremely negative experiences reported, raise concerns about how predictable totalistic treatment outcomes are. The type of harm reported in this study raises a range of ethical and legal concerns about the difference between treatment and risky experimental programs. Research in residential treatment has focused on desirable outcomes but the findings in this study suggest that the safety, regulation, and legality of totalistic programming also need to be considered as primary factors affecting youth outcomes and adult development.

Final Notes

In addition to the three research questions shaping this research, another question was raised: When is residential treatment comparable to thought reform? Since the 1960s, a handful of researchers and practitioners have asked the same thing (Beyerstein, 1992; Frankel, 1989; Gordon & Empey, 1962; Schein et al., 1961). Others have explored similar questions about coercion and persuasion in similar treatment settings (Frank, 1974; Hood, 2011; Skoll, 1992; Weppner, 1983). In 1993, the founding director of the National Institute on Drug Abuse, Robert Dupont, testified in court to explain how totalistic teen treatment programs are fundamentally different from cults. He said the main difference is that the "confrontation and the use of intensive pressure" is a short-term exposure in a totalistic program, but in a cult, members are expected to stay forever (Du Pont, 1993, 1425–1426).

Military researchers studying methods of totalitarian "brainwashing" on American civilians in China during the 1950s stated that the Chinese were actually using some of America's best methods for treating delinquency and that the difference between therapeutic influence and coercive persuasion in "brainwashing" has to do with how confined an individual is.

> What distinguishes coercive persuasion from other
> kinds of influence processes is the degree to which
> the person who is to be influenced is physically or
> psychologically confined to a situation in which he
> must continue to expose himself to unfreezing pres-
> sures (Schein et al., 1961, p.139).

The majority of adults in this study indicated that they did not
have the option of leaving and in both groups there were explicit
references to "brainwashing." For youth contained within totalistic programs and subjected to "unfreezing" pressures, if the
response is indistinguishable from the response to complex psychological trauma, the difference between treatment and coercive persuasion may be rhetorical.

Program owners and staff control the labels they give to
their methods and no program advertises itself as harmful. But
such rhetorical safeguards may pose a problem. Those who are
harmed in the name of treatment face the challenge of identifying wrongly-named aspects of "therapy." The difficulties in developing this vocabulary are barriers to healing, communication, and meaning making. Participants in this study suggest
that the experience of trauma seems to prevent the perception
and understanding of trauma, especially if complaints were
framed as a symptom of pathology or a personal failure.

Researchers, policy makers, clinicians, and concerned
parents, should consider the totalistic features of teen treatment
programs as a primary factor affecting safety and the potential
for harm. Those who have first-hand experience with totalistic
methods should be invited into the conversation about how to
improve youth outcomes. Those with more-positive experiences might have valuable information about the types of youth
for whom the benefits outweigh the risks. Those with more negative experiences are a valuable source of information about

forms of institutional abuse that are not adequately described in current scientific studies.

The data collected here say that totalistic teen treatment methods are potentially helpful to some and potentially harmful to others. But research in residential programming has focused almost exclusively on how helpful it is, even while failing to adequately explain *why* it should "help" (De Leon, 2000; Gilligan, 2015; Harder & Knorth, 2015; Harper, 2010; Nielsen & Scarpitti, 1997). Searching through peer-reviewed journals, it appears the scientific community has failed to ask much about those who have been harmed in treatment settings (Mc Cord, 2003; Mercer, 2017; White & Kleber, 2008). The evidence in this study suggests research has focused on understanding a thin slice of outcome variables removed from the full spectrum of program effects.

The United States Department of Health's National Commission for the Protection of Human Subjects of Biomedical and Behavioral Research explains in the Belmont Report Volume II, why "not all that is intended to be therapy, is therapy" (London & Klerman, 1978). Since the late 1970s, in all ethical settings, human research participants have been afforded extra protections when there is more than minimal risk (Protection of Human Subjects, 2009). Participants in this study provide empirical evidence about some of the lesser-known reasons totalistic methods can be dangerous and potentially harmful. Professional ethics assume that therapeutic intent does not a treatment make, and if the degree of risk is unknown, the methods are experimental until the outcomes can be reasonably predicted (Golddiamond, 1978; London & Klerman, 1978). There are well-established ethical protections and means of recourse afforded to human research subjects (Protection of Human Subjects, 2009). American youth who are forced to participant in unproven totalistic methods are often exposed to more than minimal risk and deserve the protections afforded to human subjects.

APPENDIX A
THERAPEUTIC COMMUNITY CONCEPTUAL MODEL
(NIELSEN & SCARPITTI, 1997)

Relationships Between Therapeutic Community Elements and Global Change in Clients

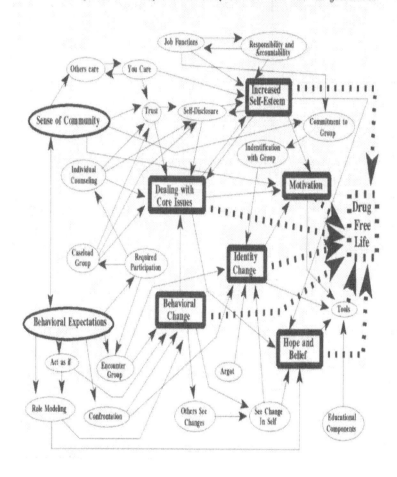

APPENDIX B
ONLINE CONSENT AGREEMENT AND QUESTIONNAIRE

Informed Consent to Participate in an Online Questionnaire

Project Title
Adult Perspectives on Totalistic Teen Treatment: Experiences and Impact

IRB Approval Number: UF-IRB201701655

Please read this consent document carefully before you decide to participate in this study. Please save a copy for your records.
This is a formal invitation to participate in research conducted by graduate student, Mark Chatfield, of the Family, Youth and Community Sciences department at the University of Florida. Mr. Chatfield is supervised in his research by his advisor, Dr. David C. Diehl.

Purpose of this study.
The purpose of this study is to explore retrospective first-hand accounts by adults who, as adolescents, were in an intensive, or totalistic, treatment program. The primary focus will be to learn how such treatment methods were experienced and how the effects and impacts of those experiences is perceived and described by research participants.

What you will be asked to do in the study.
This online questionnaire takes approximately 10 minutes to complete. It asks for demographic information and asks participants to respond to questions about their residential program, their experience in the program, and their opinions about the program. At the end of the questionnaire, participants will be asked if they would like to participate in a one-hour phone interview. If they live in the Gainesville, Florida area, they may be interviewed in-person if preferred. Participants who are interested in being interviewed will be asked to share

their first name, their phone number, and an email address where they can be reached.

Risks and Benefits.
We do not anticipate risks to participants in this study. We do not anticipate that participants will benefit directly by participating in this experiment.

Compensation.
Participants will not receive any payment for completing the online questionnaire.

Confidentiality.
Your identity will be kept confidential to the extent provided by law. Your information will be assigned a code number. There is a minimal risk that security of any online data may be breached, but since (1) no identifying information will be collected, (2) the online host uses several layers of encryption and firewalls, and (3) your data will be removed from the server soon after you complete the study, it is highly unlikely that a security breach of the online data will result in any adverse consequence for you.

At the end of this questionnaire, if you are interested in participating in an interview, you may provide a first name, phone number, and email address where you can be contacted. Interview participants will not be asked to reveal their last names at any time.

If you would like to be contacted about an interview, any contact information you provide will be assigned a code number and kept in a secure location. The list connecting your name to this number will be kept in a locked file in the research supervisor's office. When the study is completed, this list will be destroyed. Your contact information and name will not be used in any report.

Voluntary participation.
Your participation in this study is completely voluntary. There is no penalty for not participating. You may refuse to answer any question without explanation.

Right to withdraw from the study.
You have the right to stop participating at any time without consequence.

Who to contact if you have questions about the study.
Mark Chatfield
Department of Family, Youth, and Community Sciences,
University of Florida, Gainesville, Florida
P.O. Box 110180
Gainesville, FL 32611-0180
[phone number]
mchatfield@ufl.edu

Who to contact about your rights as a research participant in the study
IRB02 Office
Box 112250
University of Florida
Gainesville, FL 32611-2250
[phone number]

Who to contact in case of emergency due to any crisis arising from your participation in this research.
In case of emergency, please call 911.
In case of mental a mental health crisis you may call the Alachua County Crisis Center hotline [phone number].

Agreement
By clicking "agree to participate" I am indicating that I am at least 18 years old and I have read the procedure described above. I have received a copy of this description and I voluntarily agree to participate.

QUESTIONNAIRE

The Online Questionnaire was accessible after participants read the invitation to participate and had read the electronic consent form. Question one is the response to the informed consent and the agreement to participate in research. In the online version, the demographics section appeared at the end of the survey.

Section One – **Demographics** 4 Items (#2 – 5)	1. Consent
	Coding Keys
2. What is your age? (In years)	No Code (Actual number in years)
3. What is your race/ethnicity (Please check all that apply)	White...1 Latino, Hispanic, or Spanish origin......2 Black or African American...............3 American Indian or Alaska Native.......4 Middle Eastern or North African..........5 Asian...6 Native Hawaiian or Pacific Islander......7 Some other race, ethnicity, or origin....19 (If you would like to specify, please do so here_____) Prefer not to answer......................20
4. How do you identify your gender?	Male...............................1 Female.............................2 Transgender Male.................3 Transgender Female...............4 Non-gendered.....................5 Some other gender identity......19 (If you would like to specify, please do so here ____) Prefer not to answer.............20
5. What is your sexual orientation?	Heterosexual..............1 Homosexual..............2

301

	Bisexual...................3 Asexual....................4 Other.................19 (If you would like to specify, please do so here _____) Prefer not to answer................20

Section Two - **Treatment Over-** **view** 14 items (#6 – 17)	
	Coding
6. How many different programs did you attend before the age of 18? Skip logic…. if more than 1	No Code if 1 Two or more....................2 Don't know.....................21
TEXT This survey is designed to collect information about your experience in **one single** program. If you were in two or more programs before the age of 18, please consider which program has affected you the most, or has impacted your	

life the most, and complete the survey based on your experience in this program. If you are not sure, please consider which program you spent the most time in and complete the survey based on your experiences there. Thank You!	
7. What was the name of this program?	No Code (Actual Name)
8. Where was this program located? (City and State. If it was outside the US, what country?	No Code (Actual Location)
9. What type of program was it? (check all that apply) ***	Boot camp…………………………..1 Foster care group Home……………2 Intensive outpatient…………………3 Juvenile justice facility……………..4 Residential treatment center………...5 Therapeutic boarding school………...6 Ranch/Wilderness camp or outdoor program……………………………….7 Psychiatric hospital………………....8 Training school……………………...9 Other……………………………...19 Don't know…………………………21 (please specify)

10. Was religious conversion a fundamental goal of this program?	Yes.........1 No..........2
11. What legal authority placed you in the program? (Check all that apply)	Parent(s)...1 Other Family Member(s)..........2 Legal Guardian(s).................3 Court Order.........................4 Foster/Welfare System.............5 Other..............................19 (please specify) ____ Don't know......................21
12. Were you brought to this program by a paid escort/transport agent/company?	Yes.................1 No.................2 Don't know........21
13. How old were you when you entered this program?	No Code (Actual Age) _____ Years old
14. What year did you enter this program?	No Code (Actual Year)
15. Why were you placed in this program? (Please check all that apply).	Court ordered for criminal activity..........................1 Substance abuse............2 Behavioral problems other than criminal activity or substance abuse..3 Psychological problems.....4 Family problems............5 Problems at school..........6

	Religious reasons............7 Sexual activity...............8 Sexual orientation..........9 Gender identity..............10 Other.......................19 (please specify) _____ Don't know..................21
16. How many MONTHS were you in this program? (best estimate or exact number)	No Code (Number of Months) _____ Months
17. Did you complete the program (fulfill the requirements and/or formally graduate?)	Yes.....1 No.......2
18. How long has it been since you participated in the program or the program's aftercare?	Less than one year......1 1 – 5 years...............2 6-10 years...............3 11- 15 years.............4 16 – 20 years...........5 More than 20 years......6
19. If you would like to comment on your responses in the Treatment Overview section, please do so here.	Enter Text

Section Three - Program Experience 7 Items (#20 – 28)	
TEXT The following questions will ask you to make generaliza-tions about your program experience. At the end of this section, you may comment on your re-sponses if you would like to clarify or explain further. Please indicate the score that best describes your experience. **If your response is neutral, please select the middle circle.**	Coding Keys
20. Overall, how helpful or harmful was this program for you?	Very helpful = 5 More helpful than harmful = 4 Neutral = 3 More harmful than helpful = 2 Very harmful = 1
21. How safe or unsafe did you feel in this program?	Very safe = 5 More safe than unsafe = 4 Neutral = 3 More unsafe than safe = 2 Very unsafe = 1
22. How fair or unfair were the punishments in this program?	Very fair = 5 More fair than unfair = 4 Neutral = 3 More unfair than fair = 2 Very unfair = 1

23. How reasonable or unreasonable were the rules of this program?	Very reasonable = 5 More reasonable than unreasonable = 4 Neutral = 3 More unreasonable than reasonable = 2 Very unreasonable = 1
24T. This question tests the accuracy of the questionnaire; will you please give this one a **neutral** score?	Very accurate = 5 More accurate than inaccurate = 4 Neutral = 3 More inaccurate than accurate = 2 Very inaccurate = 1
25. How equally or unequally did the staff members treat the residents?	Very equal = 5 More equally than unequal = 4 Neutral = 3 More unequal than equal = 2 Very unequal = 1
26. How easy or how difficult was it to adjust to life after this program?	Very easy = 5 More easy than difficult = 4 Neutral = 3 More difficult than easy = 2 Very difficult = 1
27. If you would like to comment on your responses in the Program Experience section, please do so here.	No Code (actual comments)

Section Four - Opinion of Experience 10 Items (#29 – 34)	
TEXT As you read the following statements, please consider how well they describe your own general experience. How strongly do you agree or disagree with the following statements about your experience in this program? **If your response is neutral, please select the middle circle.** At the end of this section, you may comment on your responses if you would like to clarify or explain further.	Coding Keys Higher Score = More Positive Experience Lower Score = More Negative Experience
28. The program provided me with high-quality treatment.	Strongly agree = 5 Agree = 4 Neutral = 3 Disagree = 2 Strongly disagree = 1
29. I trusted the staff members to act in my best interests.	Strongly agree = 5 Agree = 4 Neutral = 3 Disagree = 2 Strongly disagree = 1
30. The program helped me to be a happier person.	Strongly agree = 5 Agree = 4 Neutral = 3 Disagree = 2 Strongly disagree = 1

31R. I experienced negative side-effects from treatment while I was in this program.*	Strongly agree = 1 Agree = 2 Neutral = 3 Disagree = 4 Strongly disagree = 5
32R. Overall, I had a negative treatment experience in this program.*	Strongly agree = 1 Agree = 2 Neutral = 3 Disagree = 4 Strongly disagree = 5
33R. In this program, my basic physical needs were neglected.*	Strongly agree = 1 Agree = 2 Neutral = 3 Disagree = 4 Strongly disagree = 5
34. The program's long-term impact on my life has been positive.	Strongly agree = 5 Agree = 4 Neutral = 3 Disagree = 2 Strongly disagree = 1
35. I received an appropriate and adequate education while in the program.	Strongly agree = 5 Agree = 4 Neutral = 3 Disagree = 2 Strongly disagree = 1
36R. I often felt a sense of dread while I was in the program.*	Strongly agree = 1 Agree = 2 Neutral = 3 Disagree = 4 Strongly disagree = 5
37. If you would like to comment on your responses in the Opinion of Experience section, please do so here.	No Code (Actual Comments)

Section Five - Program Characteristics 8 items (#35 – 42)	Coding Continuum Direction 1 = Least totalistic 5 = Most totalistic
TEXT How strongly do you agree or disagree with the following statements about your program? **If your response is neutral, please select the middle circle.**	Coding Keys
38. Almost all forms of communication between residents, and with people in the outside world, were controlled or governed by rules.	Strongly agree = 5 Agree = 4 Neutral = 3 Disagree = 2 Strongly disagree = 1
39. The program had a detailed and strict system of rule enforcement and punishment procedures.	Strongly agree = 5 Agree = 4 Neutral = 3 Disagree = 2 Strongly disagree = 1
40. Residents in the program were expected to hold each other accountable and/or report on each other for rule infractions.	Strongly agree = 5 Agree = 4 Neutral = 3 Disagree = 2 Strongly disagree = 1
41. Everyone was required to participate in group sessions that involved confessions and/or confrontations.	Strongly agree = 5 Agree = 4 Neutral = 3 Disagree = 2 Strongly disagree = 1

42. The program philosophy emphasized a need to totally change, to be completely saved, or to be transformed.	Strongly agree = 5 Agree = 4 Neutral = 3 Disagree = 2 Strongly disagree = 1
43. Progress through the program required the completion of prescribed stages, phases, or levels of treatment progress.	Strongly agree = 5 Agree = 4 Neutral = 3 Disagree = 2 Strongly disagree = 1
44. For at least some amount of time in the program, all aspects of life, such as school, therapy, meals, and recreation, took place in the program or by permission of the program.	Strongly agree = 5 Agree = 4 Neutral = 3 Disagree = 2 Strongly disagree = 1
45. If you would like to comment on your responses in the Program Characteristics section, please do so here	No Code (Actual comments)

Section Six - Participation in an Interview 6 items (#43 – 48)	
Text	Coding Keys
46. In your opinion, are your memories of your time in this program clear enough to participate in a one-hour interview?	Yes = 1 No = 2 Skip Logic – if yes, go to #44 if no, go to end
47. Are you interested in participating in a one-hour interview	Yes = 1 No = 2

about your program experiences and the impact they have had on your life?	If yes, go to interview consent. If no, go to thank you page.
48. Interview Consent	Yes = 1 No = 2 If yes on consent, go to contact information. If no on consent, go to thank you page.
TEXT Thank you for your interest in participating in an interview. Please provide your first name, a phone number, and an email address where you can be reached. Based on the design of this research, a small number of potential interviewees will be selected and contacted. If you are selected for an interview, you will first be provided with a copy of the interview questions and further information about the study.	
49. First Name	No Code (Actual Name)
49. Email Address (identifier)	No Code (Actual Email Address)
49. Phone Number (alternative identifier)	No Code (Actual Number)

TEXT Thank you for participating in this survey!	
50. [Did they participate in interview?]	Entered later

APPENDIX C
INVITATION TO PARTICIPATE IN RESEARCH

Invitation to Participate in Research

Project Title: Adult Perspectives on Totalistic Teen Treatment: Experiences and Impact

IRB Approval Number: UF-IRB201701655

This is an invitation to participate in research conducted by graduate student, Mark Chatfield, of the Family, Youth and Community Sciences department, at the University of Florida. Mr. Chatfield is supervised in his research by his advisor, Dr. David Diehl.

Who is eligible to participate
Adults, aged 18 and over, who were in an intensive treatment program in the United States while under the age of 18, are eligible to participate.

For the purposes of this study, intensive programs have been defined by the following qualities:
- Communication between residents, and with the outside world, was under strict control and contingent on good behavior.
- Youth in the program were expected to monitor each other and/or report each other if they broke the rules.
- The program philosophy emphasized the need to totally change or be completely saved.
- To progress through the program, residents were required to complete a series of prescribed stages, phases, or levels of treatment.
- Youth were required to participate in group sessions that involved confessions and/or confrontations.

- The program had a strict system of rule enforcement, punishments, and/or inflexible consequences.
- For some length of time, all aspects of life occurred under the authority, supervision, or permission of the program.

Adults who were in a treatment program that could be described by these characteristics are eligible to participate no matter how good or bad their experience was. This study is designed to assess a wide range of opinions and perspectives among adults who, for ANY reason, were placed in a program of this nature before the age of 18.

Purpose of the research.
The purpose of this study is to learn how such treatment methods were experienced and how the effects and impacts of those experiences are perceived and described by research participants.

What you will be asked to do.
This is a two-stage research project.

Online Questionnaire
In the first stage, all who are eligible are invited to participate in a brief online questionnaire that takes approximately 10 minutes to complete. No compensation will be provided for participation in this stage of the project.

Phone or In-Person Interview
In the second stage of the study, a small number of participants who completed the questionnaire and are interested, will be invited to participate in a one-hour interview that will be audio recorded with their permission. Most of the interviews will be conducted by phone but participants who live in the Gainesville, Florida area may choose to be interviewed in-person if they prefer. After the interview, participants who would like to receive a $15 gift card will be asked to provide a mailing address.

Confidentiality.

Your identity will be kept confidential to the extent provided by law. You may complete the questionnaire without providing your name. If you are interested in participating in an interview, you will be asked to provide your first name, phone number, and email address. You will not be asked to reveal your last name. Any identifying information you provide, such as your email address and phone number, will be assigned a code number and no one other than Mr. Chatfield and his faculty supervisor will have access to the code's key. When the study is completed and the data have been analyzed, the list of codes will be destroyed. Your name and your contact information will not be used in any report. Any future publications about this research will not personally identify or disclose your identity.

Voluntary participation.

Your participation in this study is completely voluntary. There is no penalty for not participating. You may refuse to answer any question without explanation.

Right to withdraw from the study.

You will have the right to withdraw from the study at any time without consequence.

If you would like to participate.

If you would like to participate, you may review the informed consent form and access the online survey at [LINK]. If you know of others who might be interested in participating in this research, please share this entire invitation without editing. If you have any technical problems with accessing the survey, or if you would like more information about this project, please contact:

Mark Chatfield
Graduate Student
Department of Family, Youth, and Community Sciences
University of Florida
mchatfield@ufl.edu
[phone number]

APPENDIX D
INTERVIEW CONSENT AGREEMENT READ OUTLOUD
PRIOR TO INTERVIEW

Informed Consent to Participate in a Recorded Interview
This is to be read out loud to interviewees as an introduction

The title of this project is:
Adult Perspectives on Totalistic Teen Treatment: Experiences and Impact
IRB Approval Number: UF-IRB201701655

This is a formal invitation to participate in research conducted by graduate student, Mark Chatfield, of the Family, Youth and Community Sciences department at the University of Florida. Mr. Chatfield is supervised in his research by his advisor, Dr. David C. Diehl.

The purpose of this study is to explore retrospective first-hand accounts by adults who, as adolescents, were in a totalistic treatment program. The primary focus will be to learn how such treatment methods were experienced and how the effects and impacts of those experiences are perceived and described by research participants.

You have been selected to participate based on the design of this study and if you agree to be interviewed, you will be asked about your experience in this program, the immediate effects it had on you, and the long-term impact the program has had on your life.

You have already been provided with a copy of this consent agreement and a copy of the interview questions, but I am required to read this document out loud to you before we begin the interview.

In order to ensure the accuracy of this research, the interviews in this study will be audio recorded with participants' permission. After the interview, if there is anything you would like to follow-up on, or add to, you may do so via email. After the recordings are transcribed they will be destroyed.

We do not anticipate risks to participants in this study. We do not anticipate that you will benefit directly by participating in this experiment.

Interview participants will receive a $15 gift card as a gesture of gratitude for their participation.

Confidentiality. Any information you provide will be kept confidential to the extent provided by law. If you would like to receive the $15 gift card after the interview, you will be asked to provide a mailing address. You will NOT be asked to reveal your last name at any time.

Your first name, email address, and phone number have been assigned a code number and will be kept in a secure location. The list connecting this information to your code number will be kept in a locked file in my research supervisor's office. When the study is completed, this list will be destroyed. Your contact information and name will not be used in any report.

As mentioned above, this interview will be audio-recorded for accuracy in data analysis purposes. All recordings will be transcribed and then destroyed. Transcriptions will be given a confidential code that is not linked to you, personally. They will be kept private and shared only with a small team of trained personnel working directly in this research. You will not be asked to reveal your name or contact information in the interview. Any future publications resulting from this research will not identify your name or contact information.

Voluntary participation. Your participation in this study is completely voluntary. There is no penalty for not participating. During the interview, you may refuse to answer any question at any time. If you refuse to answer a question you will not be asked to explain why.

You have the right to withdraw from the study at any time without consequence. If you have questions about this study you may contact me by mail, email, or by phone.

Mark Chatfield
Department of Family, Youth, and Community Sciences,
University of Florida, Gainesville, Florida
P.O. Box 110180
Gainesville, FL 32611-0180
mchatfield@ufl.edu

If you have questions about your rights as a research participant in the study you may contact the Institutional Review Board office at:
IRB02 Office
Box 112250
University of Florida
Gainesville, FL 32611-2250
[phone number]

In case of emergency due to any crisis arising from your participation in this research please call 911.

In case of mental a mental health crisis you may call the Alachua County Crisis Center hotline at [phone number].

Thank you for going over this consent agreement with me, now I have to formally ask:
Are you at least 18 years old and do you voluntarily consent to participate in this research?

Adult Perspectives on Total-istic Teen Treatment: Experi-ences and Impact	Questionnaire Scores: Section 3
UF IRB Approval Number: UF-IRB201701655	Section 4 Section 5
Consent Date:	Subgroup: H / L
Name of Interviewer:	Location of Interviewer:
Participant's Code Number:	Location of Participant:
Date and Time interview started:	Interview Mode:
Time ended:	Cover Sheet is Completed: Yes / No
Participant's FIRST name:	Identifier and Key Code is Recorded: Yes / No

Introduction

READ TO PARTICIPANT

First, I want to thank you for allowing me to interview you today and I want to emphasize that this is also your interview, I have 12 main questions but you can steer it the way you want. I really do appreciate you being willing to participate in this research.

Did you happen to read over the interview questions I sent you? And do you feel comfortable with them? If we only get part way through and you want to reschedule, that's totally fine. And if you forget to mention something that's important to you, you can write it to me in an email. If there is a problem with audio quality, I will have to ask you to repeat anything that is unclear so that I'm able to get an accurate transcript.

Before we begin, even though you already indicated your consent to participate in this research interview when you completed the online questionnaire, I'm required to read the consent form out loud again and ask for your verbal consent to participate in research. [READ CONSENT TO THEM].

Do you have any questions before we begin recording?

Ok, great, the recorder is now on. If you'd like me to turn it off at any time just let me know. And just to make a note to myself, today's date is _____
and the time is_____.
This is an interview with [first name of participant] _____
who entered the _____ program
at age _____.
[Participant]_____ is now ____ years old
and _____ 's questionnaire code is number _____.

Section One

[RQ1: How are totalistic teen treatment methods experienced?]

READ

Throughout this interview, I'd like to hear what it is about your time in this program that is most important to you.

(Before reading each question, note the minute placemark on the recording)

_____*1. When you think back and remember your time in the program, what are some of strongest memories?*

_____*2. What were some of your <u>first impressions</u> of the program?*

a. What about first impressions of the staff members working there?

Follow up: Their ages, what they were like?

b. What about first impressions of other residents?

Follow up: Any differences between newcomers and more-experienced residents?

c. How was it to learn what the expectations were (stated and unstated)?

Follow up: Level system

_____*3. When you first got there, did they explain the way the program was supposed to work?*

a. How were the rules and expectations conveyed to you?

b. How did they explain the reason for the rules?

c. Did you have the option of leaving?

Check-in, ask how they are doing, are they comfortable with continuing?

_____**4. What was your daily life like there?**

a. What was the daily schedule like?

Follow up: 5) group therapy

_____**5. What did it feel like to live in that environment?**

a. How did you make sense of it at the time?

Follow up: How did you understand/how did they explain reasons for
6) rules, petty compliance, punishments/consequences

7) all aspects of life under one central authority

[Clarification]
READ
OK, so it sounds like_____, is that right?

Check-in, ask how they are doing, are they comfortable with continuing?

Now I'd like to ask how you think the program affected you while you were in there. And with these questions, what I'm trying to get a sense of is how you think about the ways you may have changed during your time there - How you adapted to the program and <u>how you may have changed in the process of adapting.</u>

Section Two
[RQ2: How do participants describe the immediate effects of the program?]

_____ *6. What was your life like before the program?*

a. Where did you live and what was your family relationship like?

b. Why did you end up in this program?

_____ *7. When you were in the program, what did your* [parents or guardian] *know about your daily life there?*

*a. Did your **family relationship change** while you were in the program? If so, how?*

b. Did you have to earn the privilege of speaking with your parents?
c. What was it like to talk to them while you were in the program?

Follow up: Communication / emotional bond with family [or guardian, or foster family].

_____*8. Can you give some examples of how the program did/did not help you with the things you needed help with?*
[Summarize. Then prompt: Anything else?]

Do you remember noticing changes in yourself? If so, what were they?

Check-in, ask how they are doing, are they comfortable with continuing?

Section Three
[RQ3: How do participants describe the long-term impact of the program?]

READ
I'd like to ask about the way your life has been **since you've been out**. I'd like to hear your thoughts about the long-term impact the program has had on different areas of your life. So, these are really questions about the way you reflect on things and the **things that seem significant to you**.

_____*9. When you think about the way your life has played out, has your program experience impacted your life? If so, in what ways?*

Do you know people from your program who have a really different perspective? If so, why do you think your perspective is different from theirs?

_____*10. If we'd had this discussion right after you got out of the program, would you answer my questions in the same way?*

If not, how would they compare?

Follow up: How does your current perspective on the program compare with the way you saw the program when you first exited?

_____**11. Are there any other ways the program has influenced the person you've become? If so, in what ways?**

Follow up: the way you feel about yourself, any central themes they've mentioned.

_____**12. This is the last question – why were you interested or willing to participate in this interview?**

Transition to Closure: [Acknowledge their experiences appropriately.] Thank you so much for taking the time to participate in my research project. I really appreciate it immensely. We've come to the end of the interview.

Are there any other pieces to your story that you want to add?

Closing question – **Are you an alumni, former student – how would you like to be identified?**

OK, I'm turning off the recorder now.

In the next few days, if you think of anything else you'd like to add, please feel free to write it in an email so I can include it in the study. And as a small token of gratitude for your time and effort in helping with this research, I'll be sure to mail you this $15 gift card right away, I'll just need to know what address to send it to. [Small talk, thanks again, and goodbyes].

Make contact after 2 days. Thank them again.

APPENDIX F
CODING STRUCTURE OUTLINE

This outline shows the coding structure in a hierarchy
of primary code categories and subcategories. The purposes of this
appendix are:

1) to clarify the original coding structure
2) to define and show the contents of the five primary code categories
3) to show the codes each topic heading is based on.

The Five Primary Code Categories:

PRE-PROGRAM CONTEXT
STRUCTURE (RQ1)
LIVED EXPERIENCE (RQ1)
IMMEDIATE EFFECT (RQ2)
IMPACT (RQ3)

Primary Category of <u>PRE-PROGRAM CONTEXT</u>
Background information about life before the program.

PRE-PROGRAM CONTEXT coding SUBCATEGORIES

REASON FOR PLACEMENT (Topic Heading Number C1)
PARENTS and HOME LIFE (Topic Heading Number C2)
PRIOR PLACEMENTS (Topic Heading Number C3)
**EDUCATIONAL CONSULTANT/ TRANSPORT SERVICE/
DECEPTIVE INTAKE** (Topic Heading Number C4)
ATTITUDE TOWARD PLACEMENT (Topic Heading Number C5)

RQ1: HOW WERE TOTALISTIC TEEN TREATMENT METHODS EXPERIENCED?

Primary Category of STRUCTURE (RQ1)
What they experienced in the program; overlaps with LIVED EXPERIENCE.

STRUCTURE coding SUBCATEGORIES and Sub-Subcategories)

PROGRAM PHILOSOPHY (Topic Heading Number 1.4)
PROGRAM DESIGN
 Outdoor Component
 Daily Schedule (Topic Heading Number 1.6)
 Level System (Topic Heading Number 1.6)
 Buddy System
 Social Environment (Topic Heading Number 1.3)
 Group Sessions (Topic Heading Number 1.6)
 Seminars/ Intensive Practices (Topic Heading Number 1.6)
 Physical Contact (Topic Heading Number 1.6)
 Home Communication (Topic Heading Number 1.8a)
 Staff (Topic Heading Number 1.2a)
 Home Visit/ Graduation (Topic Heading Number 1.6)
RULES AND CONSEQUENCES
 1st Phase and Demotion
 Communication/ Connection/ Content (Topic Heading Number 1.8a)
 Physical and Crazy Punishment/ Rules (Topic Heading Number 1.14a)
 Restraints
 Isolation (Topic Heading Number 1.8a)
 Learning the Ropes (Topic Heading Number 1.5a)
 Walking, Eating, Bathing, Bathroom, Sleep, Time, Minutia (Topic Heading Number 1.7a)
 Group Contingencies/ Peer Police/ Self Reports (Topic Heading Number 1.3)
 Means of Recourse/ Fairness (Topic Heading Number 1.6)

329

SETTING AND CONDITIONS
>Location (Topic Heading Number 1.6)
>Social Environment (Topic Heading Number 1.3)
>Time
>Staff (Topic Heading 1.2a)
>Peers (Topic Heading Number 1.3)
>Parent Knowledge (Topic Heading Number 1.8a)
>Control (Topic Heading Number 1.6)
>Deprivations/ Harm (Topic Heading Number 1.9a)

Primary Category of <u>LIVED EXPERIENCE</u> (RQ1)
How they experienced the structure of the program; overlaps with STRUCTURE.

LIVED EXPERIENCE coding SUBCATEGORIES and *<u>Sub-Sub-categories)</u>*

INTRODUCTION TO PROGRAM
>Staff (Topic Heading Number 1.2b)
>Goodness of Fit (Topic Heading Number 1.14b)
>Intake/ First few days (Topic Heading Number 1.1)
>Learning the ropes (Topic Heading Number 1.5b)

INTERNAL, FELT, SOMATIC
>Fear (Topic Heading Number 1.10)
>Anger
>Depression
>Emotional Intensity/ Overwhelm/ Devastation (Topic Heading Number 1.10)
>Fairness (Topic Heading Number 1.5b)
>Buy In (Topic Heading Number 1.5b)
>Acceptance
>Autonomy/ Privacy (Topic Heading Number 1.7b)
>Sexuality (Topic Heading Number 1.7b)
>Disorientation/Shock (Topic Heading Number 1.10)
>Fun Times

CONNECTION and COMMUNICATION

> Communication – Barriers, parents, each other, outside friends (Topic Heading Number 1.8b)
> Isolation/ Blackout (Topic Heading Number 1.8b)
> Connection/ Bonding (Topic Heading Number 1.8b)
> Parents/ Family (Topic Heading Number 1.8b)
> Witnessing (Topic Heading Number 1.11)

MEANING MAKING

> Frames of Comparative Reference, relative experience (Topic Heading Number 1.12)
> How challenging (Topic Heading Number 1.12)
> Privileges Topic Heading Number 1.3)
> Graduation

HARM, PUNISHMENT CONTEXTS, ESCAPE

> Medical Neglect/ Abuse (Topic Heading Number 1.9b)
> Punishments (Topic Heading Number 1.9b)
> Escape/ resistance (Topic Heading Number 1.13)
> Self-Harm

RQ2: HOW DO PARTICIPANTS DESCRIBE THE IMMEDIATE EFFECTS OF THE PROGRAM?

Primary Category of IMMEDIATE EFFECT (RQ2)
Descriptions about changes they went through while in the program.

IMMEDIATE EFFECT coding SUBCATEGORIES

SELF-DISCOVERY/ GROWTH/ NEW REALIZATION ABOUT WORLD (Topic Heading Number 2.2)
EXACERBATION/ MALADAPTATION (Topic Heading Number 2.4)
FAMILY RELATIONSHIP IMPROVED (Topic Heading Number 2.1)

FAMILY RELATIONSHIP WORSENED (Topic Heading Number 2.1)

BROADENED HORIZON/ PERSPECTIVE (Topic Heading Number 2.2)

TOUGHENED (Topic Heading Number 2.3)

PHYSICAL IMPROVEMENT (Topic Heading Number 2.3)

PHYSICAL COMPLICATIONS (Topic Heading Number 2.4)

TRAUMA (Topic Heading Number 2.4)

NORMALIZED IT/ ADAPTED TO SYSTEM/ FAKED IT (Topic Heading Number 2.5)

INDOCTRINATED/ BRAINWASHED (Topic Heading Number 2.4)

RESISTED/ MISBEHAVED/ RAN AWAY (Topic Heading Number 2.4)

PUT HEAD DOWN TO GET THROUGH (overlaps with LE: Buy In)(Topic Heading Number 2.5)

NEW FRIENDS/ BETTER SOCIAL SKILLS (Topic Heading Number 2.2)

RQ3: HOW DO PARTICIPANTS DESCRIBE THE LONG-TERM IMPACT OF THE PROGRAM?

Primary Category of <u>IMPACT</u> (RQ3)
Ways they describe the influence of the structure, lived experience, and immediate effects
on their lives since exiting the program.

*IMPACT coding **SUBCATEGORIES**, <u>Sub-Subcategories</u>, and Sub-Sub-Subcategories*

MEMORIES
 <u>"Good" People, Places, Things</u> (Topic Heading Number 3.1)
 <u>"Bad" People, Places, Things</u> (Topic Heading Number 3.1)
 <u>Strong but Neutral</u> (Topic Heading Number 3.1)
 <u>Reflections on Memories</u> (Topic Heading Number 3.1)

332

Explicit About Polemic Memory Types (Topic Heading Number 3.1)

Odd/ Perplexing Memories

PERSONAL* (INTERNAL) – Overlaps with Perspective and Knowledge.

Personal Meaning/ Value of Program (Topic Heading Number 3.7)

Personal Understanding/ Self Perception (Topic Heading Number 3.6)

Comparing Personal Impact to Others (Topic Heading Number 3.6)

Jargon, Habits (Topic Heading Number 3.5)

Tangible- Physical effects / Practical Skills (Topic Heading Number 3.4)

Experience of Trauma (Topic Heading Number 3.4)

Healing from Trauma (Topic Heading Number 3.4)

PERSPECTIVE* (SUBJECTIVE, EXTERNAL) – Overlaps with Personal and Knowledge.

On Program (Topic Heading Number 3.7)

On Other People (Topic Heading Number 3.7)

Changes in Perspective (Topic Heading Number 3.7)

Complicated Mix of Perspectives (Topic Heading Number 3.4)

KNOWLEDGE* (OBJECTIVE, EXTERNAL) – Overlaps with Personal and Perspective.

About Program/ Details (Topic Heading Number 3.6)

About Larger Issues (Topic Heading Number 3.6)

About Cohort (Topic Heading Number 3.2)

Suicides and ODs (Topic Heading Number 3.2)

SOCIAL

Family (Topic Heading Number 3.2)

Cohort Friends/Relations [merged with cohort status in Impact Coding Document] (Overlaps with Memories and Knowledge: About Cohort) (Topic Heading Number 3.2)

Improving Skills – Interpersonal/ Social (Topic Heading Number 3.5)

Impaired Skills/ Barriers – Interpersonal Social (Topic Heading Number 3.5)

TRAJECTORY – Explicit about **internal** processes over time/ and **external** events marking a way forward.

> Internal Processes (Topic Heading Number 3.6)
> Reentry (Topic Heading Number 3.3)
> Substance Use (Topic Heading Number 3.3)
> School/ Subsequent Placements (Topic Heading Number 3.3)
> Career (Topic Heading Number 3.3)
> Advocacy (Topic Heading Number 3.3)

THE INTERVIEW

> Their Reasons for Participating (Topic Heading Number 3.3)
> Their Observations
> My Observations
> How they identify or label themselves

CASUAL SUMMARIES/ PATHWAYS - Links, cascades, and explanations that participants describe in ways that refer to multiple categories at the same time.

PEARLS – Of wisdom, insight, and healing experiences related to context, structure, lived experience, immediate effects, and impact.

334

Codebook Entry Template/Key

Topic Heading Number	Topic Heading	Name of Code, listed as: Primary Code Category Code Subcategory Code Sub-Subcategory			
Code definition, overlaps, examples					
Notes. (Four cells to the right in this row indicate the number of participants counted in the code subcategory).		Group H	Group L	Difference	Total

Codebook Entries

C1	Reasons for Placement	Pre-Program Context Reasons for Placement			
Participant understanding, beliefs, opinions, reflections on why they were put in this program. Related to "Parents and Home Life."					
Interview questions invited discussion, or directly, or indirectly asked about this topic.		11	12	1	23

C2	Parents and Home Life	Pre-Program Context Parents/ Home Life			
Contextual factors about parents and home life identified explicitly or implicitly by participants as relevant to explaining why they ended up in the program, how their life events led up to placement. Related to "Reasons for Placement."					
Interview questions invited discussion, or directly, or indirectly asked about this topic.		6	5	1	11

335

| C3 | **Prior Placements** | Pre-Program Context |
| | | Prior Placements |

Mentions, in passing, or details about prior program experiences (prior to the program they were reporting on); relevant to life events leading up to placement. May or may not be related to C1 and C2.

Bobbi (LBB1333) mentioned a prior placement and that her drug use escalated after her first program. This was coded both, as "C:Prior Placement" and IM:Substance use even though it was a reference to a program she was not reporting on in the interview. If this code were removed from IM, the difference in escalating substance use between groups would be even more exaggerated. It was left as Impact to help counter negativity bias.

Participant-driven topic.	7	5	2	12

| C4 | **Educational Consultant/ Forcible transport service/ Deceptive Intake** | Pre-Program Context Educational Consultant/ Forcible transport service/ Deceptive Intake |

This code is primarily the mentions of forcible parent arranged kidnappings by "escort services" but it also includes other questionable ethics related to recruitment, deceptive marketing, or questionable practices by educational consultants or lies, trickery, and deception by parents.

Participant driven topic.	5	10	5	15

| C5 | **Attitude toward placement** | Pre-Program Context Attitude toward placement |

Mentions about positive or negative attitudes, expectations about, assumptions, pre-conceived notions about what it would be like.

Participant driven topic.	4	3	1	7

336

1.1	**Intake and Introduction**	Lived Experience Introduction to Program: **Intake, First Few Days**			
First impressions, first experiences, when it was new. Overlaps with "Learning the Ropes" but differs in that mentions are not specific to the process of adapting.					
Interview questions asked about this topic.		8	12	4	20

1.2a(1) "a" indicates Primary Code of *Structure*	**The Staff**	Structure **Settings and Conditions**: Staff			
More-objective details about staff, therapists, teachers and their role in shaping the **tone** and environment.					
Interview questions specifically asked about first impressions of the staff, how staff explained things, ages and qualifications of staff.		7	11	4	18

1.2a(2)	**The Staff**	Structure **Program Design**: Staff			
More-objective details about staff, therapists, teachers and their role in shaping the **structure** of the environment.					
Interview questions specifically asked about first impressions of the staff, how staff explained things, ages and qualifications of staff.		4	5	1	9

1.2b "b" indicates Primary Code of *Lived Experience*	**The Staff**	Lived Experience **Introduction to the program**: Staff			
Subjective opinions, feelings, judgements about staff, therapists, teachers and how participants perceived them. Emphasis was more about the subjective experience.					
Interview questions specifically asked about first impressions of the staff, how staff explained things, ages and qualifications of staff.		7	9	2	16

1.3(1)	**Social Environment**	Structure **Settings and Conditions**: Social Environment			
Participant descriptions about the culture, mood, resources, and dynamics between residents within the structure.					
Interview questions asked about the daily schedule, design, and experience of daily life.		11	13	2	24

1.3(2)	**Social Environment**	Structure **Program Design**: Social Environment			
Participant descriptions about **the way the structure shaped** the culture, mood, resources, and dynamics between residents within the structure.					
Interview questions asked about the daily schedule, design, and experience of daily life.		9	9	0	18

338

1.3(3)	**Social Environment**	Structure Settings and Conditions: **Peers**			
Participant descriptions about the other residents. General statements about age ranges, reasons for placements, how "intact" or "damaged" the other residents were, the spectrum of others, often referred to as "a mixed bag."					
Interview questions asked about first impressions of the other residents.		7	5	2	12

1.3(4)	**Social Environment**	Lived Experience Meaning Making: **Privileges**			
Participant references to significance of privileges, even small privileges, relief that came with increased privileges, what it took to earn privileges. Some overlap with level system but the emphasis here was on explicit references to privileges.					
Interview questions asked about the daily schedule, design, and experience of daily life.		3	5	2	8

1.3(5)	**Social Environment**	Structure Rules and Consequences: **Group Contingencies/ Peer Police/ Self-Reports**			
Stated in the context of Rules and Consequences: References to group culture, practices, expectations - peers deciding punishments, conducting restraints, confession reports, explanations about reporting/policing others, group-wide punishments.					
Interview questions asked about the daily schedule, design, and experience of daily life.		3	4	1	7

1.4	**Program** **Philosophy**	Structure **Program Philosophy**			
Participant descriptions about what others said about the program philosophy and what they understood about the program philosophy. Emphasis was on more-objective, less subjective statements about how it worked, why it worked, what it was supposed to do.					
Interview questions asked if the staff or residents explained the way the program was supposed to work.		11	12	1	23

1.5a	**Learning the Ropes**	Structure **Rules and Consequences:** Learning the ropes			
Participant descriptions about the way the expectations and rules were conveyed. How learning was structured. With an emphasis on more-objective mentions and perspectives that did not emphasize the subjective experience of learning.					
Interview questions asked what it was like to learn about the expectations and rules and how the expectations and rules were explained.		6	5	1	11

1.5b(1)	**Learning the Ropes**	Lived Experience **Introduction to the program**: Learning the ropes			
Participant descriptions about the way it felt to **begin learning** about the expectations and rules. With an emphasis on more-subjective mentions and emphasis on the personal subjective experience of getting the hang of things.					
Interview questions asked what it was like to learn about the expectations and rules and how the expectations and rules were explained.		7	7	0	14

1.5b(2)	**Learning the Ropes**	Lived Experience **Internal, Felt: Fairness**			
Participant descriptions about the way it felt **in general** to live up to the expectations and rules. With an emphasis on more-subjective mentions and emphasis on the personal subjective experience of getting the hang of things.					
Interview questions asked what it was like to learn about the expectations and rules and how the expectations and rules were explained.	7	6	1	13

1.5b(3)	**Learning the Ropes**	Lived Experience Internal, Felt, Somatic: **Buy In**			
References to struggle with authenticity, seeing it as a game, realizing that some had bought-in completely but new arrivals were not yet committed/serious. "My disclosures were empty" meaning lip service; questioning self, indignant response "who is going to instantly get with the program?" And conflicts between what they had to say and what they knew was true. All references with this code are windows into understanding barriers to buy in, struggle with buy in – distinct from the change process, these are references to one aspect of the pressure to change by buying in.					
Interview questions asked about first impressions of others – largely participant driven.	2	5	3	7

1.6(1)	**Program Design**	Structure Program Design: **Daily Schedule**			
Participant responses to the question "Can you tell me about a typical day?" or "What was a typical day like?" Almost all participants started with wake up, and then went through the schedule, some described the whole day, others get sidetracked and began discussing things that they were reminded of while going through descriptions of the typical day's events.					
Interview questions asked about the daily schedule.	13	13	0	26

1.6(2)	**Program Design**	Structure Program Design: **Group Sessions**			
Descriptions about group therapy, and group dynamics in encounter groups.					
Interview questions asked about group session if participants did not already describe them at length. Partly participant-driven, partly protocol-driven.		10	9	1	19

1.6(3)	**Program Design**	Structure Settings and Conditions: **Control**			
Explicit references that were framed with the word control that don't easily fit elsewhere or that demonstrate the concept of control. No option to leave, controlled content of conversations, controlled movement, lights kept on at night, abusive restraints (immediate bodily control), lack of control of possessions/program control over possessions, daily bra and panty checks.					
Interview questions asked about the daily schedule and rules.		10	8	2	18

1.6(4)	**Program Design**	Structure Program Design: **Level System**			
Descriptions about the passage from one level to the next; privileges and requirements; status changes; stated as more-objective matter-of-fact statements. Overlaps with "Structure: Program Design: Controlled Communication."					
Interview questions asked about the daily schedule. Some emphasized issues, highpoints, low points, aspects of level system. Partly participant driven, partly protocol driven.		8	7	1	15

1.6(5)	**Program Design**	Structure Settings and Conditions: **Location**			
Participant descriptions about the facility, where it was, what its surroundings were like, qualities about the buildings, grounds, geography, and quality of living environments.					
Interview questions asked about the daily schedule.		9	5	4	14

1.6(6)	**Program Design**	Structure Rules and Consequences: **Means of Recourse/ Fairness**			
Positive and negative assessments of the means of recourse, how much sense the rules made, whether rule changes and expectations were described before punishments were applied. Fairness here was not described as a personal emotional sense but as common sense in reference to punishments for rules that were not stated beforehand, for uneven distribution of punishments to same violation because of staff inconsistencies, or for receiving someone else's punishments because of defending a fellow resident against unfairly extreme punishments. This code was applied when the participant was stating such imbalances of power as a matter of fact, rather than emphasizing the way it affected them.					
Interview questions asked about the daily schedule and rules.		4	7	3	11

1.6(7)	**Program Design**	Structure Program Design: **Home Visit/ Graduation**			
Descriptions of higher-level privilege of visiting home prior to graduation, and graduation, and what was required to graduate. Also includes references to after-care, transition to home visits, home internships, life contracts, and parent visitation days.					
Interview questions asked about the daily schedule and rules.		7	4	3	11

1.6(8)	**Program Design**	Structure Program Design: **Seminars/ Intensive Practices**				
Descriptions about marathon group therapy, seminar rituals, extreme catharsis, other unusually intense methods. These were statements characterized the way the structure was designed, not the subjective experience of these methods.						
Interview questions asked about the group sessions. Some emphasized issues, highpoints, low points, aspects of seminars/intensive practices associated with group sessions. Partly participant driven, partly protocol driven.			6	5	1	11

1.7a(1)	**Personal Autonomy**	Structure Rules and Consequences: **Walking, eating, bathing, bathroom, sleep, personal space, boundaries**				
Participant descriptions about rules governing personal function, control over personal space, fundamental aspects of biology, appearance, sense of time. More objective.						
Participant driven topic.			1	8	7	9

1.7a(2)	**Personal Autonomy**	Structure Program Design: **Physical Contact**				
Participant descriptions or references to rules forbidding touch, affection, or contact, and rules/expectations requiring touch, affection, and contact whether it is wanted or not in "Smooshing." Smooshing occurred in 5 different therapeutic boarding schools. Each night, youth were expected/encouraged to lay down and snuggle with each other and with adult staff members as part of the daily therapy practices.						
Interview questions asked about the daily schedule and rules.			6	4	2	10

1.7b(1)	**Personal Autonomy**	Lived Experience Internal, Felt: **Autonomy/Privacy**			
Descriptions about intrusion of personal psychological space, boundaries, experience of violation. More subjective.					
Participant driven topic.		7	6	1	13

1.7b(2)	**Personal Autonomy**	Lived Experience Internal, Felt, Somatic: **Sexuality**			
Participant descriptions about the experience and meaning of sexuality while in the program. One reference was positive, all others were how sexuality was a problem, was taboo, was exploited, unhealthy, controlled.					
Participant driven topic.		4	4	0	8

1.8a(1)	**Controlled Communication**	Structure Rules and Consequences: **Communication, Connection, Content**			
Descriptions about what was allowed and not allowed, relevant to the flow of information and ability to access information and make contact within the program and with the outside world. Emphasis on external controls, more objective statements.					
Interview questions asked about the daily schedule, experience of daily life, and communication with parents.		9	14	5	23

1.8a(2)	**Controlled Communication**	Structure Settings and Conditions: **Parent Knowledge**			
Participant responses to the question "How much did your parents know about - the program, daily life, or what it was like?" Responses range from "she knew the schedule but that's it" to "they didn't know anything, they had no idea what it was really like." Responses to this question were also given other codes if the response was more relevant to *Lived Experience* or another facet of *Structure*.					
Interview questions asked about parent knowledge.		5	7	2	12

1.8a(3)	**Controlled Communication**	Structure Rules and Consequences: **Isolation**			
These codes are not under the category of *Lived Experience* and do not emphasize the subjective magnitude – these are more matter of fact, more objective descriptions of the program *structure*. To be exact, this code includes 7 participant reports of direct experiences with being put on isolation as a punishment, 3 references (by Elsa, Pat and Joan) to strong impact of witnessing isolation practices, 8 others indicate direct experience with Yellow Zone, being slept, "ISS," ghost challenge, CAT5 Detention – formal isolation practices by design, and many references to modified isolation methods. Participant descriptions stated as more-objective, matter of fact, not emphasizing the emotional importance or importance of subjective meaning. Overlaps with controlled Communication and LE: Isolation. Only one participant, Bobbi, was not represented here but was represented in the LE code for isolation experiences.					
Interview questions asked about the daily schedule, experience of daily life.		5	6	1	11

1.8b(1)	**Controlled Communication**	Lived Experience Connection: **Barriers, Parents, each other, outside world**			
Descriptions about how it was to experience the program's structure relevant to barriers to flow of information and ability to access information and make contact within the program and with the outside world. Emphasis on internal experience of external controls, more subjective.					
Interview questions asked about the daily schedule, experience of daily life, and communication with parents.		4	7	3	11

1.8b(2)	**Controlled Communication**	Lived Experience Connection and Communication: **Parents/Family**			
Descriptions about the sense of betrayal, isolation, devastation, abandonment, loneliness, meaning of family status.					
Interview questions asked about the daily schedule, experience of daily life, and communication with parents.		5	5	0	10

1.8b(3)	**Controlled**	Lived Experience Connection:			
	Communication	**Bonding**			
Descriptions about the experience of strong emotional ties, the need for them, issues of trust in vulnerability and explicit mentions of connection as an experience within the experience of having highly controlled communication. Emphasis on the experience in the program, with less emphasis on current reflections about the experience.					
Participant driven topic. Several mentions relevant to this topic were coded as impact because they were framed as memories, as current relationships that lasted. Overlaps with IM:Friends.		4	2	2	6

1.8b(3)	**Controlled Communication**	Lived Experience Connection: **Isolation, blackout**			
This code overlaps with two structure codes (see note below). Descriptions about what it was like to experience long-term or short-term restrictions, extreme restrictions, or total restrictions on talking, information, and all communication with others or with the outside world.					
Overlaps with Structure:Rules and Consequences and Structure:Settings and Conditions		3	4	1	7

1.9a	**Deprivation of Basic Needs and Harm**	Structure Settings and Conditions: **Deprivations**			
Descriptions about denied sleep, clean water, adequate food, medical care, access to time keeping/calendars, and extreme physical danger as the deprivation of safety. The emphasis is on the more-objective, matter-of-fact description. Some mentions were intertwined with Lived Experience and were coded as both or as the other because they were stated more in a way that emphasized the subjective "I felt." Structure: Settings and Conditions codes emphasize "it was like" not "I felt."					
Participant driven topic. One of the biggest numerical coding contrasts between subgroups.		1	6	5	7

1.9b(1)	**Deprivation of Basic Needs and Harm**	Lived Experience Harm, Punishment Contexts: **Medical Neglect/Abuse**			
Explicit mentions of the occurrence of institutional abuse or medical neglect with an emphasis on what it was like. Domains of institutional abuse/neglect outlined by Rabb and Rindfleisch (1985) are the parameters defining this code. For example: failure to protect, serious physical harm, medical neglect, public humiliation, psychological cruelty, withholding of food, clean water, denial of sleep, inadequate bathing, lack of hygiene/filthy living conditions, complex abuse.					
Participant driven topic.		3	8	5	11

1.9b(2)	**Deprivation of Basic Needs and Harm**	Lived Experience Harm, Punishment Contexts: **Punishment Contexts**			
Descriptions about the contexts of punishments that help to reveal the subjective experience of harm, neglect, and deprivations or in one case, the spiteful threat of extreme punishments as a punishment in and of itself (HW994). These are complex or extreme descriptions about the indefinite nature of punishments as "the worst part," miserable group contingencies, contexts of group punishments.					
Participant driven topic.		6	3	3	9

1.10(1)	**Emotional Intensity**	Lived Experience Internal, Felt: **Overwhelm, Devastation**			
Explicit descriptions of overwhelming emotional/psychological pressure, constant intensity, extreme states of stress in intensive practices, feeling "poked at, destroyed, shattered, panicked."					
Participant driven topic.		4	6	2	10

1.10(2)	**Emotional Intensity**	Lived Experience Internal, Felt: **Disorientation, Shock**			
Descriptions about extremely weird, surprising, surreal, confusing, methods, protocols, scenarios. Explicit use of the word disorienting, shock, stunned, tricked; experiences of realizing they had been tricked. Experiences of being strip searched by strangers but also not being told that would happen. Helps to characterize unpredictable nature of some lived experiences.					
Participant driven topic.		4	6	2	10

1.10(3)	**Emotional Intensity**	Lived Experience Internal, Felt: **Fear**			
Descriptions about dread, constant fear, intense fear, terror, horrible fear, most terrifying, and "so afraid." "Pretty scary because whole life could fall apart if given consequences." That was coded as lived experience, not consequences because the emphasis is on the experience of fear, and the design of the structure and system of rules and consequences is secondary to the experience of them, or in this case, the fear of receiving them.					
Participant driven topic.		6	4	2	10

1.11	**Witnessing**	Lived Experience Connection, Communication: **Witnessing**			
Descriptions that emphasize vicarious experience. The one positive case/code is Nathan's reference to a strikingly positive display of vulnerability, but all other references were negative. Feeling afraid the same thing would happen to them, feeling helpless to intercede, feeling disturbed by bizarre behaviors, seeing others harmed through abuse/medical neglect, seeing others suffer.					
Interview questions asked about first impressions, but this is mostly a participant driven topic.		8	9	1	17

1.12(1)	**Ultimate Terms/Frames of Reference**	Lived Experience Meaning Making: **How Challenging**			
Participant use of terms such as "the hardest, really hard, almost impossible, the worst" that convey the experience of being pushed to the limit. Some overlap with emotional intensity but codes here emphasize the degree of emotion more than the emotion itself, and emphasize how they saw that intensity in processing its meaning at the time.					
Participant driven topic.		6	4	2	10

1.12(2)	**Ultimate Terms/Frames of Reference**	Lived Experience Meaning Making: **Frames of Comparative Reference**			
Descriptions that explain what frames of reference they had, what prior experiences they referred to in orienting themselves; comparing the new to the old. How staff members or the campus compared to prior programs, who the rules compared to rules at home.					
Participant driven topic.		4	2	2	6

1.13	**Escape**	Lived Experience Harm, Punishment Contexts, Escape: **Escape/Resistance**			
Descriptions of running away from the program, the feeling of having no option to leave, or that "it wasn't voluntary." Escape as a non-option; punishments for joking about escaping. Resistance in the form of internal escaping, clinging to old memories. In reporting findings, the topic of resistance is not included in this topic but the code does include a few references to escape as resistance. Primarily these codes refer to actual escape and the experience of having no option to leave					
If it wasn't clear, interview question asked if they had the option of leaving. Partly interview protocol driven, partly participant driven topic.		8	6	2	14

1.14a	**Program Fit**	Structure Rules and Consequences: **Physical and Crazy Punishments/Rules**			
Descriptions of extreme or unusual punishment practices or restrictions stated with an emphasis on explaining the structure without emphasizing the emotional importance or relevance. Definitely some judgement involved in what they reported but these statements were presented in the interview as explanations about the structure, the program, the more-objective. This code was included in the topic of Program Fit because the qualitative differences between the two groups are important.					
Largely driven by interview protocol, partly participant driven.		3	8	5	11

1.14b	**Program Fit**	Lived Experience Introduction to Program: **Goodness of fit**			
Explicit descriptions about their sense of how they fit in socially, how well the design suited their abilities, and their capacity to catch on and make progress. Wondering why it was so ill-suited to their needs, noticing that they had a positive attitude until they were introduced to the extreme rituals, feeling unprepared, not-well matched, naïve.					
Largely driven by interview protocol, partly participant driven.			9	8	1	17

2.1(1)	**Changing Relationships with Family**	Immediate Effect Family Relationship **Improved**			
How communication, honesty, relationship changed for the better while they were in the program.					
Interview protocol driven topic.		8	1	7	9

2.1(2)	**Changing Relationships with Family**	Immediate Effect Family Relationship **Worsened**			
How communication, honesty, relationship changed for the worse while they were in the program. Broken trust, lies told by program staff and complications due to exaggerations.					
Interview protocol driven topic.		5	9	4	14

2.2(1)	**Personal Growth**	Immediate Effect **Self-Discovery, Growth, New Realizations**			
Participant descriptions about new learning, new powers, abilities, the sense of growing as a person, while they were in the program.					
Interview driven – questions asked about personal changes.		11	3	8	14

2.2(2)	**Personal Growth**	Immediate Effect **New Friends/Better Social Skills**			
Descriptions about changes in empathy, ability to connect, communicate, socialize, listen, be emotionally intimate while in the program.					
Interview protocol driven topic.		8	3	5	11

2.2(3)	**Personal Growth**	Immediate Effect **Broadened Horizons**			
Descriptions about the way they changed for the better by meeting new people, learning about a wider range of mental health issues, seeing beyond their immediate concerns – while in the program.					
Participant driven topic/ Interview protocol driven topic.		4	3	1	7

2.3	**Practical Benefits**	Immediate Effect 1) **Toughened** 2) **School, practical skills, physical improvement**			
This topic is a combination of two code subcategories that describe tangible improvements/changes such as learning camping skills, becoming able to do 100 push-ups, getting a lifeguard certificate, passing classes or improving grades in school – while in the program.					
Interview protocol driven topic.		9	7	2	16

2.4(1)	**Negative Changes**	Immediate Effect **Exacerbation, Maladaptation**			
Descriptions of ways participants became worse-off while in the program. Dropped out of school, lost all confidence in parents, more manipulative, inappropriate expressions of anger, unhealthy thinking habits, stunted social skills, sexual impairment/maturity, loss of filters/brutal honesty, cynicism, channeling of violence, more withdrawn.					
Interview protocol driven topic.		4	10	6	14

2.4(2)	**Negative Changes**	Immediate Effect
		Indoctrinated, Brainwashed

Explicit references to "brainwashing," indoctrination, false confessions, Stockholm Syndrome, pressure to internalize values that seemed wrong, learning to self-blame even when it seemed inappropriate to do so. Over laps with LE:Buy In but this code refers to change, emphasis on change rather than more descriptive references that may not emphasize the change process.

Participant driven topic.		3	6	3	9

2.4(3)	**Negative Changes**	Immediate Effect
		School or Physical Complications

Tangible changes in the way their bodies changed or ways their education suffered. The emphasis is on the fact that these changes are tangible, not simply emotional, felt, or psychological changes. Stopped eating, reactions to lack of medicine, grades dropped. As opposed to 2.3.

Interview protocol driven topic.		2	7	5	9

2.4(4)	**Negative Changes**	Immediate Effect
		Resisted, Misbehaved, Ran Away

Overlaps with LE: Escape but this code emphasizes changes due to resistance and the process of resisting the program. Only two participants with this code "ran away" while on home pass and did not return when they were supposed to. This is different from an escape attempt or the experience of thinking about escape or the experience of not having the option to leave. One escape attempt by Tony is coded with this code but he describes this in terms of changes he had gone through in resisting the demands of the program.

Participant driven topic.		1	4	3	5

2.4(5)	**Negative Changes**	Immediate Effect
		Trauma

Explicit descriptions where participants discuss change while in the program that they believe was specifically due to trauma, traumatizing events, being traumatized, or retraumatized while in the program. A large number of descriptions of psychological trauma and changes due to trauma were not coded with this code because they were not explicitly framed as change while in the program - often because the understanding that it was traumatic unfolded over time after exiting. In reporting findings, trauma is an important topic even though a smaller number of statements were specifically coded as Immediate Effect: trauma. This reflects a more conservative approach to identifying trauma codes - only when it was more explicitly indicated in the context of changes participants went through and that they noticed going through while in the program. In reporting findings, participant reflections on harm and trauma symptoms, reported as *impact,* inform the way findings are presented. These reflections, understandings, perspectives were coded as *Impact* because they were reflections on traumatic events and traumatic stress that occurred or affected them even though they did not understand trauma in the moment, while in the program.

Numbers in parentheses are numbers of participants who explicitly discuss trauma experienced in the program from the past tense, as current or after-program symptoms/effects.

Participant driven topic.	2(5)	3(10)	1(5)	5(15)

2.5	**Making Progress:** **A slippery slope**	Immediate Effect 1) Normalized it, Adapted, Faked it 2) "put head down to get through"

This topic includes two similar code subcategories under *immediate effect*. Similar to descriptions about "brainwashing" and indoctrination but these two codes were applied when participants described the process of realizing there was no option but to make progress and get with the program. 1) refers to getting used to it, seeing it as a game, and learning how to find ways to please staff and comply. These changes were described as learning to adapt, to operate, for the sake of earning points toward release. 2) is a phrase used by more than one participant, similar to bite tongue, hold your tongue, suck it up, giving in, and acceptance that progress requires long term compliance. The slippery slope was a phrase used by a participant describing how these changes can lead to loss of self and later confusion about one's authenticity.

Participant driven topic.	8	13	5	21

3.1(1)	**Memories**	Impact Memories: **Reflections On**

Participant responses to questions about their strongest memories. Broad comments on amount of memories, how they have changed over the years, reactions to memories when they come up, thoughts about why some memories are strong, distinguishing between amount and strength when discussion types.

Interview protocol driven topic.	5	11	6	16

3.1(2)	**Memories**	Impact Memories: **"Bad"** people, places, things

Participant responses to questions about their strongest memories. Descriptions about strong painful emotions, injustice, being the target of "witch hunts" and then being broken open.

Interview protocol driven topic.	9	11	2	20

3.1(3)	**Memories**	Impact Memories: **"Good"** people, places, things			
Participant responses to questions about their strongest memories. Strong memories about good friendships, how precious human connection was, small pleasures.					
Interview protocol driven topic.			9	5	4	14

3.1(4)	**Memories**	Impact Memories: 1) **Strong but neutral** 2) Explicit about **polemic** memory types			
Participant responses to questions about their strongest memories. 1) These were descriptions stated without emotional investment, tending to be about physical elements of the facility, work, the design of the program. 2) these were descriptions like "my memories are all really good or really bad" or "there are two types, good or bad."					
Interview protocol driven topic.			9	7	2	16

3.2(1)	**Social Impact**	Impact Social: **Family**			
Participant descriptions about the way they believe, understand, and question the way the program has influenced their relationships with family members. Primarily relationships with parents, but one reference to a spousal relationship, a sibling, a niece, children. How they are different with family members because of what they learned or what the program did to them or said to their parents. Processing their own emotions, the quality of parent relationships.					
Interview protocol driven topic.			10	10	0	20

357

3.2(2)	**Social Impact**	Impact Personal: Understanding/Self-Perception/**Sexu- ality/Intimate relationships**			
Participant descriptions about the way they understand how the program influenced or influences their personality, sexuality, attitudes, beliefs, spirituality, and development. This code is included here because of the relevance here to intimate relationships.					
Participant and Interview protocol driven topic.		11	10	1	21

3.2(3)	**Social Impact**	Impact Knowledge: **Cohort**			
Participant descriptions about the current or past connections they have or had that were made in the program. Anecdotes about friends from the program, the cohort's role in healing from the program, how different cohort friendships are; forged in the program vs. friendships not formed in the program. How participants are affected currently by witnessing the lives of others from the program. References to "it's a mixed bag." Knowledge and judgements about them, differs from IM:Social:Cohort/Friends because these are more general statements, less personal statements. Emphasis on Knowledge rather than social relationships.					
Participant driven topic; interview asked about impact in general terms.		12	8	4	20

3.2(4)	**Social Impact**	Impact Knowledge: Cohort; **Suicides and ODs**			
Mentions or emphasis on the emotional impact, the gravity, and the grappling with witnessing or knowing about close friends or acquaintances from the program who have committed suicide or died by drug overdose.					
Participant driven topic; interview asked about impact in general terms.		3	7	4	10

358

3.2(5)	**Social Impact**	Impact Social: **Cohort Friends/Relations**				
Statements about how their cohort is doing, whether they are friends with people from their cohort, how they interact with cohort, how their cohort members relate to each other. Emphasis on relations rather than knowledge						
Interview asked if they were in touch or how perspectives compared with cohort if participant had not already mentioned it.			10	4	6	14

3.3(1)	**Trajectory**	Impact Trajectory: **Reentry**				
Participant descriptions about the transition from the program to the outside world.						
Participant driven topic; interview asked about impact in general terms.			6	9	3	15

3.3(2)	**Trajectory**	Impact Trajectory: **Substance Use**				
Participant descriptions about the way the program experience influenced their relationship with illicit substances and alcohol after exiting. Includes reflections on the way the program made them curious about drug use because they heard stories or heard about certain drugs for the first time. Some references to labeling, or self-fulfilling prophecies due to having to admit they were a drug addict, even though they weren't, in order to make progress.						
Participant driven topic; interview asked about impact in general terms.			6	3	3	9

359

3.3(3)	**Trajectory**	Impact Trajectory: **School/Subsequent Placements**			
Participant descriptions about the experience, role, and meaning of school, education, and subsequent placements and how the program experience influenced events, meaning, and decisions related to school and goals.					
Participant driven topic; interview asked about impact in general terms.		6	10	4	16

3.3(4)	**Trajectory**	Impact Trajectory: **Career**			
How the program experience influenced career goals and preferences. Includes barriers to employment but primarily direct references to how negative experiences led to determination to work in human services, often specifically to work with troubled youth.					
Participant driven topic; interview asked about impact in general terms.		4	9	5	13

3.3(5)	**Trajectory**	Impact Trajectory: **Advocacy**			
Participant mentions about concerns related to teen programs, interest in promoting programs, interest in working to expose abusive programs, working to gather information, network with others to raise awareness, and interest in criminal justice. Ranges from mentions to emphasis on advocacy as priority in life.					
Participant driven topic; interview asked about impact in general terms.		6	8	2	14

3.3(6)	**Trajectory**	Impact The Interview: **Reasons for Participating**			
Participant responses to the question about why they were willing or interested in being interviewed. This code is included here because almost all participated for advocacy type reasons. Their participation in this research is conceptualized as trajectory because if they had not been in a program, they would not be interested in participating in this type of research.					
Interview protocol driven topic.			9	14	5	23

3.4(1)	**Personal Impact**	Impact Personal: Understanding/Self-perception: **Tangible – Physical** and Practical Skill			
Participant reflections on the way program experiences shaped interests, skills, abilities as well as physical harm, chronic pain, missed opportunities.					
Participant driven topic; interview asked about impact in general terms.		1	6	5	7

3.4(2)	**Personal Impact**	Impact Personal: Experience of **trauma**			
Reflections on the experience of traumatic stress symptoms after exiting the program. Can be references to the discovery of trauma as in the realization that negative symptoms are attributable to traumatic stress. Almost all are explicit references to trauma symptoms.					
Participant driven topic; interview asked about impact in general terms.		4	12	8	16

3.4(3)	**Personal Impact**	Impact Personal: **Healing** from trauma			
Specific references and descriptions about healing from PTSD, the process of healing, coming to terms, making sense as recovery from trauma.					
Participant driven topic; interview asked about impact in general terms.		4	4	0	8

3.4(4)	**Personal Impact**	Impact Perspective: **Complicated mix** of perspectives			
These are participant statements that simultaneously reference good/bad, positive/negative at the same time. Also includes statements that seem self-contradictory, difficult to reconcile, or impossible to reconcile and rather than labeling such statements as inconsistent or unethical justifications of abuse or harm, they are labeled in the more-neutral, as "it's complicated." Also, statements where participants are explicitly grappling with the mix of harm and help they received in unethical or questionable program settings.					
Participant driven topic; interview asked about impact in general terms.		5	3	2	8

3.5(1)	**Social Skills: Improved and Impaired**	Impact Social: **Improving Skills**			
Participant descriptions about the way program experience led to improved communication skills, conflict resolution skills, ease with disclosing personal details, ability to participate in community, understand others, express self, and better ability to help others after exiting and currently.					
Participant driven topic; interview asked about impact in general terms.		5	4	1	9

3.5(2)	**Social Skills: Improved and Impaired**	Impact Social **Impaired Skills**			
Participant descriptions about the barriers created by their experiences in the program. Difficulty being understood, stigma, disrupted friend-ships, aftercare interfering with romantic relationships, learning by mis-take/learning not to talk about it too much, being in a constant state of yelling. Some descriptions were how the impairment lasted for years but is now in the past. Social awkwardness, inability to trust, feeling like an alien, having to resocialize to norms in the outside world. Allowing sex-ual assault or over-reacting to sexual assault as learned responses or re-actions to what was learned in the program.					
Participant driven topic; interview asked about impact in general terms.		3	10	7	13

3.5(3)	**Social Skills: Improved and Impaired**	Impact Personal: Understanding/Self-Perception: **Jargon, Habits**			
Overlaps with Impact: Interview: My observations – however, almost all codes in this subcategory are participant mentions about their own use of jargon after the program, and their own habits that were difficult to unlearn. Almost all participants unwittingly slipped into using jargon during the interview, but it was coded here, as this code, when they acknowledged it, or described their awareness of using it.					
Participant driven topic; interview asked about impact in general terms.		3	2	1	5

3.6(1)	**Knowledge**	Impact Knowledge: **About program**			
Participant descriptions about the history, current events, changing prac-tices, details about staff, rule changes, legal issues, and reasons for pro-gram closures. The impact of being currently influenced by information content.					
Participant driven topic; interview asked about impact in general terms.		8	12	4	20

3.6(2)	**Knowledge**	Impact Knowledge: **About larger related issues**			
Participant descriptions about policy, how programs work in general, knowledge about teen treatment in general, knowledge about social dynamics, regulation, history of cults, programs, educational consultant practices, and research related to the larger topic.					
Participant driven topic; interview asked about impact in general terms.		4	13	9	17

3.6(3)	**Knowledge**	Impact Personal: Understanding/Self-perception: **Comparing Personal Impact**			
Participant descriptions, reflections on why or how their program experience was or is so different from others in their cohort or others from other programs. Contrasted differences that they are grappling with, not how similar they are when compared. Impact of grappling with knowledge that conflicts with their own experience.					
Participant driven topic; interview asked about impact in general terms.		9	1	8	10

3.6(4)	**Knowledge**	Impact Trajectory: **Internal Processes**			
Reflections on their trajectory, self-knowledge, and inner changes. Gaining the ability to articulate the experience, learning how to compartmentalize it, journey through anger to maturity, their relationship with traumatic memories, the journey leading up to healing. Statements of how their self-knowledge has led to insights, realizations, disillusionment, self-forgiveness.					
Participant driven topic; interview asked about impact in general terms.		9	10	1	19

3.7(1)	**Perspective**	Impact Perspective: **On Program**			
Participant judgements, opinions, and their assessment of the way the program worked, how well it worked, "what it really did," and this perspective is assumed to be based on their years of looking at the entire picture of their experience, other's experience, through their own lens of knowledge, impact, and identity.					
Participant driven topic; interview asked about impact in general terms.		7	9	2	16

3.7(2)	**Perspective**	Impact Perspective: **On Other People**			
Different from comparing their experience to the experiences of others, this code was applied to statements judging, opining, and questioning what others in the program felt, did, or are doing now. These are other-oriented opinion statements, stated as objective fact or belief about others' experiences.					
Participant driven topic; but interview asked about impact in general terms and occasionally asked about their opinions on others' experiences.		8	8	0	16

3.7(3)	**Perspective**	Impact Perspective: **Changes In**			
Participant reflections about the ways their attitudes, judgements, and opinions have changed or have not changed, over the years.					
Interview protocol driven topic and participant driven as well. Some were asked if their perspective has remained constant, some brought up the topic on their own.		4	9	5	13

3.7(4)	**Perspective**	Impact Perspective: **Meaning and Value of the Program**			
Participant descriptions about the way they currently understand what they gained from it. Can be "positive" things as well as "bad" things but these were explicit statements about how they see, how they value, what they took from it. Summary statements, windows into their perspective.					
Participant driven topic; but interview asked about impact in general terms as well as questions closely related to this topic.		11	4	7	15

Codes not presented in topic heading summary tables.

		Structure Program Design: **Buddy System**			
Some programs use a mentoring system where one upper-level is responsible for mentoring a new arrival for a certain period of time to introduce them to the program.					
RQ1a		3	4	1	7

		Structure Rules and Consequences: **1st Phase and Demotion**			
This code is relevant to privileges and the level system and these statements could recoded if there was a reason to.					
RQ1a		3	4	1	7

		Structure Rules and Consequences: **Restraints**			
References to physical restraint procedures. 2 in group H are vicarious references, 2 in group L are direct experience of being restrained. All stated as matter-of-fact, little emphasis on the subjective impact.					
RQ1a		2	2	0	4

		Structure Settings and Conditions: **Time**			
This code was created during the first interview to guage how long the stays were in the program as a way to characterize the program but this information is reported in Chapter 3 from the questionnaire data and is left here as a formality – no codes were deleted. References include "so that was a long time" and "I was there for several years."					
RQ1a		1	1	0	2

		Lived Experience Internal, Felt, Somatic: **Anger**			
Mentions about being angry, so angry, really angry, rageful.					
RQ1b		2	3	1	5

		Lived Experience Internal, Felt, Somatic: **Depression**			
Mentions about depression in the program.					
RQ1b		1	2	1	3

		Lived Experience Internal, Felt, Somatic: **Acceptance**			
RQ1b		4	2	2	6

		Lived Experience Internal, Felt, Somatic: **Fun Times**			
Mentions about having fun in the program.					
RQ1b		2	2	0	4

		Lived Experience Meaning Making: **Graduation**			
The value and experience of graduation. The decision to leave this off the list is due to the fact that Structure: Graduation was the more often used code and this was left off the list of topics for simplicity sake because it doesn't add enough qualitative value to warrant it's inclusion in the counting tables in Chapter 4.					
RQ1b		3	6	3	9

		Lived Experience Harm, Punishment Contexts, Escape: **Self-Harm**			
References to two suicide attempts, and one instance by Iris, of illicit use of a bronchial dilator by participants while in the program. Could be included under Escape.					
RQ1b		2	1	1	3

		Impact Memories: Reflections on Memories: **Odd/Perplexing Memories**			
Memories of indiscretions or odd statements or actions by staff or about the program that stuck out as important and persistent, lingering, to participants when asked about strong memories.					
RQ3		2	3	1	5

		Impact The Interview: **Their Observations about themselves or the interview during the Interview**			
Their Observations about themselves or the interview during the Interview. Some were apologies to the researcher, apologies about re-telling disturbing accounts. Some were their reflections on their use of jargon, how nice it was to be understood, or how much they appreciated the chance to speak with the interviewer.					
RQ3		7	10	3	17

		Impact The Interview: **My Observations**			
Researcher notations about the tone, use of jargon, slipping into the present tense to describe past events.					
RQ3		4	3	1	7

		Impact The Interview: **How they identify or label themselves**			
During the first four interviews, 2 participants mentioned their current identity status as a survivor or as a former resident so a question to close the interview asked how they identify themselves, if they had not already done so and if there was time and it seemed appropriate. Some simply had no label, and not all were asked.					
RQ3		8	11	3	19

		Impact **Casual Summaries/Logic Pathways**			
Links, cascades, and explanations that participants described in ways that refered to multiple categories at the same time.					
RQ3		14	15	1	29

		Impact **Pearls**			
Of wisdom, insight, and healing experiences related to context, structure, lived experience, immediate effects, and impact.					
RQ3		9	8	1	17

APPENDIX H
CODE COUNTING TABLES

Pre-Program Context Summary of Topic Headings with Comparison Code Counts

Topic Heading Number C= Context	Topic Heading	Group H	Group L	Differ-ence	Total
C1	Reasons for Placement	11	12	1	23
C2	Parents and Home Life	6	5	1	11
C3	Prior Placements	6	5	1	11
C4	Educational Consult-ant/Transport Service/ Deceptive Intake	3	9	6	12
C5	Attitude Toward Placement	4	3	1	7

RQ1 Summary of Topic Headings with Comparison of Code Counts

Topic Number and Heading (Primary Code Categories in Parentheses)	Code Subcategories	Group H	Group L	Differ-ence	Total
1.1 - Intake and Intro-duction (Lived Experience)	Introduction to Program: Intake, First Few Days	8	11	3	19
1.2a - The Staff (Structure)	Settings and Conditions	7	11	4	18
	Program Design	4	5	1	9
1.2b - The Staff (Lived Experience)	Introduction to Program	7	9	2	16
1.3 - Social Environ-ment (Structure)	Settings and Conditions	11	13	2	24
	Program Design	9	9	0	18
	Peers	7	5	2	12
	Privileges	3	5	2	8
	Group Contin-gencies, Peer Policing, Self-Reports	3	4	1	7
1.4 - Program Philoso-phy (Structure)	Program Philosophy	11	12	1	23
1.5a - Learning the Ropes (Structure)	Rules and Consequences	6	5	1	11

370

1.5b - Learning the Ropes (Lived Experience)	Introduction to Program	7	7	0	14
	Internal, Felt: Fairness	7	6	1	13
	Buy In	2	5	3	7
1.6 - Program Design (Structure)	Daily Schedule	13	13	0	26
	Group Sessions	10	9	1	19
	Control	10	8	2	18
	Level System	8	7	1	15
	Location	9	5	4	14
	Means of Re-course	4	7	3	11
	Home Visits/ Graduation	7	4	3	11
	Seminars/ Inten-sive Practices	6	5	1	11
1.7a - Personal Autonomy (Structure)	Rules and Conse-quences: Walk-ing, eating, bath-ing, bathroom, sleep	1	8	7	9
	Physical Contact	6	4	2	10
1.7b - Personal Autonomy (Lived Experience)	Internal, Felt: Autonomy/ Privacy	7	6	1	13
	Sexuality	4	4	0	8
1.8a - Controlled Communication (Structure)	Communication, Connection, Content	9	14	5	23
	Parent Knowledge	5	7	2	12
	Consequences: Isolation	5	6	1	11
1.8b - Controlled Communication (Lived Experience)	Connection: Barriers, Parents, Each other, Outside World	4	7	3	11
	Communication: Parents and Family	5	5	0	10
	Connection: Bonding	4	2	2	6
	Connection: Iso-lation, Blackout (overlaps with S: RC and S: SC)	3	4	1	7

1.9a - Deprivation/ Harm (Structure)	Settings and Conditions	1	6	5	7
1.9b - Deprivation/ Harm (Lived Experience)	Medical Neglect/ Abuse	2	8	6	10
	Punishment Contexts	6	3	3	9
1.10 - Emotional Intensity (Lived Experience)	Internal, Felt: Overwhelm, Devastation	4	6	2	10
	Internal, Felt: Disorientation, Shock	4	6	2	10
	Internal, Felt: Fear	6	4	2	10
1.11 - Witnessing (Lived Experience)	Connection, Communication	8	9	1	17
1.12 - Ultimate Terms/ Comparative References (Lived Experience)	Meaning Making: How Challenging	6	4	2	10
	Meaning Making: Frames of Comparative Reference	4	2	2	6
1.13 - Escape (Lived Experience)	Harm, Punishment: Resistance	8	6	2	14
	Self-Harm	2	1	1	3
1.14a - Program/Social Fit (Structure)	Physical and Crazy Punishments, Rules	3	8	5	11
1.14b - Program/Social Fit (Lived Experience)	Introduction to Program: Goodness of Fit	9	8	1	17

RQ2 Summary of Topic Headings with Comparison of Code Counts

Topic Heading (Code Categories in Parentheses) 2=RQ2	Code Subcategories	Group H	Group L	Difference	Total
2.1 - Changing Relationships with Family	Improved	8	1	7	9
	Worsened	5	9	4	14

Topic Number and Heading	Code Subcategories	Group H	Group L	Difference	Total
2.2 - Personal Growth	Self-Discovery, Growth	11	3	8	14
	Better Social Skills	8	3	5	11
	Broadened Horizons	4	3	1	7
2.3 - Practical Benefits	Improvements in School/ Practical Skills and Physical Improvements	6	5	1	11
	Toughened	3	2	1	5
2.4 - Negative Changes	Exacerbation, Maladaptation	4	10	6	14
	Indoctrinated, Brainwashed	3	6	3	9
	Physical Complications	2	7	5	9
	Resisted, Misbe-haved, Ran Away	1	4	3	5
	Trauma	2(5)	3(10)	1(5)	5(15)
2.5 - Making Progress: A slippery slope	Normalized it, Adapted, Faked it	5	10	5	15
	Put Head Down to Get Through	3	3	0	6

RQ3 Memories - Summary of Topic Subheadings with Comparison of Code Counts

Topic Number and Heading	Code Subcategories	Group H	Group L	Differ-ence	Total
3.1 - Memories					
	Reflections On	5	11	6	16
	Bad	9	11	2	20
	Good	9	5	4	14
	Strong & Neutral, Polemic	9	7	2	16
3.2 - Social Impact					
	Family	10	10	0	20
	Intimate Relationships	11	10	1	21
	Knowledge: Cohort	12	8	4	20
	Suicides and ODs	3	7	4	10
	Social: Cohort Friends and Relations	4	2	2	6

373

3.3 - Trajectory					
	Reentry	6	9	3	15
	Substance Use	6	3	3	9
	School/Subsequent Placements	6	10	4	16
	Career	4	9	5	13
	Advocacy	6	8	2	14
	Reason for Interview	9	14	5	23
3.4 - Personal Impact					
	Tangible/ Physical	1	6	5	7
	Trauma	4	11	7	15
	Healing	4	4	0	8
	Complicated Mix	5	3	2	8
3.5 - Social Skills					
	Improved	5	4	1	9
	Impaired	4	9	5	13
	Jargon/ Habits	3	2	1	5
3.6 - Knowledge					
	About program	8	12	4	20
	About larger related issues	4	13	9	17
	Compared to Others	9	1	8	10
	Internal Processes	9	10	1	19
3.7 - Perspective					
	On Program	7	9	2	16
	On Other People	8	8	0	16
	Changes In	4	9	5	13
	Meaning and Value of Program	11	4	7	15

SUBJECTIVITY STATEMENT

Bias, Reflexivity, and Heuristic Scaffolding

This thesis was informed by personal interest in the topic and a desire to help prevent harm. Since these biases could threaten the quality of my work, I'd like to explain my interests and how I believe they shaped my research. I can't know the full extent of my unconscious motives and preferences, but I care enough about the topic to do what I can to help the reader judge the value of this work.

When I was an undergraduate student, I attended an international conference for researchers and clinicians in the social sciences. Soon after arriving, I was flattered to hear that a researcher from Europe had seen one of my short essays online. She said I should be careful when publishing op-ed articles because if I am labeled as an advocate who wants to prevent harm, my credibility as a scientist will never be taken seriously.

Her words were like the unresolvable Zen koan, "what is the sound of one hand clapping?" I still don't know how anyone can research social problems without wanting to address them. I resented these words, then dismissed them, and then revisited them as a graduate student because I've heard similar comments from other professors.

Some of my professors have explained that the urge to solve social problems can interfere with objective scientific inquiry. Other professors have cautioned me because it is hard to do qualitative research in your own backyard when you are too close to the topic. Some suggested I consider a thesis topic I could pursue with objective disinterest. These mentors were hard to hear but I took their comments to heart and slowly began to appreciate them as I studied qualitative methodology.

These rude awakenings kept me awake at night and helped me to understand how my blind assumptions might insulate me from perceiving accurately and questioning well. Such conversations were frustrating but they forced me to question the lenses I was looking through. I still look at empirical evidence through biased lenses, but I have a better sense of how they have skewed my vision in the past.

By understanding how researchers can engage with their subjectivity in a way that can prompt more rigorous engagement with their data (Roulston & Shelton, 2015), I slowly let go of the urge to defend my interests and began working to explore the ways my blind spots and dogmatic convictions could weaken my study. My passion for understanding this topic and my interest in producing good work, forced me to develop ways to check my biases and examine my assumptions while accepting that there are no magic methods; validity through rigor is a recursive process that is never simply right and done (Cho & Trent, 2006).

During my first semesters as a graduate student, as I was learning about my prejudices and emotional investments, part of my problem was that I had set out to study the contentious, uncomfortable topic of institutional child abuse. In Europe, Australia, and Canada, there are experts, organizations, and government inquiries devoted to the history, dynamics, and prevention of harm to youth residing in out-of-home settings. In the United States there seems to be less interest. Here, interest in the prevention of institutional maltreatment swelled in the early 1980s and again in the mid to late 2000s, but there is very little research in this type of prevention.

If you search the internet for specialists in this field, you'll find that in the United States, current experts in residential treatment tend to avoid the term, "institutional abuse." In the US, the prevention of institutional child abuse is reframed to the more palatable phrase, "improving quality of care." According to the scientific literature, the topic I had chosen didn't really exist in this country.

Also, I was unqualified. As a new graduate student, when I was asked how I would operationalize the concept of abuse and how I would distinguish the objective fact of maltreatment from the subjective experience of harm, I realized that I did not know. The validity of the concept of institutional child abuse is questionable because what is directly observable is often at odds with what is experienced. The opinions of the victims, often years after the fact, are subjective, difficult to measure, and always imperfectly accurate to some unknown degree. To extend the allegory of "twitches or blinks" (Yin, 2016, p. 281), there is no way for researchers to know if they are observing intentional winks, automatic twitches, deliberate blinks, or deceptive fake-blinks, because the observable fact is never more than the motion of an eyelid.

Experts in the field of institutional maltreatment say that intention is an invalid assessment criterion. They say it is the foreseeable risk and potential for impairment that defines abuse. But if abuse is identified by the foreseeable risk of impaired development, perhaps it is a topic best suited for lawyers, journalists, and well-funded teams of researchers working in countries where such concepts are less contentious.

In this project, I reported multiple forms of institutional abuse but I attempt to remain neutral and suspend judgement. In some instances, participants described methods of treatment that have been defined as institutional abuse in the literature but they described these methods as benevolent. If I were reporting any other type of abuse and participants spoke freely about how much it helped them, a researcher taking a neutral stance might be accused of being an apologist, or worse. If I am guilty of slanting my findings, it may be that I have put a neutral slant on highly unethical practices.

I went into this project feeling challenged, afraid I would be dismissed because of my background and concerns about social justice. I was afraid that by challenging whatever paradigm has contributed to the general lack of interest in totalistic treatment programs, such an agenda would automatically disqualify me from "real" science. The large amount of time and energy I put into this study was me hoping to prove I was capable of a rigorous study. In addition to the 300+ pages of thesis presented here, another 1,000+ pages of transcriptions, notes, tables, and matrices were generated. As one professor told me, "good qualitative research takes an insane amount of time." And it's true. Without being crazy-interested in the topic and deeply concerned about the project, the participants, and the data, a large qualitative study would be an impossible act of self-torture by tedium. Because of my genuine interest, I was able to persevere, but

377

now I must explain why you should trust that my agendas and passions had a beneficial effect on my thesis methods.

I realize that time and energy alone do not ensure high-quality research. I feel confident about the quality of this research because of the methods I chose and the work I produced, but also because of the ways I changed while engaging in this project. By questioning my own assumptions, by catching subtle ways my articulation strayed from the evidence, and by working to build in safeguards against the biases I have difficulty seeing, I have developed new skills and have changed with new learning. Through this process, I started to hear some of the ways my own voice can prevent me from listening and reporting faithfully the voices of others. Yvonne, Uriah, and Lawrence taught me that ethics are subjective and distinct from subjective judgements about the degrees of totalism.

I am an "insider" with 33 years of experience with this topic. My personal experiences, trajectories, perspectives, and beliefs have informed my interest in the topic. My interests have affected the way I conceptualized the design, communicated with participants, and the way I collected, organized, interpreted, and reported my findings. Because of my personal experience in a totalistic teen treatment program during the 1980s, and because of my ability for rapport and comradery, I was able to collect data from people who are skeptical of outsiders that "don't know what it was like." Many participants in this study reported they were more comfortable speaking with me because they knew I had experienced something similar. I believe an outsider could conduct an equal number of interviews using the same interview questions but almost everything else would be at least a little bit different. The participants who self-selected into the study, the scope of the interviews, and the analytical frameworks would be valuable in different ways.

The qualitative researcher is the primary instrument that filters, selects, organizes and processes a limited range of information (Maguire & Delahunt, 2017; Yin, 2016). I made design choices I could defend if questioned by a skeptical expert, and these decisions, combined with my fear of being dismissed, resulted in an "insane" amount of work. In analysis, I kept notes that document the forks in the road as my understanding evolved. I followed the examples of my professors who taught me that data is golden. With care, data is the link that allows us to perceive and comment on something real. What surprised me the most in this study is the feeling I had after each interview, and the feeling that grew during my weeks of data collection. I felt as if some sacred piece of life had been given to me. These participants trusted me with their personal experiences and still trust that I will do right. If good data are gold, then the data I collected are sacred and reflect something unique about the essence of what it is to be human.

I am happy for those who reported being saved by their program, but I am sympathetic to those who have been harmed, dismissed, and not believed. Since 2012, in searching for peer-reviewed articles that describe my own experience and the experiences of others I know, I became concerned about absent voices. From what I could tell, those who have experienced harm in totalistic teen programs are underrepresented in scientific research. Also underrepresented are the voices of the true believers; those who actively participated in extreme forms of treatment and proudly proclaim the effectiveness of unethical, or even illegal methods of change. Their perspectives are complicated because the methods that "saved their lives" have proven harmful to others. My agenda in exploring the full range of experiences was driven by a genuine interest in the compelling divide between those who were saved and those who were harmed by the same set of methods. As a graduate of a totalistic program, I was absolutely convinced I had been saved, but I also experienced the trauma of maltreatment in a closed environment. After exiting in 1987, I experienced a profound disillusionment as I began to hear about the ways others were negatively affected by their treatment experience.

In 2004, as I got in touch with friends from the program, I began to reflect on the ways I hurt others while enforcing the rules to please staff. I thought of the potentially harmful things I said and did in the name of therapy so that I could make it to the next level, and graduate. And although I was once extremely grateful for the way my program experience stretched me and forced me to grow, such gratitude often seems inappropriate because my own progress through the program helped perpetuate a social system that harmed others.

I realize that many people perceive those same dynamics differently. Many people did not perceive harm and for them, the only "problem" might be the struggle to justify the help they received in programs others label "abusive." In their case, the only negative aspect of the experience is perpetrated by vocal critics who are convinced their program was harmful. As a former graduate, I understand feeling grateful and saved, and I understand the vocal criticism of unethical programs. I appreciate all of these perspectives and emotions as real, subjective, valuable experiences. And I believe we all have a limited view. I believe that treatment providers, parents, researchers, legislators and law enforcement personnel will want to know about the experiences, effects, and impacts reported by all of the participants in this study.

In the interviews, I felt happy to hear examples of genuinely therapeutic experiences. I felt happy for the participants reporting them and I felt happy because it confirmed something I intuitively want to believe. As rare as these accounts were, I felt they demonstrated that totalistic methods were neutral, to be used for good or ill, as some experts have claimed (Schein et al., 1961; Gordon & Empey, 1962). During the last 25 years of learning about cults, "brainwashing," and teen programs, I have gone back and forth with the question of whether highly totalistic methods are value-free and whether it is possible for adults to use them on youth in ways that can be purely beneficial. I suspect it may be possible, and I want to believe, but the evidence seems to say the benefits are often tinged with harm and the risks have yet to be fully explored.

What was most challenging to me is the ethical conflict I felt in reporting potentially harmful practices without commenting on them as such. During the interviews, I was caught up and enthused by the moving accounts by some of the participants in group H and I felt a genuine connection based on my own personal experiences. But in a couple of the interviews, participants said things I disagreed with strongly, and instead of speaking up, I focused on the things I could agree with. It is not my job to make sure everyone knows my opinions, but I was uncomfortable at times with taking a neutral stance and remaining silent with my opinions when participants described benefiting from practices I associate with institutional abuse. I do hope that after reading this thesis, all 30 participants will still feel glad they took the time to be interviewed. My fear is that those who had the most negative experiences and those who had the most positive experiences, might feel as if I've neglected their perspectives by focusing on the most common trends.

Taking it down a notch

Perhaps a better way to explain my relationship to the data might be to "take it down a notch" (Saldaña, 2014) and describe some of the choices and actions I took to guard against my own biases and ensure quality. The fancy term for this is "heuristic scaffolding" (Gerstl-Pepin & Patrizio, 2009, p. 301). To me, this means I took deliberate, concrete steps to develop a structure of practices to support the development of meaningful, useful knowledge that readers can have some amount of confidence in.

I started with the goal of privileging the counter narrative. In this case, it meant including all of the highest scoring participants *because* they were the outliers with a unique perspective. Their positive experiences were vastly outnumbered by more-negative scoring participants, but since they represent perspectives that potentially contradict my own biases, I designed the sampling methods to ensure that their experiences represented half of the amount of data collected. In reporting findings, I often included their accounts even if they were the lone exception. I presented their accounts with limited interpretation because some of their descriptions include references to program methods that I question from an ethical standpoint. If I had fewer opinions about unethical practices, there is a chance it would have been more appropriate for me to extend my interpretations. Instead, I chose to present such findings while keeping my own perspective in check. For this reason, I expect to be criticized for not taking a strong-enough stance against abusive programs.

In developing the research instruments, I sought expert and peer-review in the phrasing of questionnaire items. In pilot testing I got a good sense of how my assumptions limited the interview questions. During interviews, I kept this in mind and in each interview, I checked my understanding with participants, asking them to confirm or clarify my interpretation of their statements. This immediate form of reality testing was not possible after the interviews, but in all subsequent steps of the project, I regularly referred back to the transcripts to challenge my first interpretation.

Transcription was approached as a way to compare my first impressions and initial notes with what was actually said. By reviewing the recordings and written dialogue numerous times, I saw how my emotional impressions were sometimes quite different from the content emphasized by participants. The first transcripts were coded with a research partner who invested a large amount of time talking through her coding decisions, comparing them to my own and giving me important points in developing the code categories. After coding, I checked for biases by counting the number of words and codes in each transcript, and in each subgroup.

Throughout these processes I kept track of my thoughts and decisions in a research journal and checked in with my research supervisor on a weekly basis. In analysis, I used a comparative method of intentionally stepping into different perspectives in order to identify the way my assumptions might limit my range of interpretation. Throughout the writing processes, I referred back to the participants' own words to make sure I was not overstating, exaggerating, or misrepresenting them. I studied the way experts write about qualitative methods and I referred to their insights throughout the project. I feel confident that I did my best to stay aware of how my thumb print winds up in the picture and then I went back to look for places that had happened.

A note on my worldview

I've read in several places that qualitative researchers must be explicit about their ontological and epistemological stances. Although I do not yet have a label for my philosophical stance, I do I wish I could tell you with certainty what my stance is named because researchers who know their stance, and maintain it consistently throughout a report, might be deemed more credible (Glesne, 2011). In my thesis, I tried to use a logical approach to collecting subjective data. I interpreted these data with a knowledge of rigorous research design using my own subjective, imperfect lens. I've done by best to explain what my lens is like so you will have enough information about me to judge in your own way what parts of my research might be weak and what parts might be more trustworthy.

I've written a thesis on the way complex social dynamics are perceived and described over time, but I do not have a firm grasp on the neurological and philosophical mechanisms that drive and frame those processes. In that sense, this thesis is weak because it is built on a foundation of meaning I don't fully grasp. I don't know what my thoughts and my consciousness are made of and yet I relied on something I assume to be rational thought and consciousness throughout this entire project and claim that they are useful in creating knowledge.

I am skeptical of isms and I tend toward the middle of the road when it comes to knowing what knowledge is. For several semesters, I thought this meant I was a "critical realist." Then, I encountered a book that told me realists were less tolerant of subjective realities. I am pretty sure I am pretty tolerant of subjective realities because I think that's one of the best types of reality there is. I believe there are some very real things that cannot be directly observed by scientists. I also believe there are probably real things that exist whether anyone perceives them or not but I am comfortable not knowing for sure. Also, I assume that the number of things that can be conveyed in words is a lot smaller than the number of things affecting any one of us in any given instant. I don't think we all have the same abilities for perception. I do think internal experiences are real but I don't feel comfortable calling them things because I don't know what perceptions are made of. I don't know if non-physical phenomena are things, or actions, or strictly imaginary. I don't see how there can be such a thing as unbiased knowledge or research. I certainly do not understand why knowledge for its own sake would be any sort of a good or pure ideal for a human being to strive for. And, if I were asked to describe my stance tomorrow, I would probably write something different. I know I've done my best and it could be a lot better. I am sure there are numerous blind spots in my vision that others will note as fundamental problems, and I can only hope they will find something useful and improve the work I've done here by developing more accurate studies on the topic.

APPENDIX J
DEFINITIONS OF TERMS

Coercion	"Refers to an array of strategies that shape behavior by responding to specific actions with external pressure and predictable consequences." Interchangeable with "compulsory treatment," "legal pressure into treatment," "involuntary treatment," "criminal justice referral to treatment" (Satel, 1999, p. 2).
Cult	"A cult is a group or movement that, to a significant degree, (a) exhibits great or excessive devotion or dedication to some person, idea, or thing, (b) uses a thought-reform program to persuade, control, and socialize members (i.e., to integrate them into the group's unique pattern of relationships, beliefs, values, and practices), (c) systematically induces states of psychological dependency in members, (d) exploits members to advance the leadership's goals, and (e) causes psychological harm to members, their families, and the community....cults may be religious (with seemingly orthodox or bizarre beliefs), psychotherapeutic, political, or commercial" (Langone, 1993, p. 9).
Iatrogenic	Harm in the name of help. May be directly due to treatment or arising within the treatment setting. White and Kleber identify several categories in their review of the literature tailored to iatrogenesis in addictions treatment: flawed theories of change, improper diagnosis, harm from treatment dosage or treatment type, lack of fidelity to protocol, harm from using established therapeutic protocol, and harm from the milieu (White & Kleber, 2008).

Institutional "In the narrow sense, as abuse occurring in residen-
abuse tial group care settings; in the broad sense, as flow-
ing accidentally from or as an intrinsic element in
the operation of our governmental or other social
institutions affecting young people; and in other
ways, between these extremes" (Beker & Hanson,
1982, p. 5).

"The rearing of children in residential care must assure their progression along the developmental
pathways toward adulthood. Conversely, acts that
distort children's pathways or impede their progress
are abusive or neglectful" (Thomas, 1982, p. 25).

"Institutional abuse is…a symptom of much else
that is wrong in facilities with serious patterns of
abuse. Solutions addressing this symptom, while
they may have great value, are unlikely to have a
significant impact on those conditions within the facility which encourage abuse of children. Current
approaches generally stress reporting, investigation, and correction of incidents. Such approaches,
however necessary, are only means of closing the
barn door after the horse is gone, in the words of the
old saying" (Mercer, 1982, p. 127).

Physical maltreatment (potential or actual); sexual
maltreatment (direct or vicarious); failure to provide for basic needs; failure to supervise/protect
from harm; emotional maltreatment (impair or ag-
gravate existing impairment); questionable moral
behavior by caregiver; harmful restraint/control (includes isolation and medication); setting up for failure (deception, gross inconsistency, provoked failure) (Rabb & Rindfleisch, 1985, p. 286-287).

386

Institutional-ized abuse: systematic/ program abuse	"'Institutionalized' child abuse and neglect is directly derivative from the nature of institutions, and, in most cases, at least tacitly supported by them" (Harrell & Orem, 1980, p. vii).
Institutional maltreatment	Physical abuse and neglect resulting from corporal punishment, restraint, chemical restraint, isolation, sexual abuse, nutritional, hygiene, lack of supervision, medical, sleeping arrangements, clothing, crowding, sanitation. Emotional abuse with harm to the child; belittling, public ridicule of child or their family, background, culture, or race; failure to treat suicide threats as serious and to provide appropriate emotional support; consistently treating members of a peer group unequally or unfairly; group punishment for individual behavior; scapegoating; allowing group to develop its own control system without staff intervention; persistent lack of concern for welfare; inappropriate emotional physical or emotional treatment. To be considered across "four definitional variations: Is it harmful? Is it legal? Is it appropriate? Is it optimal?" (Harrell & Orem, 1980).
Intensive treatment	A continuum of varying degrees which characterize forms of treatment that are meant to facilitate a global change of the whole person within a total institution or a totalistic setting.
Maltreat-ment	Refers to abuse and/or neglect, or a combination of the two.
Mental injury	"Injury to the intellectual or psychological capacity of a child as evidenced by an observable and substantial impairment in the ability to function within a normal range of performance and behavior, with due respect to culture" (Model Child Protection Act, in Harrell and Orem, 1980, p.6).

Systematic abuse/ Program abuse	"Abuse and neglect of children in out-of-home care occurs when programs within a facility are below normally accepted standards; have extreme or unfair policies; or rely on harsh, inhumane, or unusual techniques to teach or guide children" (Gil, 1982, p.10).
Psychological maltreatment	Interchangeable or synonymous with psychological abuse and/or emotional maltreatment/abuse. "Rejection, isolation humiliation, verbal assaults, being ignored, being terrorized. At the core of all forms of child maltreatment." (Cohn, 1987, p.ix). "It has been described as a repeated pattern or extreme incident(s) of terrorizing, spurning, isolating, exploiting/corrupting, or denying emotional responsiveness; conditions which convey the message that the child is worthless, flawed, unloved, endangered, or only valuable in meeting someone else's needs (American Professional Society on Abuse of Children, 1995; United Nations Committee on the Rights of the Child, 2011). It also includes developmentally inappropriate interactions, especially disciplinary practices and exposure to domestic violence (Glaser, 2002)" (Hart & Glasser, 2010, p. 261). Verbal or nonverbal, repeated or singular, intended or not, by a person in position of power or responsibility over the child, potential to impair social, cognitive, emotional, or physical development. Characterized by behaviors which are: humiliating, degrading, terrorizing, extremely rejecting, depriving of basic needs, depriving of valued objects, inflicting marked distress, corrupting/exploiting, cognitively disorienting, emotionally blackmailing, Complex abuse. (Moran, Bifulco, Ball, Jacobs & Benaim, 2002, p. 220)

Residential treatment, also *"Therapeutic residential care"*	"Involves the planful use of a purposefully constructed, multi-dimensional living environment designed to enhance or provide treatment, education, socialization, support and protection to children and youth with identified mental health or behavioral needs in partnership with their families and in collaboration with a full spectrum of community-based formal and informal helping resources" (Whittaker et al., 2015, p. 24).
Thought reform	"A behavior change technology applied to cause the learning and adoption of an ideology or set of behaviors under certain conditions" (Singer & Ofshe, 1990, p.189). "Consists of two basic elements: confession, the exposure and renunciation of past and present "evil"; and re-education, the remaking of a man in the Communist image. These elements are closely related and overlapping, since they both bring into play a series of pressures and appeals – intellectual, emotional, and physical – aimed at social control and individual change" (Lifton, 1963, p. 5).
Total institution	"First, all aspects of life are conducted in the same place and under the same single authority. Second, each phase of the members' daily activity is carried on in the immediate company of a large batch of others, all of whom are treated alike and required to do the same thing together. Third, all phases of the day's activities are tightly scheduled, with one activity leading at a prearranged time into the next, the whole sequence of activities being imposed from above by a system of explicit formal rulings and a body of officials. Finally, the various enforced activities are brought together into a single rational plan purportedly designed to fulfill the official aims of the institution" (Goffman, 1961, p. 6).

Totalistic	Refers to qualities and characteristics of total institutions (Goffman, 1961) and autocratic treatment programs (De Leon, 2000).
	Also refers to the work of Robert Jay Lifton (1963) on ideological totalism, the psychology of totalism, and the eight conditions of thought reform in totalitarian prisons: milieu control, mystical manipulation, scared science, subordination of person to doctrine, dispensing of existence, personal confession, the need for purity, and loading the language.
	The term "totalistic" refers to the degree to which the milieu specifies and dictates the way individuals should "think, feel, and act" (Langone, 1993, p.4).
Milieu	"The daily environment of structure and interactions" (Colburn, 1990, p. 10).

APPENDIX K
SEQUENCE TIMELINE

2017

May and June – Developed proposal

July 5th - Submitted pre-proposal to committee

July 19th – Pre-proposal meeting - Received feedback on text, instruments, planning, and IRB

July 20th – August 15th - Conducted pilot tests – Revised instruments

August 17th – Presented full proposal to committee

August 31st - Submitted IRB documents

September 6th – IRB approval

September 18th - Launched Qualtrics consent form and questionnaire

September 19th - Sent inquiries to organizational contacts.

September 19th to October 15th - Sent out the Invitation to Participate to willing organizations.

November 31st – Last survey link closed, end of quantitative data collection.

December 1st – Group Assignments based on scoring rubric.

December 2017 – February 2018 – Conducted interviews, began analysis.

2018

February and March - Transcriptions, coding, created analysis matrices.

April and May – Write-up of findings, synthesis, discussion, conclusions.

June 7th - Sent thesis to committee.

June 7th to 21st – Received feedback, began revisions.

June 21st – Oral defense of thesis.

July 5th – Main revisions completed.

July 6th – Submitted first draft to editorial office.

July 25th – Submitted final draft to editorial office.

LIST OF REFERENCES

Abrahams, J. & McCorkle, L.W. (1945). Group psychotherapy in the treatment of military offenders. *American Journal of Sociology, 51*(5), 455-464.

Adams, D. W. (1995). *Education for extinction: American indians and the boarding school experience 1875-1928.* Lawrence: Univ. Press of Kansas.

Alexander, J. C. (2012). *Trauma: A social theory.* Malden, MA: Polity.

Anglin, J. P. (2006). *Pain, normality, and the struggle for congruence: Reinterpreting residential care for children and youth.* New York: Haworth Press.

Archuleta, M. L., Child, B. J., & Lomawaima, K. T. (Eds.). (2000). *Away from home: American indian boarding school experiences, 1879-2000.* Phoenix, AZ: The Heard Museum.

Aziz, D. W., & Clark, C. L. (1996). Shock incarceration in new york. *Juvenile and adult boot camps.* Lanham, MD: American Correctional Association.

Baber, K. M. (2011). Short ridge academy: Positive youth development in action within a therapeutic community. *Advances in Child Development and Behavior, 41*, 309-348.

Bach, G. R. (1954). *Intensive group psychotherapy.* New York: The Ronald Press Company.

Barnhart, R. K., & Steinmetz, S. (Eds.). (2000). *Chambers dictionary of etymology.* New York: Chambers.

Barter, C. (1999). Independent investigations into institutional child abuse: Developing theory and practice. In N. Stanley, J. Manthorpe & B. Penhale (Eds.), *Institutional abuse: Perspectives across the life course* (pp. 66-88). New York: Routledge.

Behar, L., Friedman, R., Pinto, A., Katz-Leavy, J., & Jones, H. W. G. (2007). Protecting youth placed in unlicensed, unregulated residential "treatment" facilities. *Family Court Review, 45*(3), 399-413. doi:10.1111/j.1744-1617.2007.00155.x

392

Behrens, E., & Satterfield, K. (2011). A multi-center study of private residential treatment outcomes. *Journal of Therapeutic Schools and Programs, V*(I), 29-45.

Beker, J., & Hanson, R. (1982). Introduction. In R. Hanson (Ed.), *Institutional abuse of children and youth.* (pp. 3-5). New York: Haworth Press.

Bettmann, J. E., & Jasperson, R. A. (2009). Adolescents in residential and inpatient treatment: A review of the outcome literature. *Child & Youth Care Forum, 38*(4), 161-183. doi:10.1007/s10566-009-9073-y

Beyerstein, B. (1992). Treatment, thought reform, and the road to hell. In A. S. Trebach & K. B. Zeese (Eds.), *Strategies for change: New directions in drug policy* (pp. 245-251). Washington, D.C.: Drug Policy Foundation.

Blake, A. M. (2003). *An examination of organizational factors associated with the recurrence of maltreatment in institutional care.* (Doctoral dissertation). Retrieved from Pro Quest Dissertations Publishing. http://search.proquest.com/docview/288269389?pq-origsite=summon&accountid=10920

Boel-Studt, S. M., & Tobia, L. (2016). A review of trends, research, and recommendations for strengthening the evidence-base and quality of residential group care. *Residential Treatment for Children & Youth, 33*(1), 13. doi:10.1080/0886571X.2016.1175995

Bonell, C., Jamal, F., Melendez-Torres, G. J., & Cummins, S. (2015). 'Dark logic': Theorising the harmful consequences of public health interventions. *Journal of Epidemiology and Community Health, 69*(1), 95-98. doi:10.1136/jech-2014-204671

Braun, V., & Clarke, V. (2016). (Mis)conceptualising themes, thematic analysis, and Other problems with fugard and potts' (2015) sample-size tool for thematic analysis. *International Journal of Social Research Methodology, 19*(6), 739-743. doi:10.1080/13645579.2016.1195588

Brendtro, L. K., & Longhurst, J. E. (2005). The resilient brain. *Reclaiming Children and Youth, 14*(1), 52.

Bromley, D. G. (1998). Listing (in black and white) some observantions on (sociological) thought reform. *Nova Religio: The Journal of Alternative and Emergent Religions, 1*(2), 250-266. doi:10.1525/nr.1998.1.2.250

Bryman, A. (2012). *Social research methods* (4. ed. ed.). Oxford: Oxford Univ. Press.

Burns, D., Hyde, P., & Killett, A. (2013). Wicked problems or wicked people? reconceptualising institutional abuse. *Sociology of Health & Illness, 35*(4), 514-528. doi:10.1111/j.1467-9566.2012.01511.x

Byne, W. (2016). Regulations restrict practice of conversion therapy. *LGBT Health, 3*(2), 97-99. doi:10.1089/lgbt.2016.0015

Cabral, L., & Sefton, L. (2013, March, 27). Linda cabral and laura sefton on using voice recognition software for transcription. Retrieved from http://aea365.org/blog/linda-cabral-and-laura-sefton-on-using-voice-recognition-software-for-transcription/

Cases of child neglect and abuse at private residential treatment facilities: Hearing before the committee on education and labor: House of Representatives, 110th Cong. (2007).

Casriel, D. (1963). *So fair a house: The story of synanon.* Edgewood Cliffs, NJ: Prentice Hall.

Caton, H. (1998). Reinvent yourself: Labile psychosocial identity
    and the lifestyle marketplace. In I. Eibl-Eibesfeldt, & F. K. Salter
    (Eds.), *Ethnic conflict and indoctrination: Altruism and identity in
    evolutionary perspective.* (pp. 325-343). New York: Berghan
    Books.

Chama, S., & Ramirez, O. (2014). Young people's perceptions of a
    group home's efficacy: A retrospective study. *Residential Treat-
    ment for Children & Youth, 31*(2),120-134.
    doi:10.1080/0886571X.2014.918442

Charmaz, K. (2017). The power of constructivist grounded theory
    for critical inquiry. *Qualitative Inquiry, 23*(1), 34-45.
    10.1177/1077800416657105

Chen, T. H. (1960). *Thought reform of the chinese intellectuals.*
    Hong Kong: Hong Kong Univ. Press.

Child abuse and deceptive marketing by residential programs for
    teens: Hearing before the committee on education and labor: Se-
    rial No. 110-89, U.S. House of Representatives, 110th (2008). Re-
    trieved from: https://www.gpo.gov/fdsys/pkg/CHRG-
    110hhrg41839/pdf/CHRG-110hhrg41839.pdf

Chatfield, M. (2014) *Institutionalized persuasion: The technology of
    reformation in straight incorporated and the residential teen
    treatment industry.* CreateSpace Independent Publishing Platform;
    North Charleston, SC.

Cho, J., & Trent, A. (2006). Validity in qualitative research revis-
    ited. *Qualitative Research, 6*(3), 319-340.
    10.1177/1468794106065006

Choo, H. Y., & Ferree, M. M. (2010). Practicing intersectionality in
    sociological research: A critical analysis of inclusions, interac-
    tions, and institutions in the study of inequalities. *Sociological
    Theory, 28*(2), 129-149. doi:10.1111/j.1467-9558.2010.01370.x

Clark, C. (2017). *The recovery revolution: The battle over addiction treatment in the united states*. New York: Columbia University Press.

Cohn, A. H. (1987). Foreward. In M. R. Brassard, R. Germain & S. N. Hart (Eds.), *Psychological maltreatment of children and youth*. New York: Pergamon Press.

Colburn, R. (1990). Introduction. In V. Fahlberg (Ed.), *Residential treatment: A tapestry of many therapies*. (pp. 9-13). Indianapolis, IN: Perspectives Press.

Cook, M. S. (2000). The impossible me: Misconstruing structural constraint and individual volition. *Advances in Life Course Research, 5*, 55-75. 10.1016/S1040-2608(00)80006-4

Cressey, D. R. (1976). Theoretical foundations for using criminals in the rehabilitation of criminals. In A. Bassin, T. E. Bratter & R. L. Rachin (Eds.), *The reality therapy reader: A survey of the work of william glasser, m. d.* (pp. 568-587). New York: Harper & Row.

Creswell, J. W. (2007) *Qualitative Inquiry & Research Design: Choosing among five approaches*. (2nd Ed.) Thousand Oaks, CA: Sage.

Creswell, J. W., & Poth, C. N. (2018). *Qualitative inquiry and research design: Choosing among five approaches* (4th ed.). Thousand Oaks: SAGE.

Daly, K. (2014). Conceptualising responses to institutional abuse of children. Current Issues in Criminal Justice, 26(1), 5-29.

De Leon, G. (1995). Therapeutic communities for addictions: A theoretical framework. International Journal of Addictions, 30(12), 1603-1645. doi:10.3109/10826089509104418

— (2000). *Therapeutic community: Theory, model, and method*. New York: Springer Publishing Company.

— (2015a). "The gold standard" and related considerations for a maturing science of substance abuse treatment. therapeutic communities; A case in point. Substance use & Misuse, 50(8-9), 1106. doi:10.3109/10826084.2015.1012846

— (2015b). Therapeutic communities. In M. Galanter, H. D. Kleber & K. T. Brady (Eds.), The american psychiatric publishing textbook of substance abuse treatment (pp. 511-530). Arlington, VA: American Psychiatric Association. Retrieved from http://psychiatryonline.org/doi/full/10.1176/appi.books.9781615370030.mg34

De Leon, G., & Melnick, G. (1993). Therapeutic community survey of essential elements questionnaire (SEEQ), short form. New York: Community Studies Institute. Retrieved from http://www.ndri.org/manuals-instruments/seeqshor.doc

De Leon, G., & Wexler, H. (2009). The therapeutic community for addictions: An evolving knowledge base. Journal of Drug Issues, 39(1), 167-177. doi:10.1177/002204260903900113

Dellums, R. (1997, April 10). Charles dederich sr. founder of synanon. Congressional Record Extensions of Remarks, E635. Retrieved from: http://www.gpo.gov/fdsys/pkg/CREC-1997-04-10/pdf/CREC-1997-04-10-pt1-PgE635.pdf

Dishion, T. J., McCord, J., & Poulin, F. (1999). When interventions harm: Peer groups and problem behavior. American Psychologist, 54(9), 755-764. doi:10.1037/0003-066X.54.9.755

Dozier, M., Kaufman, J., Kobak, R., O'Connor, T. G., Sagi--Schwartz, A., Scott, S., . . . Zeanah, C. H. (2014). Consensus statement on group care for children and adolescents: A statement of policy of the american orthopsychiatric association. American Journal of Orthopsychiatry, 84(3), 219-225. doi:10.1037/ort0000005

Dupont, R. (1993). Fager v. straight, inc. (Circuit court for fairfax county virginia 1993).Retrieved from http://thestraights.net/people/medical-doctors/dupont/dupont-web4.htm#dupont-%20straight%20based%20on%20synanon%20the%20cult

Dunbar-Ortiz, R. (2014). *Indigenous peoples' history of the united states*. Boston: Beacon Press.

Dye, M. H., Ducharme, L. J., Johnson, J. A., Knudsen, H. K., & Roman, P. M. (2009).modified therapeutic communities and adherence to traditional elements. *Journal of Psychoactive Drugs, 41*(3), 275-283. doi:10.1080/02791072.2009.10400538

Ebert, A., & Dyck, M. J. (2004). The experience of mental death: The core feature of complex posttraumatic stress disorder. *Clinical Psychology Review, 24*(6), 617-635. doi:10.1016/j.cpr.2004.06.002

Edelen, M. O., Tucker, J. S., Wenzel, S. L., Paddock, S. M., Ebener, P., Dahl, J., & Mandell, W. (2007). Treatment process in the therapeutic community: Associations with retention and outcomes among adolescent residential clients. *Journal of Substance Abuse Treatment, 32*(4), 415-421. doi:10.1016/j.jsat.2006.10.006

Elder, G. H., & Shanahan, M. J. (2006). The life course and human development. In R. M. Lerner (Ed.), *Handbook of child psychology volume one: Theoretical models of human development* (pp. 668-715) John Wiley & Sons, Inc.

Eliade, M. (2012). *Rites and symbols of initiation: The mysteries of birth and rebirth*. Putnam, Connecticutt: Spring Publications.

Empey, L. T., & Erickson, M. L. (1972). *The provo experiment* (2.print. ed.). Lexington, Mass: 1974.

Eppley, K. (2006). Defying insider-outsider categorization: One researcher's fluid and complicated positioning on the insider-outsider continuum. *Forum: Qualitative Social Research*, 7(3). Retrieved from http://www.qualitative-research.net/index.php/fqs/article/viewArticle/150/329.

Erickson, E. H. (1968). *Identity, youth, and crisis.* (2. print. ed.). New York: Norton.

— (1980). *Identity and the life cycle.* New York: Norton.

Fahlberg, V. (1990). *Residential treatment: A tapestry of many therapies.* Indianapolis: Perspectives Press.

Farmer, E. M. Z., Murray, M. L., Ballentine, K., Rauktis, M. E., & Burns, B. J. (2017). Would we know it if we saw it? assessing quality of care in group Homes for youth. *Journal of Emotional and Behavioral Disorders, 25*(1), 28-36. doi:10.1177/1063426616687363

Feld, B. C. (1999). *Bad kids: Race and the transformation of the juvenile court.* New York: Oxford University Press.

Festinger, L. (1957). *A theory of cognitive dissonance.* Stanford, Calif: Stanford Univ. Press.

Finlay, L. (2014). Engaging phenomenological analysis. *Qualitative Research in Psychology, 11*(2), 121-141. doi:10.1080/14780887.2013.807899

Frank, J. D. (1974). *Persuasion and healing* (Rev. ed. ed.). New York: Schocken Books.

Frankel, B. (1989). *Transforming identities.* New York: Lang.

Freeman, W. J. (2000). *How brains make up their minds.* New York: Columbia Univ. Press.

Friedman, R. M., Pinto, A., Behar, L., Bush, N., Chirolla, A., Ep-
stein, M., . . . Alliance for the Safe, Therapeutic and Appropriate
use of Residential Treatment. (2006). Unlicensed residential programs: The next challenge in protecting youth. *American Journal
of Orthopsychiatry, 76*(3), 295-303. doi:10.1037/0002-
9432.76.3.295

GAO-08-146T: Residential treatment programs: Concerns regarding
abuse and deaths in certain programs for troubled youth: united
states government accountability office testimony before the committee on labor and education: House of Representatives, (2008).

GAO-08-346, House of Representatives, Report. (2008).

GAO-08-713T: Residential programs: Selected cases of death,
abuse, and deceptive marketing: United states government accountability office testimony before the committee on education
and labor. House of Representatives, (2008).

Garmezy, N., Masten, A. S. & Tellegen, A. (1984). The study of
stress and competence in children: A building block for developmental psychopathology. *Child Development, 55*(1), 97-111.
10.1111/j.1467-8624.1984.tb00276.x

Gerstl-Pepin, C., & Patrizio, K. (2009). Learning from dumbledore's
pensieve: Metaphor as an aid in teaching reflexivity in qualitative
research. *Qualitative Research, 9*(3), 299-308.
doi:10.1177/1468794109105029

Giddens, A. (1984). *The constitution of society.* University of California Press.

Gil, E. (1982). Institutional abuse of children in out-of-home care.
In R. Hanson (Ed.), *Institutional abuse of children and youth* (pp.
7-13). New York: Haworth Press.

Gilligan, R. (2015). Foreword. In Whittaker, J. K., del Valle, J. F. & Holmes, L. (Ed.), *Therapeutic residential care for children and youth: Developing evidence-based international practice* (pp. 11-20). London and Philadelphia: Jessica Kingsley.

Glesne, C. (2011). *Becoming qualitative researchers* (4. ed.). Boston: Pearson.

Goffman, E. (1959). *The presentation of self in everyday life.* New York: Anchor Books.

Goffman, I. (1961). *Asylums.* New York, NY: Anchor books.

— (1963). *Stigma: Notes on the management of spoiled identity.* Englewood Cliffs, N.J: Prentice-Hall.

Goldiamond, I. (1978). *On the usefulness of intent for distinguishing between research and practice, and its replacement by social contingency: Implications for standard and innovative procedures, coercion and informed consent, and fiduciary and contractual relations. Chapter 14 in, The belmont report: Ethical prinicples and guidelines for the protection of human subjects research: Appendix volume II.* Washington, D. C.: United States Department of Health, Education, and Welfare. Retrieved from https://videocast.nih.gov/pdf/ohrp_appendix_belmont_report_vol_2.pdf

Gordon, W. H., & Empey, L. T. (1962). Communist rectification programs and delinquency rehabilitation programs: A parallel?. *American Sociological Review, 27*(2), 256-258.

Gowan, T., & Whetstone, S. (2012). Making the criminal addict: Subjectivity and social control in a strong-arm rehab. *Punishment & Society, 14*(1), 69-93. doi:10.1177/1462474511424684

Grant, J. D., & Grant, M. Q. (1959). A group dynamics approach to the treatment of nonconformists in the navy. *The Annals of the American Academy of Political and Social Science, 322*(1), 126-135. doi:10.1177/000271625932200116

Hanson, R. (1982). *Institutional abuse of children & youth*. New York: Haworth Press.

Harder, A. T., & Knorth, E. J. (2015). Uncovering what is inside the 'black box' of effective therapeutic residential youth care. In Whittaker, J. K., del Valle, J. F. & Holmes, L. (Ed.), *Therapeutic residential care for children and youth: Developing evidence-based international practice* (pp. 217-230). London & Philadelphia: Jessica Kingsley Publishers.

Harding, J. (2013). *Qualitative data analysis from start to finish*. Los Angeles: SAGE.

Harrell, S. A., & Orem, R. C. (1980). *Preventing child abuse and neglect: A guide for staff in residential institutions*. U.S. Government Printing Office, Washington, D.C.: U.S. Department of Health and Human Services, Office of Human Development Services.

Harper, N. J. (2010). Future paradigm or false idol: A cautionary tale of evidence-based practice for adventure education and therapy. *Journal of Experiential Education, 33*(1), 38-55. doi:10.5193/JEE.33.1.38

Hart, S. N., & Glaser, D. (2011). Psychological maltreatment – maltreatment of the mind: A catalyst for advancing child protection toward proactive primary prevention and promotion of personal well-being. *Child Abuse & Neglect, 35*(10), 758-766. doi:10.1016/j.chiabu.2011.06.002

Haynes, C., Eivors, A., & Crossley, J. (2011). 'Living in an alternative reality': Adolescents' experiences of psychiatric inpatient care. *Child and Adolescent Mental Health, 16*(3), 150-157. doi:10.1111/j.1475-3588.2011.00598.x

Heimlich, J. (2011). *Breaking their will: Shedding light on religious child maltreatment*. Amherst: Prometheus Books.

Herman, J. L. (1992). Complex PTSD: A syndrome in survivors of prolonged and repeated trauma. *Journal of Traumatic Stress, 5,* 377–391.

— (1997). *Trauma and recovery.* New York: Basic Books.

Herman, N. J.(1996). Return to sender: Reintegrative stigma-management strategies of ex-psychiatric patients. In D. H. Kelly (Ed.), *Deviant behavior: A text-reader in the sociology of deviance* (pp. 615-632). New York: St. Martin's Press.

Hitlin, S., & Kramer, K. W. O. (2014). Intentions and institutions: Turning points and adolescents' moral threshold. *Advances in Life Course Research, 20,* 16-27. 10.1016/j.alcr.2014.01.003

Holden, M. J., Anglin, J. P., Nunno, M. A., & Izzo, C. V. (2015). Engaging the total therapeutic residential care program in a process of quality improvement: Learning from the CARE model; In J. K. Whittaker, J. F. del Valle & L. Holmes (Eds.), *Therapeutic residential care for children and youth: Developing evidence-based international practice* (pp. 301-313). Philadelphia: Jessica Kingsley Publications.

Holden, M. J., Izzo, C., Nunno, M., Smith, E. G., Endres, T., Holden, J. C., & Kuhn, F. (2010). Children and residential experiences: A comprehensive strategy for implementing a research-informed program model for residential care. *Child Welfare, 89*(2), 131.

Holstein, J. A., & Gubrium, J. F. (1994). Phenomenology, ethno methodology, and interpretive practice. In N. K. Denzin, & Y. S. Lincoln (Eds.), *Handbook of qualitative research* (pp. 262-272). Thousand Oaks: SAGE.

Hood, D. (2011). *Addiction treatment: Comparing religion and science in application.* New Brunswick: Transaction Publishers.

H. R. 3024, Stop child abuse in residential programs for teens act of 2017. 115th cong. (2017).

Interstate Consortium on Residential Child Care. (1980). *Residential child care guidebook*. Trenton, NJ: The Interstate Consortium, Department of Human Services.

Izzo, C. V., Smith, E. G., Holden, M. J., Norton, C. I., Nunno, M. A., & Sellers, D. E. (2016). Intervening at the setting level to prevent behavioral incidents in residential child care: Efficacy of the CARE program model. *Prevention Science, 17*(5), 554-564. doi:10.1007/s11121-016-0649-0

James, S. (2011). What works in group care? — A structured review of treatment models for group Homes and residential care. *Children and Youth Services Review, 33*(2), 308-321. doi:10.1016/j.childyouth.2010.09.014

— (2015). Commentary by sigrid james on: engaging the total therapeutic residential care program in a process of quality improvement: Learning from the CARE model. In J. K. Whittaker, J. F. del Valle & L. Holmes (Eds.), *Therapeutic residential care for children and youth: Developing evidence-based international practice* (pp. 314-315). Philadelphia: Jessica Kingsley Publications.

James, S., Thompson, R., Sternberg, N., Schnur, E., Ross, J., Butler, L., . . . Muirhead, J. (2015). Attitudes, perceptions, and utilization of evidence-based practices in residential care. *Residential Treatment for Children & Youth, 32*(2), 144-166. doi:10.1080/0886571X.2015.1046275

Jöhncke, S. (2009). Treatmentality and the governing of drug use. *Drugs and Alcohol Today, 9*(4), 14-17. 10.1108/17459265200900036

Kerig, P., Moeddel, M., & Becker, S. (2011). Assessing the sensitivity and specificity of the maysi-2 for detecting trauma among youth in juvenile detention. *Child & Youth Care Forum, 40*(5), 345-362. doi:10.1007/s10566-010-9124-4

Knapp, J.L. & Weitzen, F. (1945). A total psychotherapeuitc push method as practiced in the fifth service command rehabilitation center, fort knox, kentucky. *The American Journal of Psychiatry, 102*(3), 362-366.

Lalich., J. (2004). *Bounded choice: True believers and charismatic cults*. Los Angeles, CA: University of California Press.

Langone, M. D. (1993). Introduction. In M. D. Langone (Ed.), *Recovery from cults: Help for victims of psychological and spiritual abuse* (pp. 1-21). New York: Norton.

Leach, J. (2016). Psychological factors in exceptional, extreme and torturous environments. *Extreme Physiology & Medicine, 5*(1), 7. doi:10.1186/s13728-016-0048-y

LeBel, J., & Kelly, N. (2014). Trauma-informed care. In G. M. Blau, B. Caldwell & R. E. Lieberman (Eds.), *Residential interventions for children, adolescents, and families: A best practice guide* (pp. 78-95). New York: Routledge.

Lee, B. R., Bright, C. L., Svoboda, D. V., Fakunmoju, S., & Barth, R. P. (2011). Outcomes of group care for youth: A review of comparative studies. *Research on Social Work Practice, 21*(2), 177-189. doi:10.1177/1049731510386243

Lepselter, S. (2016). *The resonance of unseen things: Poetics, power, captivity, and ufos in the american uncanny*. University of Michigan Press.

Lewin, K. (1947). Frontiers in group dynamics: Concept, method and reality in social science; social equilibria and social change. *Human Relations, 1*(1), 5-41.

Lewis, D. (2008). Using life histories in social policy research: The case of third sector/public sector boundary crossing. *Journal of Social Policy, 37*(4), 559-578. doi:10.1017/S0047279408002213

Liegghio, M., Nelson, G., & Evans, S. (2010). Partnering with children diagnosed with mental health issues: Contributions of a sociology of childhood perspective to participatory action research. *American Journal of Community Psychology, 46*(1), 84-99. doi:10.1007/s10464-010-9323-z

Lifton, R. J. (1957). Psychiatric aspects of chinese communist thought reform. *Symposium of the Group for the Advancement of Psychiatry,* New York. 234-252.

— (1963). *Thought reform and the psychology of totalism: A study of "brainwashing in china.* New York: Norton.

London, P., & Klerman, G. (1978). *The boundaries between research and therapy, especially in mental health. chapter 15, in: The belmont report: Ethical principles and guidelines for the protection of human subjects research, appendix volume II.* Washington, D. C.: The united states department of health, education, and welfare. Retrieved from https://videocast.nih.gov/pdf/ohrp_appendix_belmont_report_vol_2.pdf

Lovern, J. D. (1991). *Pathways to reality: Erickson-inspired treatment approaches to chemical dependency.* New York: Brunner/Mazel, Inc.

Lipsey, M. W. (2009). The primary factors that characterize effecttive interventions with juvenile offenders: A meta-analytic overview. *Victims & Offenders, 4*(2), 124-147. doi:10.1080/15564880802612573

Luthar, S. S. (1991). Vulnerability and resilience: A study of high-risk adolescents. *Child Development, 62*(3), 600-616. 10.1111/j.1467-8624.1991.tb01555.x

Maguire, M., & Delahunt, B. (2017). Doing a thematic analysis: A practical, step-by-step guide for learning and teaching scholars. *The All Ireland Journal of Teaching & Learning in Higher Education, 3,* 3351-3364.

Masten, A. S., Hubbard, J. J., Gest, S. D., Tellegen, A., Garmezy, N., & Ramirez, M. (1999). Competence in the context of adversity: Pathways to resilience and maladaptation from childhood to late adolescence. *Development and Psychopathology, 11*(1), 143-169. 10.1017/S0954579499001996

Matthews, C., & Salazar, C. (2014). Second-generation adult former cult group members' recovery experiences: Implications for counseling. *International Journal for the Advancement of Counselling, 36*(2), 188-203. doi:10.1007/s10447-013-9201-0

Maxwell, J. A. (2012). *A realist approach for qualitative research.* Thousand Oaks, CA: Sage.

McCord, J. (2003). Cures that harm: Unanticipated outcomes of crime prevention programs. *The Annals of the American Academy of Political and Social Science, 587*(1), 16-30. doi:10.1177/0002716202250781

McCorkle, L. W. (1952). Group therapy in the treatment of offenders. *Federal Probation, 16*(22), 22-27.

Mercer, J. (2017). Evidence of potentially harmful psychological treatments for children and adolescents. *Child & Adolescent Social Work Journal, 34*(2), 107. doi:10.1007/s10560-016-0480-2

Mercer, M. (1982). Closing the barn door: The prevention of institutional abuse through standards. *Child and Youth Services, 4*(1-2), 127

Moran, P., Bifulco, A., Ball, C., Jacobs, C. Benaim, K. (2002). Exploring psychological abuse in childhood: Developing a new interview scale. Bulletin of the Menninger Clinic, Vol. 66 (3), p. 213-241

Neville, L., Miller, S., & Fritzon, K. (2007). Understanding change in a therapeutic community: An action systems approach. *Journal of Forensic Psychiatry & Psychology, 18*(2), 181-203. doi:10.1080/14789940601108439

Nielsen, A. L., & Scarpitti, F. R. (1997). Changing the behavior of substance abusers: Factors influencing the effectiveness of therapeutic communities. *Journal of Drug Issues, 27*(2), 279-298. doi:10.1177/002204269702700207

Nunno, M. (2009). Invited commentary on CAPTA and the residential placement: A survey of state policy and practice. *Child & Youth Care Forum, 38*(2), 69-73. 10.1007/s10566-009-9068-8

Nunno, M. A., Holden, M. J., & Tollar, A. (2006). Practice implications learning from tragedy: A survey of child and adolescent restraint fatalities. *Child Abuse & Neglect, 30*(12), 1315-1316. doi:10.1016/j.chiabu.2006.10.005

Ofshe, R., & Singer, M. T. (1986). Attacks on peripheral versus central elements of self and the impact of thought-reforming techniques. *Cultic Studies Journal, 3*(1), 3-24.

OJJDP (Office of Juvenile Justice and Delinquency Prevention). (2014). Statistical briefing book. Retrieved from https://www.ojjdp.gov/ojstatbb/corrections/qa08201.asp?qaDate=2014

Overcamp-Martini, M., & Nutton, J. (2009). CAPTA and the residential placement: A survey of state policy and practice. *Child & Youth Care Forum, 38*(2), 55-68. 10.1007/s10566-009-9067-9

Palareti, L., & Berti, C. (2009). Different ecological perspectives for evaluating residential care outcomes: Which window for the black box? *Children and Youth Services Review, 31*(10), 1080-1085. doi:10.1016/j.childyouth.2009.07.011

Parent, D. G. (2003). Correctional boot camps: Lessons from a Decade of Research. *Research in practice.* U.S. Department of Justice, Office of Justice Programs, National Institute of Justice.

Parham v. J. R. (1979). 442 U.S. 503, 89 S. Ct. 733.

Penhale, B. (1999). Introduction. In Stanley, N., Manthorpe, J. & Penhale, B. (Ed.), *Institutional abuse: Perspectives across the life course* (pp. 1-15). London & New York: Routledge.

Pew Charitable Trust. (2015). Legislating evidence-based policy making: A look at state laws that support data-driven decision-making. Issue brief. Pew-MacArthur Results First Initiative. Retrieved from: https://www.pewtrusts.org/-/media/assets/2015/03/legislationresultsfirstbriefmarch2015.pdf

Pidgeon, N & Henwood, K. (2006). Grounded theory. In M. Hardy, & A. Bryman (Eds.), *Handbook of data analysis* (pp. 625-648). Thousand Oaks, CA: Sage.

Polvere, L. (2011). Youth perspectives on restrictive mental health placement: Unearthing a counter narrative. *Journal of Adolescent Research, 26*(3), 318-343. doi:10.1177/0743558410391257

Priede, C. & Farrall, S. (2011) Comparing results from different styles of cognitive interviewing: "verbal probing" vs. "thinking aloud." *International Journal of Social Research Methodology* 14(4), 271-287.

Protection of human subjects, 45 C.F.R. §46.101. (2009). United States Department of Health and Human Services. Retrieved from: https://www.hhs.gov/ohrp/regulations-and-policy/regulations/45-cfr-46/index.html

Rabb, J., & Rindfleisch, N. (1985). A study to define and assess severity of institutional abuse/neglect. *Child Abuse & Neglect, 9*(2), 285-294. doi:10.1016/0145-2134(85)90021-3

Rauktis, M. (2016). "When you first get there, you wear red": Youth perceptions of point and level systems in group Home care. *Child and Adolescent Social Work Journal, 33*(1), 91-102. doi:10.1007/s10560-015-0406-4

Reamer, F., & Siegel, D. (2008). *Teens in crisis: How the industry serving struggling teens helps and hurts our kids*. New York: Columbia University Press.

Redl, F. (1957, April). The meaning of "therapeutic milieu". *In E.K. Cannan (Chair), Symposium on Preventive and Social Psychiatry*. Symposium conducted at the Walter Reed Army Medical Center, Washington, D.C. 503-515.

Riessman, C. K. (2001). Analysis of personal narratives. In J. F. Gubrium, & J. A. Holstein (Eds.), *The handbook of interviewing research: Context and method* (pp. 695-710). Thousand Oaks, CA: Sage.

Rittel, H. W. J., & Webber, M. M. (1973). Dilemmas in a general theory of planning. *Policy sciences, 4*(2), 155-169.

Rodríguez-Carballeira, Á., Saldaña, O., Almendros, C., Martín-Peña, J., Escartín, J., & Porrúa-García, C. (2015). Group psychological abuse: Taxonomy and severity of its components. *The European Journal of Psychology Applied to Legal Context, 7*(1), 31.

Robbins, I. P. (2014). Kidnapping incorporated: The unregulated youth-transportation industry and the potential for abuse. *American Criminal Law Review, 51*(3), 563.

Roulston, K., & Shelton, S. A. (2015). Reconceptualizing bias in teaching qualitative research methods. *Qualitative Inquiry, 21*(4), 332-342. doi:10.1177/1077800414563803

Roy, K., Zvonkovic, A., Goldberg, A., Sharp, E., & LaRossa, R. (2015). Sampling richness and qualitative integrity: Challenges for research with families. *Journal of Marriage and Family, 77*(1), 243-260. 10.1111/jomf.12147

S. 3031 Stop child abuse in residential programs for teens act of 2016. 114th cong. (2016).

Saldaña, J. (2014). Blue-collar qualitative research. *Qualitative Inquiry, 20*(8), 976-980.10.1177/1077800413513739

— (2016). An introduction to codes and coding. *The coding manual for qualitative researchers* (pp. 1-42). Washington, D. C.: SAGE.

Salter, F. K. (1998). Indoctrination and institutionalized persuasion: Its limited variability and cross-cultural evolution. In Eibl-Eibsfeldt, I. & Salter, F.K. (Ed.), *Ethnic conflict and indoctrination: Altruism and identity in evolutionary perspective* (pp. 421-452). New York: Berghahn Books.

Satel, S. L. (1999). *Drug treatment: The case for coercion.* Washington, D.C.: AEI Press.

Schein, E. H. (1962). Man against man: Brainwashing. *Corrective Psychiatry and Journal of Social Therapy, 8*(1-4), 90-97.

Schein, E. H., Barker, C. H., & Schneier, I. (1961). *Coercive persuasion: A socio-psychological analysis of the "brainwashing" of American civilian prisoners by the Chinese communists.* New York: Norton.

Settersten, R. A. (2002). Socialization and the life course: New frontiers in theory and research. *Advances in Life Course Research, 7*, 13-40. 10.1016/S1040-2608(02)80028-4

Shean, M. (2015). *Current theories relating to resilience and young people: A literature review.* Melbourne, Australia: Victorian Health Promotion Foundation.

Singer, M. T., & Ofshe, R. (1990). Thought reform programs and the production of psychiatric casualties. *Psychiatric Annals, 20*(4), 188-193. doi:10.3928/0048-5713-19900401-06

Skoll, G. R. (1991). Power and repression. *The American Journal of Semiotics, 8*(3), 5-29.

— (1992). *Walk the walk and talk the talk*. Philadelphia: Temple Univ. Press.

Small, M.L. (2008) 'Lost in Translation: How Not to Make Qualitative Research More Scientific, in M. Lamont and P. White (eds) *Report from Workshop on Interdisciplinary Standards for Systematic Qualitative Research*. Washington, DC: National Science Foundation.

Smith, M. (2010). Victim narratives of historical abuse in residential child care. *Qualitative Social Work, 9*(3), 303-320. doi:10.1177/1473325010367816

Smith, C. P., & Freyd, J. J. (2013). Dangerous safe havens: Institutional betrayal exacerbates sexual trauma. *Journal of Traumatic Stress, 26*(1), 119-124. doi:10.1002/jts.21778

Staller, K. M. (2015). Qualitative analysis: The art of building bridging relationships. *Qualitative Social Work, 14*(2), 145-153. doi:10.1177/1473325015571210

Stanley, N., Manthorpe, J. & Penhale, B. (Ed.). (1999). *Institutional abuse: Perspectives across the life course*. London & New York: Routledge.

Stevens, A. (2012). 'I am the person now I was always meant to be': Identity reconstruction and narrative reframing in therapeutic community prisons. *Criminology & Criminal Justice, 12*(5), 527-547. doi:10.1177/1748895811432958

Stewart, D.W., Shamdasani, P.N. & Rook, D.W. (2007). *Focus groups. Theory and practice*. Sage Publications, London.

Substance Abuse and Mental Health Services Administration (SAMHSA). (2015). *Appropriate alternatives to conversion therapy for children and adolescents*. Special Report. Rockville, MD: Substance Abuse and Mental Health Services Administration.

Substance Abuse and Mental Health Services Administration (SAMHSA). (2016). *National Mental Health Services Survey (N-MHSS): 2014. Data on Mental Health Treatment Facilities.* BHSIS Series S-87, HHS Publication No. (SMA) 16-5000. Rockville, MD: Substance Abuse and Mental Health Services Administration. Retrieved from: https://www.samhsa.gov/data/sites/default/files/2014_National_Mental_Health_Services_Survey.pdf

Sugarman, B. (1974). *Daytop village: A therapeutic community.* New York: Holt, Rinehart and Winston.

Szalavitz, M. (2006). *Help at any cost: How the troubled-teen industry cons parents and hurts kids.* New York: Penguin Group.

Teague, C. M. (2013). Developmental trauma disorder: A provisional diagnosis. *Journal of Aggression, Maltreatment & Trauma, 22*(6), 611-625. doi:10.1080/10926771.2013.804470

Terr, L. C. (1991). Childhood traumas: An outline and overview. *American Journal of Psychiatry, 148,* 10–20.

Terry, C. M. (2003). *The fellas: Overcoming prison and addiction.* Belmont, CA: Wadsworth/Thomson Learning.

Thoburn, J., & Ainsworth, F. (2015). Making sense of differential cross-national placement rates for therapeutic residential care. In J. K. Whittaker, J. F. del Valle & L. Holmes (Eds.), *Therapeutic residential care for children and youth: Developing evidence-based international practice* (pp. 37-46). Philadelphia: Jessica Kingsley Publishers.

Thomas, B. R. (1982). Protecting abused children: Helping until it hurts. In R. Hanson (Ed.), *Institutional abuse of children and youth* (pp.139-154). New York: Haworth Press.

Thomas, G. (1982). The responsibility of residential placements for children's rights to development. *Child and Youth Services, 4*(1-2), 23-45. doi:10.1300/J024v04n01_05

413

Tracy, S. J. (2010). Qualitative quality: Eight "Big-tent" criteria for excellent qualitative research. *Qualitative Inquiry, 16*(10), 837-851. doi:10.1177/1077800410383121

Turner, S. A. (1989). Parham v. J.R.: Civil psychiatric commitment of minors. *The Journal of Contemporary Health Law and Policy, 5*, 263. Retrieved from http://www.ncbi.nlm.nih.gov/pubmed/10293011

Turner, V. (1969). *The ritual process: Structure and anti-structure.* Chicago: Aldine.

— (1987). Betwixt and between: The liminal period in rites of passage. In L. C. Mahdi, S. Foster & M. Little (Eds.), *Betwixt and between: Patterns of masculine and feminine initiation* (pp. 3-19). La Salle, IL: Open Court.

Ungar, M. (2011). The social ecology of resilience: Addressing contextual and cultural ambiguity of a nascent construct. *American Journal of Orthopsychiatry, 81*(1), 1-17. 10.1111/j.1939-0025.2010.01067.x

— (2013). Resilience, trauma, context, and culture. *Trauma, Violence, & Abuse, 14*(3), 255-266. 10.1177/1524838013487805

United Nations Human Rights. (1989). *Convention on the Rights of the Child.* [online] Available at: http://www.ohchr.org/en/professionalinterest/pages/crc.aspx

Urban, J. B., Osgood, N. D., & Mabry, P. L. (2011). Developmental systems science: Exploring the application of systems science methods to developmental science questions. *Research in Human Development, 8*(1), 1-25. 10.1080/15427609.2011.549686

U.S. Department of Health and Human Services (USDHHS). (1999). *Mental Health: A Report of the Surgeon General.* Rockville, MD: U.S. Department of Health and Human Services. Retrieved from: http://profiles.nlm.nih.gov/ps/access/NNBBJC.pdf

U. S. Department of Health and Human Services. (2010). The Child
Abuse Prevention and Treatment Act, including Adoption Opportunities & The Abandoned Infants Act, as amended by P. L. 111-
320, The CAPTA Reauthorization Act of 2010. Retrieved from:
https://www.acf.hhs.gov/sites/default/files/cb/capta2010.pdf

U.S. Senate. (1974). *Individual rights and the federal role in behave
ior modification: A study prepared by the staff of the subcommit-
tee on constitutional rights of the committee on the judiciary.*
(93rd Cong., 2nd sess.). Washington: U.S Government Printing
Office.

Usher, J., & Jackson, D. (2014). Phenomenology. In J. Mills, & M.
Birks (Eds.), *Qualitative methodology: A practical guide* (pp.
181-197). Washington, D. C.: SAGE.

van der Kolk, B A. (2005). Developmental trauma disorder: To
wards a rational diagnosis for children with complex trauma histories. *Psychiatric Annals, 35*(5), 401.

Volkman, R., & Cressey, D. R. (1963). Differential association and
the rehabilitation of drug addicts. *American Journal of Sociology,
69*(2), 129-142. doi:10.1086/223542

Walker, S. C., Bumbarger, B. K., & Phillippi, S. W. (2015). Achiev-
ing successful evidence-based practice implementation in juvenile
justice: The importance of diagnostic and evaluative capacity.
Evaluation and Program Planning, 52, 189-197.
doi:10.1016/j.evalprogplan.2015.05.001

Weppner, R. S. (1983). *The untherapeutic community: Organizational behavior in a failed addiction treatment program.* Lincoln:
University of Nebraska Press.

Westervelt, S. D., & Cook, K. J. (2012). *Life after death row.* New
Brunswick, NJ: Rutgers Univ. Press.

White, W. L. (2014). *Slaying the dragon : The history of addiction treatment and recovery in america* (2nd ed.). Bloomington, IL: Chestnut Health Systems.

— (2016). Bridging the worlds of harm reduction and addiction treatment: An interview with andrew tatarsky, PhD. *Counselor, Nov-Dec* Retrieved from http://www.counselormagazine.com/detail-pageoverride.aspx?pageid=1729&id=15032385924

White, W. L., & Kleber, H. D. (2008). Preventing harm in the name of help: A guide for addiction professionals. *Counselor, 9*(6), 10-17.

White, W. L. & Miller, W. (2007). The use of confrontation in ad dictions treatment. *Counselor, 8*(4), 12-30.

Whitehead, K., Keshet, M., Lombrowski, B., Domenico, A., & Green, D. (2007). Definition and accountability. *American Journal of Orthopsychiatry, 77*(3), 348-349. doi:10.1037/0002-9432.77.3.348

Whittaker, J. K., del Valle, J. F. & Holmes, L. (2015). Introduction: The current landscape of therapeutic residential care. In Whittaker, J. K., del Valle, J. F. & Holmes, L. (Ed.), *Therapuetic residential care for children and youth: Developing evidence-based international practice* (pp. 23-33). London & Philadelphia: Jessica Kingsley Publishers.

Whyte, M. K. (1974). *Small groups and political rituals in China.* Berkeley: Univ. of California Press.

Willis, G.B. (2005) *Cognitive interviewing: A tool for improving questionnaire design.* Sage, Thousand Oaks, pp. 273-298.

Woodhouse, B. B. (2002). Speaking truth to power: Challenging "the power of parents to control the education of their own". *Cornell Journal of Law and Public Policy, 11*(3), 481.

Yalom, I. D., & Lieberman, M. A. (1971). A study of encounter group casualties. *Archives of General Psychiatry, 25*(1), 16-30. doi:10.1001/archpsyc.1971.01750130018002

Yin, R. K. (2016). *Qualitative research from start to finish* (Second edition ed.). New York ; London: Guilford Press.

Zablocki, B. (1997). The blacklisting of a concept: The strange history of the brainwashing conjecture in the sociology of religion. *Nova Religio: The Journal of Alternative and Emergent Religions, 1*(1), 96-121. doi:10.1525/nr.1997.1.1.96

Zimbardo, P. G. (2007). *The lucifer effect: Understanding how good people turn evil.* New York: Random House.

Zimmerman, D. P. (2004). Psychotherapy in residential treatment: Historical development and critical issues. *Child and Adolescent Psychiatric Clinics of North America, 13*(2), 347-361. doi:10.1016/S1056-4993(03)00122-6

BIOGRAPHICAL SKETCH

Marcus Chatfield is a PhD student of US History at the University of Florida. He received an Individualized Bachelor of Arts degree at Goddard College in 2013. The following year he self-published his undergraduate thesis, *Institutionalized Persuasion: The Technology of Reformation in Straight, Incorporated and the Residential Teen Treatment Industry*. Despite the typos and awkward sentences, he went ahead and put it out there "warts and all"—as one friendly critic said. Although he did his best at the time, he hopes to revise and expand that work as soon as possible. "Live and learn," they say.

In 2018 he received a Master of Science degree at the University of Florida in the Department of Family, Youth and Community Sciences. This manuscript is a paperback edition of his graduate thesis, *Adult Perspectives on Totalistic Teen Treatment: Experiences and Impact*, which is available online as a free PDF. He self-published this work to make it more accessible.

Marcus's essays about the teen program industry and the history of Straight, Inc. are online at *Op-Ed News* and *POINTS: The Blog of the Alcohol and Drugs History Society*. A summary of his graduate thesis was published in an essay collection developed by the Child Welfare League of America (CWLA) and the Field Center at the University of Pennsylvania. The collection, *Child Maltreatment in Insular & Isolated Communities* (2018), is available from the CWLA website.